DIMENSIONS OF HUMAN GEOGRAPHY:

Essays on Some Familiar and
Neglected Themes

Karl W. Butzer, *Editor*

Michael P. Conzen   Robert David Sack
Richard H. Jackson   Christopher L. Salter
Douglas L. Johnson   Joseph Sonnenfeld
Ronald Rees   Yi-Fu Tuan

THE UNIVERSITY OF CHICAGO
DEPARTMENT OF GEOGRAPHY
RESEARCH PAPER 186

1978

Library of Congress Cataloging in Publication Data

Main entry under title:
Dimensions of Human Geography.
(Research Paper—the University of Chicago, Department of Geography;
no. 186)
1. Anthropo-geography—Addresses, essays, lectures. 2. Geographical perception—Addresses, essays, lectures. I. Butzer, Karl W. II. Series: Chicago. University. Dept. of Geography. Research paper; no. 186.
H31.C514 no. 186 [GF49] 910s [301.3]
77-27874
ISBN 0-89065-093-4

Cover Photograph

Three generations of settlement in superposition, near Barkley West, South
Africa. The house foundations and other ruins belong to an abandoned European
prospectors' town of the 1870's diamond rush; the standing, triangular or rectangular walls were later built as stock-enclosures by Black pastoralists; the
metal-roofed houses represent the fringe of a modern "township" created by
Apartheid legislation. (K.W.B., August 1971).

Research Papers are available from:
The University of Chicago
Department of Geography
5828 S. University Avenue
Chicago, Illinois 60637
Price: $6.00 list; $5.00 series subscription

PREFACE

> The study of attitudes tends to
> emphasize the role of fantasy
> in transforming nature . . . it
> depicts man's <u>world</u> rather
> than man's env<u>ir</u>onment. Man's
> world is a fabric of ideas and
> dreams, some of which he man-
> ages to give visible form. [1]

Geographers have, with good reason, concerned themselves with the description and analysis of an objective universe since the time of Diodorus and
Strabo. Factual information is, after all, the mainstay of any structural framework to organize or generalize human knowledge. Although the geographer's
world is real in terms of people, objects and material, its perception, articulation, and analysis are products of the mind. The physical and social sciences
generally focus on elements of the physical environment and on human subjects,
respectively, but the geographer has traditionally been interested in both. This
makes explanation or the attribution of causality doubly difficult to achieve, but
it also has the salutary effect of repeatedly drawing the geographer's attention
to subjective as well as objective phenomena. I believe that few geographers
have ever ignored the one or the other, despite the formal constraints to broader intellectual discussion imposed by specialized publications.

Reviews and obituaries frequently lament, by implication, the paucity of
"Renaissance scholars" in modern academia. Yet the accelerating search for
objectivity and scientific method selects against intellectual breadth, commonly
relegating the role of synthesis and speculation to senior individuals who have
"proven" themselves on other ground or to an external group of opportunistic
popularizers who seek to mediate between science and the general public. Disciplines would be better served if they encouraged a healthier mix of specializa-

---

[1] Yi-Fu Tuan: Attitudes toward Environment: Themes and Approaches, in
Environmental Perception and Behavior, University of Chicago, Department of
Geography, Research Paper No. 109 (edited by David Lowenthal; Chicago, 1967),
pp. 16-17.

tion and generalization, and of objectivity and subjectivity. Frequent alternations between application and reflection are not only good for the individual, but promote intra- and interdisciplinary dialog.

It seems to me that geographers have applied themselves with commendable zeal and an admirable range of methods for a little too long. There appears to be a certain restlessness, a concern about relevance or direction that suggests it may be time for an intellectual breathing spell. Many of our best scholars have become disillusioned with the narrow specialization and isolation of the sub-fields, drifting into other fields in the absence of useful reinforcement and communication within geography. Others have been appalled with the sterility of economic determinism and thus encouraged to explore phenomenological dimensions previously neglected. I myself have discovered some of the same dissatisfaction, in research and teaching focused on prehistoric man-nature systems or settlement archeology that inevitably emphasized cultural materialism and ecology. Admittedly, the application of geographical methodologies to archeology is an exciting venture, and ecology seeks to model a dynamic interplay between biological, cultural and environmental forces. But I continued to regret the relegation of human idiosyncrasy, initiative and ingenuity to a secondary role. For the sake of balance, I emphasized the role of perception, and concluded one course with lectures that underscored the human perspective. It was while speculating on the significance of societal attitudes to the environment that I became conscious that other geographers entertained many similar sentiments.

In this way, a lecture theme called to mind many of the anthropological and geographical contributions to environmental perception and behavior. The notion of a symposium, on what was provisionally called Culture and Geographical Space, subsequently appealed to a range of geographers contacted. It was their enthusiasm that made possible a double, special-session at the Salt Lake City meetings of the Association of American Geographers (April 26, 1977). We presented a series of personal views, some of them mildly iconoclastic, and above all tried to convey our own spirit of enthusiasm to the loyal audience that had filled up the conference room even before we ourselves arrived for the early, 8:30 AM start. The talks were linked by their collective yearning for change, their re-thinking of old paradigms, and their rejection of the mechanical model-building approach as an overarching goal rather than as a means to an end. The generous response has encouraged us to revise the papers and prepare them for publication. In our more optimistic moods we felt that these essays might point towards new directions in human geography. More realistically, perhaps, we hope that they may stimulate the search for a logic and coherence within the widely spreading reach of what has grown from the older sprouts of geography.

Several individuals have contributed substantially to making our common efforts a reality. Marvin W. Mikesell's feedback and advice helped implement what began as an idea, and through many hours of discussion he helped clarify my thinking. Sarah K. Myers provided much stimulus in the initial planning and while co-chairing the sessions. Helpful analyses of the collection of papers were made by Peter G. Goheen and William D. Pattison. Finally, I owe a personal debt of gratitude to my co-authors, for their responsiveness at all stages of a collaborative effort.

KARL W. BUTZER

Chicago and Flossmoor, IL
July, 1977

TABLE OF CONTENTS

CHAPTER 1

CULTURAL PERSPECTIVES ON GEOGRAPHICAL SPACE

Karl W. Butzer
University of Chicago

Paradigms of Geographical Inquiry

Self-analysis is a periodic ritual of academic disciplines. The nature of intellectual endeavor dictates that phases of analytical progress are first followed by integration of new information into broader and often holistic frameworks. Eventually the promethean advances of the human mind give way to introspective reassessments of the validity of results, if not of underlying concepts. These inevitable reevaluations frequently trigger a radiation of new research directions. Novel fields of inquiry evolve that are intended to derive more valid conclusions. For a time the new field is conveniently compact and coherent, but ultimately it too is subject to centrifugal trends. Several intellectual generations later the daughter fields of study remain basically interrelated, but their methodological components and approaches vary. They differ as much among themselves as they all differ from the ancestral discipline.

Much of the problem of defining geography has been one of attempting to retain a strict patrilineal tradition between classical and modern geography. In fact, the discipline has been repeatedly metamorphosed by quantum evolutionary changes. Geography today is related to the geography of Strabo[1] no more or less than Homo sapiens is linked to some Tertiary primate ancestor. However, geography is also related to a disparate host of contemporary fields such as geology, meteorology, anthropology or sociology, in much the same way as various members of a family are interrelated. A century after Darwin's The

---

[1]The Geography of Strabo (translated by H. L. Jones; 8 vols.; Heinemann, London, 1917-32). See, also, Fred E. Lukermann: The Concept of Location in Classical Geography, Annals, Association of American Geographers, Vol. 51, 1961, pp. 194-210; Clarence Glacken: Traces on the Rhodian Shore (Berkeley, University of California Press, 1967).

<u>Descent of Man</u>, people are no longer embarrassed by the facts of biological evolution, having become increasingly aware of the nature of their own identity. The expansiveness of geography since 1960 has also provided a greater sense of confidence. Analytical advances have been rapid in response to diversification or improvement of technology, and one may even sense that a new conceptual framework is just on the horizon. It can be claimed that the so-called quantitative revolution has not only generated a new methodology but has also whetted a critical awareness of process, form, and function. Also within the 1960's, a groundswell of public interest in environmental quality has served to redirect the attention of geographers from introverted concern with human artifacts towards the overarching problem of man as part of the ecosystem.[2]

New configurations are difficult to discern in a time of flux. But a fresh sense of identity may well be emerging among the broad spectrum of geographical practitioners. If this assessment is correct, such a sense of identity may owe much both to an improved ability to articulate traditional problems, and the application of a more sophisticated technology, acquired from the physical and social sciences. I emphasize traditional, but not in rhetorical affirmation of patrilineal continuity. The idealized apposition of "man and nature" espoused by Ritter,[3] Marsh,[4] and Richthofen[5] remains the crucial ingredient. However, the modern concept of "society and environment" differs in more than words, by suggesting complex interaction--involving all components and several hierarchies. The leading geographers of the 19th century anticipated these goals but ultimately found the prerequisite tasks of earth description all-consuming. This primal effort of basic recording and analysis also brought into being those

[2]Marvin W. Mikesell: Geography as the Study of Environment: An Assessment of Some Old and New Commitments, in Perspectives on Environment (edited by Ian R. Manners and M. W. Mikesell; Association of American Geographers, Washington, D. C., 1974), pp. 1-23.

[3]Carl Ritter: Einleitung zur allgemeinen vergleichenden Geographie und Abhandlungen zur Begründung einer mehr wissenschaftlichen Behandlung der Erdkunde (Berlin, 1852).

[4]George Perkins Marsh: Man and Nature; or, Physical Geography as Modified by Human Action (1864) (edited by David Lowenthal; Harvard University Press, Cambridge, Ma., 1965), chap. 1.

[5]Ferdinand v. Richthofen: Aufgaben und Methoden der heutigen Geographie, Akademische Antrittsrede, Universität Leipzig, 1883; Vorlesungen über allgemeine Siedlungs- und Verkehrsgeographie (edited by Otto Schlüter; Reimer, Berlin, 1908).

sibling disciplines, such as geophysics and anthropology, that have shared this burden with geography. A century later, geographers are fortunate that they are far better prepared to approach once again the fundamental question of society and environment.

Change calls for extra circumspection. Geography must look forward if it is to regain its former prominence in the intellectual ferment of the times. But I feel that it should also search its past for virtues and legacies that can be usefully applied today. It should be axiomatic that a new and better paradigm include the best of tradition while optimizing on the experience of cognate disciplines. By exploiting these vertical and horizontal planes, geography may be better able to maintain the identity of its goals and to profit from the pluralism of its practitioners.

Towards a Broader Spatial Paradigm?

The surface of Earth comprises the totality of geographical space. Such space includes physical, cultural, and economic attributes and can be examined from both ideographic and nomothetic viewpoints. Each of the three thematic attributes has dominated the prevailing paradigm of a generation of geographers: the physical from Richthofen[6] to Davis, [7] the cultural from Schlütter[8] to Sauer, [9] and the economic since the implementation of Christaller's[10] and Loesch's[11] spatial concepts within geographical research. This succession of thematic

---

[6]Ibid. (1883).

[7]W. M. Davis: An Inductive Study of the Content of Geography, Bulletin, American Geographical Society, Vol. 38, 1906, pp. 67-84.

[8]Otto Schlütter: Die Ziele der Geographie des Menschen (Oldenbourg, Munich, 1906); Die Erdkunde in ihrem Verhältnis zu den Natur- und Geisteswissenschaften, Geographischer Anzeiger, Vol. 21, 1920, pp. 145-152, 213-218.

[9]See, for example, Carl O. Sauer: The Morphology of Landscape (1925), in Land and Life (edited by John Leighly; University of California Press, Berkeley, 1967), pp. 315-350; Foreword to Historical Geography, ibid., pp. 351-379. Also Philip Wagner: The Human Use of the Earth (Collier-Macmillan, New York, 1960); and P. L. Wagner and M. W. Mikesell, Readings in Cultural Geography (University of Chicago Press, Chicago, 1962), pp. 1-24.

[10]Walter Christaller: Central Places in Southern Germany (1933) (translated by C. W. Baskin; Prentice-Hall, Englewood Cliffs, 1960).

[11]August Loesch: The Economics of Location (1940) (translated by W. H. Woglom and W. F. Stolper; Wiley, New York, 1954).

orientations, as well as the traditional dichotomy of topical and areal dimensions, [12] has served to promote the organic growth of geography. Each conceptual trend, within its own time context and motivated by its own group of adherents, has been developed with enthusiasm and conviction, sometimes to its logical extreme. Ultimately hypothesis leads to antithesis, as the limitations of a
dominant paradigm are perceived.

There are indications today that many geographers have recognized the
intellectual limitations of the economic paradigm of spatial organization. Edward Taaffe forecast a return to "cautious and pragmatic pluralism," [13] urging
that the spatial view be better articulated with ecological and chorological approaches in geography. Similarly, Sack [14] has argued that the spatial and chorological views are complementary rather than irreconcilable. Unnecessary fragmentation and occasional excesses of quantification are not the only issues. At
the very time that many geographers have turned their concern to pressing
social questions, mathematical exuberance has reduced the human component to
dot maps of artifacts or clusters of people. Considered in strictly numerical
terms, artifactual aggregates or material attributes lose much of their cultural
or symbolic value. Unlike anthropologists, many geographers have tended to
overlook that people do not generally act as individuals, but as members of a
community. It is the community that collectively shapes attitudes or makes fundamental decisions, [15] the result of which are the material components that
most commonly lend themselves to successful computerization. Communities
in their turn are the integral components of the pervasive but heterogeneous
matrix that constitutes cultures.

The prevalent spatial-economic paradigm in geography has developed
within the experiential framework of European and North American society, one
in which it is axiomatic that social forms emerge from the practical activities
of individuals. [16] However, in the traditional values systems of "developing" or

---

[12] See Richard Hartshorne: Perspective on the Nature of Geography (Rand McNally, Chicago, 1959), especially chap. 9.

[13] Edward J. Taaffe: The Spatial View in Context, Annals, Association of American Geographers, Vol. 64, 1974, pp. 1-16.

[14] R. D. Sack: Chorology and Spatial Analysis, Annals, Association of American Geographers, Vol. 64, 1974, pp. 439-452.

[15] Robert Redfield: The Little Community (University of Chicago Press, Chicago, 1960).

[16] Marshall Sahlins: Culture and Practical Reason (University of Chicago Press, Chicago, 1976).

non-Western societies, production and material effectiveness are often of subordinate importance. It would seem that many leading geographers have failed to appreciate that cultures also are idiosyncratic or particularistic, that the imprint of culture on the landscape includes factors other than profit and loss, or distance decay, and that culture, by definition, is cumulative.

Intellectual communities are maintained by a salutory system of checks and balances, and even a very casual review of the broader field during the last decade or so shows that a refreshing number of geographers has remained duly sensitive to the pervasiveness of culture. In part this can be recognized in what might be described as a humanistic resurgence, emphasizing symbolic values, [17] aesthetic norms, [18] the artistic component of landscapes, [19] or even existential phenomenology. [20] Symptoms of the rapid growth of interest by geographers in these seemingly esoteric pleasures can be identified in the massive attendance of the Landscape in Literature session at the 1974 geography meet-

---

[17] David Lowenthal: Geography, Experience, and Imagination: Towards a Geographical Epistemology, Annals, Association of American Geographers, Vol. 51, 1961, pp. 241-260; Yi-Fu Tuan: Topophilia: A Study of Environmental Perception, Attitudes and Values (Prentice-Hall, Englewood Cliffs, 1974); Space and Place: Humanistic Perspective, Progress in Geography, Vol. 6, 1974, pp. 212-252; R. D. Sack: Magic and Space, Annals, Association of American Geographers, Vol. 66, 1976, pp. 309-322.

[18] David Lowenthal and H. C. Prince: The English Landscape, Geographical Review, Vol. 54, 1964, pp. 309-346; Lowenthal and Prince: English Landscape Tastes, ibid., Vol. 55, 1965, pp. 186-222; Lowenthal: The American Scene, Geographical Review, Vol. 58, 1968, pp. 61-68; Gerhard Hard: Arkadien in Deutschland, Die Erde, Vol. 94, 1965, pp. 21-41; D. W. Meinig, Environmental Appreciation: Localities as a Humane Art, Western Humanities Review, Vol. 25, 1971, pp. 1-11. For the counterpoint of blighted environments, see P. F. Lewis, D. Lowenthal and Yi-Fu Tuan, Visual Blight in America, Association of American Geographers, Commission on College Geography, Resource Paper No. 23, Washington, 1973.

[19] See, for example, Herbert Lehmann: Formen landschaftlicher Raumerfahrung im Spiegel der bildenden Kunst, Erlanger Geographische Arbeiten No. 22, 1968, pp. 1-24; R. L. Heathcote: The Artist as Geographer: Landscape Painting as a Source for Geographical Research, Proceedings Royal Geographical Society of Australasia, South Australian Branch, Vol. 73, 1972, pp. 1-21; Ronald Rees: Geography and Landscape Painting: An Introduction to a Neglected Field, Scottish Geographical Magazine, Vol. 89, 1973, pp. 147-157; Rees: Landscape in Art, this volume.

[20] Ranging from Yi-Fu Tuan: Geography, Phenomenology, and the Study of Human Nature, Canadian Geographer, Vol. 15, 1971, pp. 181-192, to Anne Buttimer: Grasping the Dynamism of Life-world, Annals, Association of American Geographers, Vol. 66, 1976, pp. 277-292.

6

ings in Seattle, [21] in the revival of the periodical Landscape, in the urban vignettes of the Comparative Metropolitan Analysis Board, [22] and in the Atlas of American Culture project. Simultaneously, there has been extensive exploration of the realms of perception, as pertinent to several directions of geographical research. [23] Collectively these complex strands of subjective and often humanistic writing can perhaps be interpreted as an implicit criticism of many fundamental assumptions in a "scientific" geography[24] increasingly preoccupied with the formulation and testing of "laws" or the generation of systems models.

The founders of the spatial school certainly did not subscribe to blatant materialism. Christaller explicitly saw his own work as complementary to traditional regional studies, [25] and his triad of central-place organizing principles included an administrative factor with no necessary economic rationale. More recently, spatial concepts have been increasingly incorporated into cross-cultural and even anthropological studies. So, for example, spatial models for nomadic mobility patterns have been explained from ecological and cultural premises. [26] At the systematic level, Christaller's model has been expanded to

[21]C. L. Salter and W. J. Lloyd, eds.: Landscape in Literature, Association of American Geographers, Commission on College Geography, Resource Paper 76-3 (Washington, 1977); Salter: Signatures and Settings: One Approach to Landscape in Literature, this volume.

[22]M. P. Conzen and G. K. Lewis: Boston: A Geographical Portrait (Ballinger Publishing Co., Cambridge, Ma., 1976).

[23]Including cultural, social and economic perspectives. See, for example, H. C. Brookfield: On the Environment as Perceived, Progress in Geography, Vol. 1, 1969, pp. 51-80; Joseph Sonnenfeld: Geography, Perception, and the Behavioral Environment, in Man, Space, and Environment (edited by P. W. English and R. C. Mayfield; Oxford, New York, 1972), pp. 244-251; Sonnenfeld: Resource Perceptions and the Security of Subsistence, this volume; T. F. Saarinen: Environmental Planning: Perception and Behavior (Houghton-Mifflin, Boston, 1976).

[24]See J. N. Entrikin: Contemporary Humanism in Geography, Annals, Association of American Geographers, Vol. 66, 1976, pp. 615-632.

[25]Christaller, op. cit. [note 10], p. 9.

[26]D. L. Johnson: The Nature of Nomadism: A Comparative Study of Pastoral Migrations in Southwestern Asia and Northern Africa, University of Chicago, Department of Geography, Research Paper 118, Chicago, 1969, pp. 1-200; Johnson: Nomadic Organization of Space: Reflections on Pattern and Process, this volume; for other examples of this incipient fusion of traditional concerns with spatial concepts, see Marvin W. Mikesell, Tradition and Innovation in Cultural Geography, Annals, Association of American Geographers, Vol. 68, 1978, in press.

7

do better justice to the organization of space in developing countries by E. A. J. Johnson,[27] who explicitly recognized 5 key organizing principles: market hierarchies, administrative or military control, juridical institutions, and sacerdotal groups. The long-neglected role of ritual and cosmology in defining sacred space has been explored in some depth.[28] Attempts have also been made to apply central place theory to prehistoric settlement patterning.[29] Most recently, a group of cultural anthropologists has collaborated to provide an impressive compendium of papers that utilize spatial concepts in analyzing regional economic and social systems.[30]

These examples may serve to show that spatial theory has both greater flexibility and broader applicability than some of its proponents or opponents may have anticipated. In fact, the value of spatial concepts for the organization of materials and formulation of hypotheses in cultural geography, anthropology, archeology and, of course, economics, has proven to be substantial. This suggests that an even more effective integration of economic, cultural, and ecological perspectives within a more broadly conceived paradigm of spatial organization is not only possible but desirable. Such a paradigm must be multidimensional in its approach to the organization of space, in order to provide linkages for the several trends of geographical research, and above all to stimulate more productive conceptualization in the broader realm of the social sciences.

---

[27]E. A. J. Johnson: The Organization of Space in Developing Countries (Harvard University Press, Cambridge, Ma., 1970), chap. 1.

[28]Mircea Eliade: The Sacred and the Profane (Harper, New York, 1959); D. E. Sopher: Geography of Religions (Prentice-Hall, Englewood Cliffs, 1967); Paul Wheatley: City as Symbol (Lewis, London, 1967); Wheatley, The Pivot of the Four Quarters (Aldine, Chicago, 1971); R. H. Jackson and R. L. Layton: The Mormon Village: Analysis of a Settlement Type, Professional Geographer, Vol. 28, 1976, pp. 136-141; Jackson: Religion and Landscape in the Mormon Cultural Region, this volume; Yi-Fu Tuan: Sacred Space: Explorations of an Idea, this volume.

[29]So, for example, Waldo Tobler and Samuel Winesburg: A Cappadocian Speculation, Nature, Vol. 231, 1971, pp. 39-41; for a thorough review, see G. A. Johnson: Aspects of Regional Analysis in Archaeology, Annual Review of Anthropology, Vol. 6, 1977, pp. 479-508. Spatial dimensions to prehistoric cultural innovation are suggested in K. W. Butzer: Environment, Culture and Human Evolution, American Scientist, Vol. 65, 1977, pp. 572-584.

[30]C. A. Smith, ed.: Regional Analysis, Vol. I: Economic Systems, Vol. II: Social Systems (Academic Press, New York, 1976). Emphasis is primarily on central place theory (including rank-size ordering and primacy), rural exchange and marketing systems, and the application of regional analysis concepts to social systems.

Perspectives on the Nature of Space

Perception studies have already suggested more refined views of space to a number of geographers, so for example, the distinction of geographical, operational, perceived and behavioral environments proposed by Sonnenfeld.[31] On a far more abstract level, the architect Norberg-Schulz, inspired in large measure by Parsons[32] and Piaget,[33] envisaged a different, essentially psychological hierarchy of pragmatic, perceptual, existential, cognitive, and logical space.[34] Norberg-Schulz's paradigm has been recently applied by Wheatley to improve comprehension of the traditional Islamic city.[35] A more explicitly socio-environmental approach has been suggested by Erik Cohen,[36] who attempts to integrate Parsons's four subsystems of society (economy, polity, pattern maintenance, and community)[37] into an elaborately structured paradigm of social ecology that incorporates both institutional and functional perspectives. Four societal orientations to "environment" are identified, representing a spectrum of socio-environmental attitudes ranging from the materialistic to the abstract. They are:

(1) instrumental, as a matter of resources;

(2) territorial, as military or political control;

(3) sentimental, in terms of attachment, whether as emotional "belonging" or for purposes of social prestige; and

(4) symbolic, evaluating the significance of environmental features by the degree to which they are aesthetically enjoyable or in terms of their proximity to the sacred or the extent to which they symbolize it.[38]

---

[31] Op. cit. [note 23].

[32] Talcott Parsons: Societies: Comparative and Evolutionary Perspectives (Prentice-Hall, Englewood Cliffs, 1966).

[33] Jean Piaget: The Psychology of Intelligence (Routledge and Kegan Paul, London, 1950).

[34] Christian Norberg-Schulz: Existence, Space and Architecture (Praeger, New York, 1971).

[35] Paul Wheatley: Levels of Space Awareness in the Traditional Islamic City, Ekistics, Vol. 253, 1976, pp. 354-66.

[36] Erik Cohen: Environmental Orientations: A Multidimensional Approach to Social Ecology, Current Anthropology, Vol. 17, 1976, pp. 49-70.

[37] Talcott Parsons: Systems of Modern Societies (Prentice-Hall, Englewood Cliffs, 1971).

[38] Cohen, op. cit. [note 36], Table I in particular. The discussion com-

Cohen uses "ecology" and "environment" as a sociologist, not as a biologist or geographer. Yet his basic concepts implicitly or explicitly include spatial organization, perception, symbolic landscapes, and other approaches or themes that were either first developed or subsequently adapted within the field of geography. The instrumental or economic perspective, most familiar in Western and Marxist societies, represents the basic subject matter of most geographical research into spatial organization. The political view has repeatedly received the attention of geographers, [39] while military landscapes have also been characterized. [40] The sentimental and symbolic dimensions of space were explored in seminal studies by Lowenthal and Tuan, [41] and even sacred space and aesthetic landscapes have become objects of geographical concern. [42]

Such orientations or perspectives are overlapping rather than mutually exclusive. [43] Their value lies not in the creation of categories or formal intradisciplinary structures, but in drawing attention to distinctive components that are, to some degree or other, inherent to all geographical phenomena. They can, furthermore, provide a point of departure to explore attitudes to and conceptual dimensions of geographical space.

Space as a Set of Available Resources

Depending on technology, organization, and subsistence modes, space provides a set of natural resources. These are perceived differently by hunter-

---

ments that follow Cohen (ibid., pp. 62-68) suggest that the majority of anthropologists will remain wary, if for no other reason than that conceptual approaches are frequently confused with empirical propositions. The merits of several criticisms offered to Cohen's analytical framework or conclusions are beyond the purpose of this paper.

[39] So, for example, E. W. Soja: The Political Organization of Space, Association of American Geographers, Commission on College Geography, Resource Paper No. 8, Washington, 1971, with references to earlier work.

[40] E. A. J. Johnson, op. cit. [note 27], pp. 3-8.

[41] See note 17. Not surprisingly the social-sentimental and symbolic are less clearly differentiated in geographical than in sociological or anthropological writings.

[42] See notes 18 and 28.

[43] It is relevant that Parsons's societal subsystems are believed to interact constantly (op. cit., 1971 [note 37]), while Cohen (op. cit. [note 36], especially Table 2) envisages an elaborate matrix of conflicts that actually serve to maintain complex interactions.

gatherers, by agricultural communities, or by industrialized societies, so affecting their perceived value and potential exploitation.[44] Furthermore, these resources are not distributed uniformly, but are commonly found in local concentrations or as extensive zones of low-level dispersal, only in part coincident with other resources. The distribution of the aggregate of perceived resources, their relative values, and the related inter- and intra-group competition will help to determine horizontal settlement arrangement and, in economically-differentiated complex societies, vertical or hierarchical settlement patterns as well. The interrelationships between the complex of human communities and their available resources constitutes the ecological adaptation. Such adaptations commonly but not necessarily are cumulative rather than momentary, since they may reflect all local environments in which a human group has previously learned and in which its predecessors have learned.[45]

To some degree or other an economic-environmental orientation has been fundamental for all societies at all times. Yet the nature of the resulting economic matrix is highly variable from one complex culture to another.

Space as a Matter of Control

Particularly in the case of sedentary societies, space (as an aggregate of human constructs and natural economic potentials) may become an object of military and/or political organization. Settlement sites are selected with an eye to defensibility and specific locales are deliberately converted into settlements or fortresses because of their strategic value. Implicit or explicit boundaries are drawn and political aspirations are made by groups, classes, or individuals as to limited control or general authority. Complex delimitations within the countryside may attain the intricacy of Medieval Europe, with space variously controlled by several hierarchical institutions (king, secular nobility, religious potentates and orders, chartered cities or companies, individual landholders) and according to different privileges (secular or religious suzerainty, military and juridical control, right to exact taxes or customs).

---

[44]See Brookfield ⌈note 23⌉; D. A. Davidson: Terrain Adjustment and Prehistoric Communities, in Man, Settlement, and Urbanism (edited by P. J. Ucko, Ruth Tringham, and G. W. Dimbleby; Schenkman, Cambridge, Ma., 1972), pp. 17-22; Sonnenfeld, op. cit. ⌈note 23⌉, and Resource Perceptions and the Security of Subsistence, this volume.

[45]P. L. Wagner: Cultural Landscapes and Regions: Aspects of Communication, Geoscience and Man, Vol. 10, 1974, pp. 133-142.

11

The overall effect of a sufficiently complex overlay of socio-political con-
trols is a spatial organization determined less by available resources and their
proximity, than by spatial fragmentation as imposed by socio-political boundaries and the resultant economic privileges. In an extreme case this would not
only affect settlement patterning and hierarchies, but could also favor social,
religious, or ethnic segregation within settlements. The degree to which such
political organization of space assumes prominence depends on cultural attributes such as sedentariness, social organization, class differentiation, and the
nature and complexity of authority. It would tend to assume greatest significance in multitiered, urbanized civilizations, but may also be important among
simpler agricultural or pastoral societies.

Space in Terms of Social Identification

In the words of Erik Cohen:[46]

Primordial attachment finds its most fundamental concrete expression in the
sense of belonging: points in the environment or spatial features gain intrin-
sic significance for an individual or a group, independently of either their
instrumental value or their extrinsic symbolic meaning. This sentiment is
expressed in an emotionally loaded notion that one possesses roots, has a
place in the world, or belongs to a community or a neighbourhood which is
one's home . . . The individual comes to identify more intensively with
some points or areas in space and less intensively with others.

Consequently, by encouraging solidary relationships, the sense of place serves
an integrative function in society: "it provides an emotional anchorage to individuals and groups."[47]

Social space also stimulates differentiation as places or areas acquire
prestige in the process of social evaluation, particularly as a result of the social status of the people who live there. In effect,

The hierarchy of prestige areas represents the spatial component of social
stratification . . . (leading) to integration between dissimilar groups through
the institutionalization of spatial segregation and distance between them,
expressing their social distance.[48]

The close relationship of prestige with class or craft suggests that this mechanism of differentiation would be best developed in urbanized societies, whereas
the primary, emotional attachment to space would probably play a more significant role among most rural societies.

---

[46]Op. cit. [note 36], p. 55.   [47]Ibid.

[48]Ibid., p. 56.

Space in Terms of Symbolic Value

In broad terms, a landscape is created by a society in its own image[49] and serves to express that society's ideal environment, no matter how imperfect. As expressed by Wagner,[50]

Its forms, proportions, orientation, and properties are meant to be the very map and pattern for correct, harmonious behavior, and to give the model by which such behavior may be learned . . . A place or a landscape declares its underlying intent, or its ideal meaning, when living people activate it and actualize it . . . (An) intimate fourfold relationship . . . binds together time, place, act, and man--making each, in good degree, the function and expression of the other three reciprocal determinants.

In the end, "the landscape which a society has created may become its most enduring memorial."[51] A society's impact is recorded in place names, visual symbolisms, structures, and observances, so much so that "the forms of landscape and the norms of behavior are congruent."[52]

Conversely the landscape can mold the culture. As Wagner has argued,

The roles of landscape content in symbolic discourse, and as part of what defines behavior, are of major consequence. Landscape, like and with behavior, instructs and informs. . . .[53] As even now, in former times expressive artificial features of environment played a part as well in education; but their range and reference was of vastly different magnitude. The settlement itself, the fields and gardens, houses, tools and weapons, costumes and paraphernalia, amplifying learning, brought the individual into contact with the work of vanished craftsmen and builders, the ancestors, whose presence thus, and through renown, weighed heavily on the living.[54]

Further, in many societies such as our own, the values and content of such cultural landscapes are abstracted and reformulated by painters and writers for transmission to the public.

Not all points within the landscape are of equal value on a scale of sacredness. Instead,

Points in space and environmental features are evaluated in terms of their nearness to the sacred or the extent to which they symbolize it. . . . At one extreme are the cases in which places become sanctified through a slow, nondeliberate process, as, for example, wells, trees, hills, mountains, rivers and shrines in many societies acquire sacredness in "time immemorial."

---

[49]Lowenthal, op. cit., 1968 [note 18].

[50]Wagner, op. cit. [note 45], pp. 135-136.

[51]G. C. Homans: English Villagers of the Thirteenth Century (Harvard University Press, Cambridge, Ma., 1941), p. 12.

[52]Wagner, op. cit. [note 45], p. 136.

[53]Ibid.

[54]Ibid., p. 137.

At the other are the explicit, formal processes of sanctification, typically rituals of consecration or inauguration. . . . In the cosmologies of primitive people and traditional religions, the sacred, by endowing the world with moral-religious meaning, provides it with a fundamental order and thus separates the ordered "cosmos, " focused on a sacred "center, " from the surrounding orderless and hence meaningless and threatening "chaos. "[55]

In this sense the moral-religious institutions of a society are articulated with the landscape and expressed as sacred space. It is thus, at several levels, that the landscape provides stimuli for symbolic evaluation and identification. These are images, real or perceived, that are transformed into sources of meaning.[56]

Some Advantages of a More Explicitly Cultural Approach

These different perspectives on the nature of geographical space suggest that a multidimensional and more explicitly cultural approach would have considerable methodological and empirical utility within geography.

The social and symbolic components of space complement prevailing economic and political attitudes. Potential integration of these viewpoints into a pluralistic paradigm of spatial organization would reduce the increasing polarization between the "materialistic" and "humanistic" as well as the mathematical and nonmathematical schools. A centripetal paradigm would help to reunite the quantitative, economic, social, and cultural strands of geography and refocus them to the common goal of people. This human axis, if defined in sufficiently sophisticated terms, would intersect with that of the physical environment to define a realistic sphere of ecological investigation. It is on this plane that geographers may most readily recognize their traditional, central concern: the human use of the earth.

The implementation of a pluralistic spatial paradigm that does proper credit to the true complexity of culture would allow a fresh articulation of what exactly constitutes a "cultural landscape. " This concept, so basic to what geographers do, has nonetheless proven to be elusive and, in the long run, centrifugal rather than a point of integration for geographical concerns.[57] A dynamic and integrated approach to the multiple configurations of spatial organization

[55]Cohen, op. cit. [note 36], pp. 56-57.

[56]See Sonnenfeld, op. cit., 1972 [note 23].

[57]Marvin W. Mikesell: Landscape, International Encyclopedia of the Social Sciences, Vol. 10, 1968, pp. 575-580.

would contribute to more successful analysis and formulation of human landscapes.

Geography's attempts to deal with some of the more pressing contemporary issues have not been particularly successful. In predicting social change
in large conurbations some of us have relied more on extrapolation of mechanical trends rather than on an organic understanding of the behavioral and psychological components that condition social response. In urging a more equitable
reallocation of resources or opportunities some of us have ignored the reality
of the community as the arbiter of response and possible change. In dealing
with seemingly deadlocked constellations of modern society some of us have
been oblivious of the time dimension of culture or the cumulative nature of social sentiment and symbolic value, e. g., among minority groups. Many of us
have begun to despair over the attitudinal controversies and practical contradic-
tions in the search for new economic solutions or in the development and implementation of environmental law.[58] This is but an example of the inherent conflict generated by contradictory social orientations within all societies. A
broader perspective might well help generate more effective strategies to reach
solutions.

Last but not least, a specifically cultural paradigm would allow a more
sensitive appraisal of "society and environment" in cross-cultural terms.
Societies view nature "through a screen composed of beliefs, knowledge, and
purposes"[59] that is based on the cultural sharing of experience that varies
from one society to another. Environmental adaptation is not based on economic optimization, but is conditioned by political, strategic, sentimental, social,
aesthetic, and symbolic factors. Depending on the relative values placed upon
these possible orientations, the configuration of subsistence and settlement patterns, and even of the society itself, will vary. The mix of potentially conflict-
ing, environmental purposes[60] will create many distinct sets of environmental
attitudes. As a result, the land ethic of different cultures will vary, however
subtly, with equally diverse ecological impact.

---

[58]T. O'Riordan: Environmentalism (Pion, London, 1976).

[59]R. A. Rappoport: Nature, Culture and Ecological Anthropology, in Man,
Culture and Society (edited by H. L. Shapiro; Oxford, London, 1971), p. 246.

[60]Cohen, op. cit. [note 36].

Acknowledgement. --I am grateful to Marvin W. Mikesell for suggestions during
the inception of this paper, and to Kenneth Foote for discussion of an interim
draft. The related research was facilitated by a Guggenheim Fellowship.

CHAPTER 2

RESOURCE PERCEPTIONS AND THE SECURITY OF SUBSISTENCE

Joseph Sonnenfeld

Texas A&M University

"It was great when I was young. It was during the
Depression, and there was a real closeness among
people. Nobody had anything, so what we did have we
shared."

Betty Moran, quoted in the
New Yorker (April 4, 1977)

The subsistence security so many try to achieve is in large part determined by the adequacy of resources, technology, and population control. Yet
the relationship between these elements is an inconsistent one, given the sense
of security that many traditional populations seem to enjoy, by contrast with
the sense of insecurity common among industrial populations. It is as if the
security equation were not quite complete. It is as if an adaptation function
were operating, in some perverse way transforming deficiencies to sufficiency
for some, and sufficiencies to deficiency for others. The equation of resources,
technology, and population control with subsistence security is indeed incomplete; or at least its elements require elaboration.

Resources important for subsistence have certain basic characteristics:
they are abundant or scarce; of high quality or of low quality; random in occurrence or predictable; and controlled or uncontrollable. So characterized, they
may also be so perceived, though most will acknowledge that there is no necessary consistency between the reality and the perception of such characteristics
as quality, predictability and controllability; and neither is there any necessary
relationship between the simple availability of raw materials and the subsistence security that any population enjoys.

Conventional wisdom relates the disparity between resource availability
and subsistence security to differentials in technology and population control;

and for some groups, also to inequities in the ownership and distribution of essential raw materials. But there is another kind of inequity that affects subsistence security: that which results from the random occurrence of critical resources and related environmental events. For many traditional populations, environmental uncertainties were sufficiently common to have generated reciprocal subsistence relationships, involving a form of sharing in times of need which some have characterized as altruism or reciprocal altruism.[1]

Altruism is commonly defined as an "unselfish concern for the welfare of others";[2] generally the more the cost or risk to the doing-of-good, the more altruistic the behavior is considered to be. In survival terms, altruistic behavior is likely to be selected against, unless it is able to elicit reciprocated favors, the payoffs of which are greater than the costs (Fig. 1).[3] Reciprocal altruism generally assumes such payoffs, which is the reason why it is sometimes considered to be simply another form of selfish behavior;[4] but this is so only in biologic terms. When viewed as culturally conditioned rather than as biologically determined behavior, individuals share because it is the right thing--the moral thing--to do.[5] Cultural conditioning does not permit otherwise; or, at

---

[1]An alternative sharing response is through the "pooling" of resources or production. While such pooling is common at the family level, it also occurs at the community level, in which all give their produce to a chief or headman who subsequently redistributes this to community members. Reciprocity implies a one to one relationship between contributor and receiver, and is the kind of "giving" which permits the development of a selfless altruism. The surrendering of produce implicit in "pooling" seems to assume no ownership of produce to begin with, which would appear to preclude altruism. See Marshal Sahlins: Stone Age Economics (Aldine, Chicago, 1972), especially Chapter 5, for a discussion of both pooling and reciprocity concepts.

[2]Richard D. Alexander: The Search for a General Theory of Behavior, Behavioral Science, Vol. 20, 1975, pp. 77-100.

[3]Robert L. Trivers: The Evolution of Reciprocal Altruism, Quarterly Review of Biology, Vol. 46, 1971, pp. 35-57.

[4]Richard Symanski and Nancy Burley: Geography and Natural Selection--Revisited (unpublished paper, 1976); see also F. Paulsen: A System of Ethics (Scribner's, New York, 1903), pp. 379 ff.

[5]There is a conflict inherent in a concept of altruism as culturally conditioned behavior which is not generally recognized. Cultural conditioning implies, in this case, that society conditions the behavior of its members to conform to group norms for sharing. By definition, the altruist is expected to give freely, without expectation of return, even if at considerable cost or risk to his own welfare. But what if such altruism does not conform to what group norms also define as responsible behavior, which requires one to be responsible to

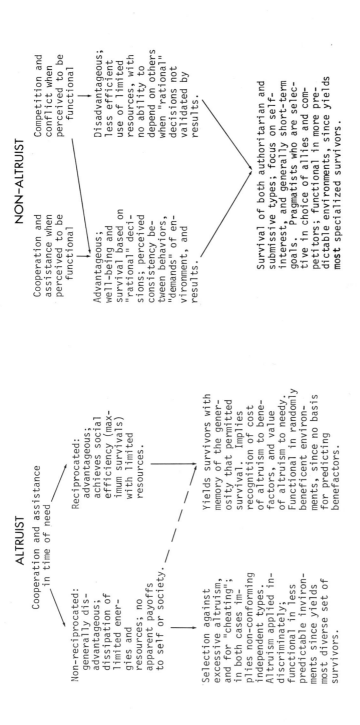

Fig. 1.--Responses to subsistence pressure

18

least, not unless a stress or change occurs which the culture is not able to accommodate for. Both stress and change are common when new technology or economy is introduced among traditional societies. From the perspective of the individual, the change which overrides cultural conditioning is one which may be perceived as either for the better or worse, but both are capable of producing a breakdown in sharing relationships.

As an example of such an effect, data from a study of northern Alaska Eskimo[6] suggested a curious differential in the perception of environmental risk and in the sense of subsistence security. Generally, those who had gone furthest in adopting western life styles and work habits were the ones who seemed the less secure and the more sensitive to risk in environment. In part, insecurity was the result of loss in subsistence skills; but associated changes in social relationships with kin and community had been replaced by less dependable relationships with government, shopkeepers, employers and others who had their own standards of what constituted appropriate supportive behavior in time of need.

The beginning of the breakdown in community subsistence relationships among the Eskimo could in fact be traced back to the introduction of new weapons--firearms--which made it easier for hunters to operate independently. Similar introductions of new technology among other subsistence oriented populations had similar effects on community relationships,[7] with an equivalent impact on the perception of security, quite apart from any change in the levels

---

those for whom one has culturally-prescribed obligations? Altruism applied broadly can include behavior directed to those outside one's system of responsibility, which may conceivably be at risk to those within that system. See, for example, Abram W. Gouldner: The Norm of Reciprocity: A Preliminary Statement, American Sociological Review, Vol. 25, 1960, pp. 176-177. This possibility for a generalized (open-ended) altruism therefore raises the question of whether the "morality" which is culturally conditioned should be characterized as altruism; or whether, instead, it is the helping for which there is no "need" and which may even be contrary to cultural prescription that constitutes altruism, and provides the selective advantage that explains its persistence. There is also the question of whether the persistence of altruism--its survival--need be even explained in functional terms (Gouldner, ibid., pp. 162-163). Whether altruism is in fact of long-term advantage for any group's survival can only be determined retrospectively. Figure 1 traces possible outcomes of altruistic and non-altruistic responses to subsistence pressure.

[6]J. Sonnenfeld: Social Stress in Extreme and Remote Environments (Paper, annual meeting, Association of American Geographers, Milwaukee, April, 1975).

[7]Abram Kardiner: The Individual and His Society (Columbia University Press, New York, 1939), pp. 329 ff. Also Sahlins, op. cit. [see note 1 above].

of production that resulted from technologic introductions.

To _feel_ secure is not necessarily to _be_ secure, but it is the measure of security which has behavioral significance. People feel secure about their subsistence when the resources required for subsistence are available when needed, either directly from their environment, or indirectly from others willing to share surplus resources from another environment. Subsistence sharing occurs for a variety of reasons, [8] but it is especially functional when there is randomness in the availability of critical resources, or in the environmental events which influence these. Individual hunters, fishermen, and farmers are not always fortunate enough to be where the conditions are best, but if they are willing to share with others when they are the more successful, they can expect others to help when necessary in return. [9] This kind of sharing relationship breaks down (1) when a persistent differential in subsistence success develops, in which case reciprocal relationships are reduced to unilateral ones, always with the same "givers" and the same "receivers"; or (2) when scarcity affects all for an extended period of time, in which case the pressure for survival transcends other obligations. [10]

Sharing assumes, therefore, a reasonable equivalence in the probability of scarcity and of abundance over time, so that all can expect to benefit over time. Sharing relationships persisted among subsistence populations because resources, though occasionally or even regularly scarce, were also renewable; and technology was not so efficient as to yield to individual hunters, fishermen, or farmers the control over resources able to convert randomness in subsis-

---

[8] For example, Sahlins, _ibid._, suggests an important status value for generalized reciprocity--which does not require reciprocation in kind--for chiefs or headmen, or for those seeking "big man" status.

[9] To emphasize the significance of such relationships, Kardiner describes, by contrast, the sense of insecurity common among the Chukchi who lacked dependable social relationships. He attributes this in part to a "shifting economy, which permits no sense of control, and in which skill and hardiness do not always reap their reward . . ."; but also in part to a social system "in which mutual responsibility is underplayed, so that there is no expectation of help, but only the necessity of bowing to fate" (Kardiner, _op. cit._ [see note 7 above], p. 125); this, in effect, is the opposite of what the Eskimo developed to accommodate for an essentially equivalent environmental situation.

[10] One additional explanation for a breakdown in sharing relationships is the introduction of money as a basis for exchange, the sharing of which falls outside the sharing norm established for foodstuffs (see Sahlins, _op. cit._ [see note 1 above], pp. 215 ff.).

tence success to consistency in such success. When new technology offered
assurance that the successful would continue to be successful, individuals had
little to gain from continuing a reciprocal subsistence relationship; and if there
were no substitute favors to be reciprocated, it lapsed, despite the availability
of a variety of behavioral safeguards intended to sustain such relationships.[11]
Unfortunately, the changes brought about by the introduction of new technology
were sometimes premature, given the impact of new technology on resources
still essential for subsistence.

Resource Perceptions and Reciprocal Relationships

Where reciprocal subsistence relationships prevail, populations appear
not to deplete their resources; the same technology which sustains reciprocity
also seems to constrain, by its inefficiency, the overexploitation of resources.
And since surplusses are expected to be shared by all, there is no incentive for
accumulations beyond immediate needs, which is at least part of the reason for
what has been described as the waste of underutilization of resources
and technology by primitive economies.[12] But a sharing ethic is also associated with waste of a kind. For the Eskimo, at least, an abundance of game
could produce gluttonous consumption; which is wasteful when future food supplies are expected to be deficient, which they often were. But a willingness to
engage in wasteful consumption helps reduce the personal cost of sharing surplusses, which is less during periods of abundance than of scarcity. The alternative to immediate consumption is the storing of one's surplusses; but if others are still in need, this suggests that priorities are personal rather than
social, which is enough reason for a culture not to discourage such waste (consumption beyond needs for the many rather than storing of surplus for the few):
it is a generous waste which values social obligations even at the expense of
future security. However, one result of such practice is that when a more efficient technology is developed or introduced, there is little basis in tradition for

---

[11]See, for example, Herbert Barry, Irvin L. Child, and Margaret K. Ba-
con: The Relation of Child Training to Subsistence Economy, American Anthro-
pologist, Vol. 61, 1959, pp. 51-63, which elaborates on culture-specific child-
training procedures designed to yield socialized adults with appropriate values
and behaviors. That a breakdown in sharing relationships can develop within a
single generation, despite conditioning during childhood to the contrary, suggests that a sharing norm may have to be continually reinforced; in turn implying conflict with the satisfaction of more basic needs.

[12]Sahlins, op. cit. [see note 6 above], p. 41.

constraint in the exploitation of limited resources; one "gets while the getting is good." Given limits to the supply and renewability of limited resources, the benefits of new technology may be short-lived. The end product may be a poorer resource base and a less secure subsistence than existed prior to the new technology, with no guarantee of an option to revert to traditional practices.

Resource depletion has not only been a problem for Eskimo and other traditional populations in process of change; it has also been a problem for western populations whose normal state has been one of change. When constraints are removed from resource exploitation, involving a technology which permits exploitation of resources beyond a people's or nation's needs, to satisfy also the fabricated needs of commerce, it is the cost of exploitation rather than of conservation which is the primary determinant of waste. New resources are sought from almost anywhere, the friction of distance and even the demands of security notwithstanding. This behavior almost suggests that a waste ethic is inherent in the human mentality; or at least that the gratification which results from immediate satisfaction is a more effective conditioner than that which results from self-denial.

Insensitivity to resource limits derives not only from an optimism in the potential of technology, but also from a mobility which permits expansion into new environmental settings. While there might have been sensitivity to ecological relationships in more familiar home environments, an equivalent understanding of resource-sustaining relationships is less likely in new settings. Also unlikely is a commitment to the ecological well-being of the place not intended as home, especially when there are other places to escape or return to. But even when resources are obviously being depleted, and there are no more places to go, there is often still lacking the sense of an option to conserve resources if this means reduction in standard of living or social well-being. Among developing nations, in particular, rapidly expanding populations make it difficult to establish long-term ecological priorities which require restrictions on resource use when these appear to be at the expense of the shorter-term survival of close social relations.

Variations in Value Orientation

Much of what has been discussed above may be viewed as a system of differentials in the valuation of resources, technology, and people. A rather simple view of changing combinations of valuations is indicated in Figure 2.

Historically, priorities seem to have "progressed" from a high valuation

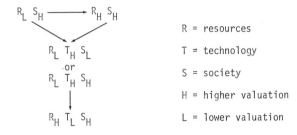

$$R_L \, S_H \longrightarrow R_H \, S_H$$

$$R_L \, T_H \, S_L$$
or
$$R_L \, T_H \, S_H$$

$$R_H \, T_L \, S_H$$

R = resources

T = technology

S = society

H = higher valuation

L = lower valuation

Fig. 2.--Differentials in value orientation

of people by traditional societies (implying a social conscience); to an increase
in valuation of resources, as environmental and technological limits became
apparent (implying a concern for long-term survival); through an industrial age
shift to high valuation of technology (implying optimism in technological solutions to economic and political problems); to a post-industrial recognition of
the overriding significance of people and resources (implying an ultimate concern for social welfare and environmental quality).

A more symmetrical analysis of contemporary types is depicted in Figure
3, with some rather arbitrary labels attached to characterize them.[13] These
groups are likely to perceive their security differently, but they also differ in
their security potential. Those with an engineering ethic are likely to feel less
and less secure over time, since short of constraints on the use of technology
they risk having neither the security of close relationships nor an adequate
resource environment to fall back on, given a dependence on non-renewable or
depletable resources. The residual traditionals may be the most secure, if
they can keep from being overrun by the developing world and the socialist de-

---

[13]This set does not include all possible combinations, for example,
$R_L \, T_L \, S_H$ and $R_H \, T_H \, S_L$; the former--low resource and technology evaluators--
might include members of non-materialistic religious sects, and the latter--
high resource and technology evaluators--might include scientists/engineers
dedicated to the preservation of environment at all costs; both groups require
some form of subsidy to survive.

R_L T_L S_L - "other-worldly"

R_H T_L S_L - eco-isolates (homestead mentality)

R_H T_L S_H - residual traditionals (eschew "progress")

R_L T_H S_L - engineering ethic

R_L T_H S_H - developing world

R_H T_H S_H - socialist democracies

Fig. 3.--Valuation types

mocracies; the latter have commitments to social welfare, and with denser populations and associated political vulnerability, are likely to be especially sensitive to inefficiencies in the use of any domestic environment, their respect for minority rights notwithstanding. Of the remainder, security for the eco-isolates is contingent on their remaining isolated; and for the "other worldly, " on their faith.

Implicit in all of this is a relationship between concerns for the security of subsistence, the survival or non-survival of certain populations, and the protection or preservation of environment; and since these are not always compatible, this raises the question of priorities. Concern for preserving environment implies a concept of the finiteness of resources, and this derives either from the experience of depletion, or from a sense--for whatever reason--of vulnerability to the forces and limits of nature. Aesthetics or morality (our obligations to nature) constitute a less compelling basis for a preservation ethic, since these appear to emphasize the welfare of the environment for the few versus the needs of subsistence for the many: aesthetics and obligations to nature can be compromised when the security of subsistence is at stake.

This issue of priorities, interestingly enough, also constitutes a basis for conflict between competing systems of altruism, which focus alternately on long-term and short-term social needs, the satisfaction of the one appearing to be at the expense or risk of the other. There is implicit too an almost unresolvable conflict between that altruism generated by a compassion for people and that directed instead toward nature. The welfare of nature seems to require a regulation and control that are contrary to the satisfaction of expanding human needs for land and resources; but others contend that a commitment to the preservation of what nature still remains is also necessary for man's survival.

Perhaps what is most surprising is that so few seem concerned about either the welfare of nature or the well-being of those who are in need, whether members of their own or others' societies. Curiously, we appear to have evolved out of a condition in which social obligations and social forms of altruism were viable group norms, at least partly selected for their survival value in an unpredictable environment. With increasing control over environment, altruism still persists, but with loss of its reciprocal value, it has become a random personality function instead.

In summary, I have attempted to include in a concept of subsistence security not only the elements of resource perception and technology, but also of subsistence sharing, based on a form of reciprocal altruism which involves obligated social relationships. I have elaborated on the environmental dimensions of such sharing relationships, and also on the impact of new technology on the maintenance of these relationships among traditional societies. An equally critical impact of technology was suggested for western societies, one which has been compounded by the effects of expansion into new ecological settings, where resource values and ecological well-being have too often been inversely related. In addition, I have outlined a system of differential valuation--of people, resources and technology--and of the security and survival implications of these, suggesting also that there are inherent conflicts in the assignment of priorities: between short-term and long-term social well-being, and between the welfare of people and the welfare of nature. As a final observation, I suggested that changes in the conditions selecting for altruism have affected both its form and distribution.

Altruism now exists primarily as a personal system of values; which is perhaps why we appear increasingly dependent, both for the welfare of environment and for society-at-large, on the activism of a few committed individuals, who are only variably consistent in the direction that their altruism leads them.

CHAPTER 3

NOMADIC ORGANIZATION OF SPACE:
REFLECTIONS ON PATTERNS AND PROCESS

Douglas L. Johnson
Clark University

Nomadism connotes aimless movement and random ordering of space. Jules Verne understood this well when he derived the name of his fictional character, Captain Nemo, from the Greek root for an unknown wanderer. For in popular imagination, be he pastoralist or merchant seaman, gypsy or hunter, the nomad is perceived to be a footloose and unpredictable individual, a fierce, independent, proud, and prickly personality capable of the ultimate in both hospitality and vindictiveness. At one and the same time the nomad is a social outcast and a rebel against the constricting confines of conventional behavior. Conventionally viewed as being rootless in space, free to come and go at will, the nomad elicits from more sedentary contacts an array of contradictory emotions ranging from romantic idolatry to a bewildered incomprehension that verges on outright hostility. Those seeking alternatives to industrialized society often find nomads attractive; a presumed propensity for antisocial behavior makes nomads anathema to tax collectors and their ilk. Yet neither contrasting perspective is particularly accurate.

Coming to grips with the essential nature of mobile livelihoods without exhibiting either excessive romanticism or uncritical bias has proven to be a formidable task. Those in the forefront of development planning often have viewed such mobile ways of life as pastoral nomadism from an urban, industrial perspective, have found them to be regressive, parasitic anachronisms best consigned to oblivion, and have urged their demise.[1] Re-evaluations of pastoral life styles in anthropology have taken an ecological perspective and

---

[1]Many of the articles in the International Social Science Journal, Vol. 60, 1959, special issue on nomadism exhibit this perspective.

have emphasized the nomad's rational perception and utilization of agriculturally marginal resources, [2] although some of the traditional fascination with the
romance of an austere life and its attenuated material culture continues. [3] Similar reappraisals analyze hunting societies, numerically minuscule but culturally significant mobile livelihoods. [4] Attempts to analyze mobile livelihoods
cross-culturally and comparatively have been infrequent, [5] perhaps because the
magnitude of such an integration is daunting. This paper focuses largely on pastoral nomads as an example of a sophisticated spatial organization, examines
the underlying principles that structure their spatial behavior, and suggests
how this structured universe facilitates their adaptation to the pressures and
opportunities of contemporary social and economic relationships.

Pattern in Pastoral Spatial Organization

While several approaches to understanding the spatial behavior of mobile
livelihoods have been followed, cartographic techniques have been particularly
favored in geographic studies. If a group moves through space over time as
part of its livelihood activities, a geographer's initial tendency is to map the
spatial movement patterns that result.

Use of cartographic analysis to investigate the migration pattern and ecological setting of pastoral nomads indicates that rationality and regularity characterize their organization of space. This runs counter to the conventional mys-
tique that pastoral nomads engage in aimless wandering. Yet within a general

---

[2] Two notable examples are Neville Dyson-Hudson and William Irons, eds.:
Perspectives on Nomadism (E. J. Brill, Leiden, 1972) and Brian Spooner: The
Cultural Ecology of Pastoral Nomads, Addison-Wesley Module in Anthropology
No. 45, 1973.

[3] Donald P. Cole: Nomads of the Nomads: The Al Murrah Bedouin of the
Empty Quarter (Aldine, Chicago, 1975) gives a flavor of a rapidly disappearing
way of life, while Shelagh Weir's The Bedouin: Aspects of the Material Culture
of the Bedouin of Jordan (World of Islam Festival Publishing Company Ltd.,
London, 1976) is a splendid text and photo account on which an exhibit at the
Museum of Mankind, London, is based.

[4] Richard B. Lee and Irven DeVore, eds.: Man the Hunter (Aldine, Chicago, 1968).

[5] A promising exception to this generalization is the recent examination of
shifting agriculturalists, pastoral nomads, and periodic market peddlars reported by Richard Symanski, Ian R. Manners and R. J. Bromley: The Mobile-
Sedentary Continuum, Annals, Association of American Geographers, Vol. 45,
1975, pp. 461-471.

framework of rational and explicable movement, considerable variation in pattern exists. This occurs because pastoral nomads, like all other traditional mobile livelihoods, exploit resource niches that are environmentally, socially, and, most generally, politically marginal. It is into the gaps in the system undesired or ignored by more favored groups that the mobile livelihoods insert themselves.

Pastoral nomads, for example, exist by exploiting seasonal grass and water resources that are too far removed spatially to be reached by more sedentary livelihood modes. The pastoral mode of production occupies the more arid end of a moisture gradient where the prospects for sedentary farming are highly localized and limited or are too variable and risk-prone to be subjected to continuous exploitation. Regular movement between dry-season well sites and seasonal rain-fed pastures underlies the nomadic pastoral adjustment. The specifics of routes followed, the regularity of areas visited, the amplitude of displacement undertaken, the ecological systems exploited, and the degree of contact with agriculturalists involved varies from group to group depending on the local setting. Detailed examination of twenty African and Southwest Asian pastoral groups suggests that three major patterns of nomadic adjustment can be discerned. [6]

Vertical Nomadism

Altitudinal variation in the seasonal occurrence of pasture and water results in a vertical pattern of nomadic spatial organization. Movement between winter pastures in the lower elevations and summer pastures in higher elevations characterizes this type. Wherever moisture conditions are relatively good and topographic relief considerable, the resulting patterns can be characterized as constricted-oscillatory. Figure 1A depicts this pattern in generalized form.

Seasonal movement between pastures at differing elevations is essential to the survival of the nomadic group. Herding sheep and goats for their basic subsistence, the nomads and their flocks would be unable to survive on the desiccated summer pastures of the lowlands or withstand the rigors of year-round exposure to the frigid temperatures of high altitude meadows. Not only are the highlands and lowlands too harsh for successful year-round exploitation, but

---

[6] Douglas L. Johnson: The Nature of Nomadism: A Comparative Study of Pastoral Migrations in Southwestern Asia and Northern Africa, University of Chicago, Department of Geography, Research Paper No. 118, 1969.

they also are seasonally productive environments. Movement between highland and lowland enables the pastoralist to exploit each area's best features while avoiding its worst. Where sedentarization has taken place, as much as 80 percent of the stock has been lost.[7] Yet these same animals, vulnerable as they are to conditions at the extremes of the environmental gradient exploited, are more productive than the animals kept by settled agriculturalists located throughout the pastoralist's range. Thus mobility constitutes a key ingredient in the pastoral nomad's ability to wrest a living from the resources at his disposal.

Movement between winter lowland and summer highland pastures is ecologically rational and astute as well as spatially regular. This regularity is based on the seasonal rhythm of spatial differentiation in available grass and water as well as on the constraining influence of topography. The existence of mountain passes and valleys serves to channel migrating herds and herders and to confine them to definite routes. But spatial regularity is a product of more than just physical environment; it also flows from a complex web of social relationships between pastoral groups of varying degrees of political and economic power as well as with the sedentary farming groups through which the migrating herds must move and with whom their masters are enmeshed. Pressure exerted by other mobile pastoral populations tends to hold any migrating community to a fairly rigid schedule, while well-defined regulations and customary law govern rights of passage, the timing of movements, and interaction with sedentary communities.

In exchange for dung, animals pasture on stubble in harvested village fields during the autumn return to winter pastures; seasonal wage labor in village agriculture, especially for poorer pastoralists, constitutes a welcome income supplement. Trade of animals and animal products for agricultural commodities constitutes an additional set of farmer-pastoralist linkages. Insufficient unto itself, these exchanges are essential to the well-being of constricted oscillatory nomads. Highly specialized producers of animals that assure basic nutrition, their ultimate survival is hostage to the economic forces and political strength of settled society. It is in response to such concerns that the highly evolved and integrated tribal structures of the altitudinal pastoralists have emerged, for only strong leadership effectively linked to the larger social and political environment can guarantee viability.

---

[7]Fredrik Barth: Nomads of South Persia: The Basseri Tribe of the Khamseh Confederacy (Humanities Press, New York, 1965), p. 6.

29

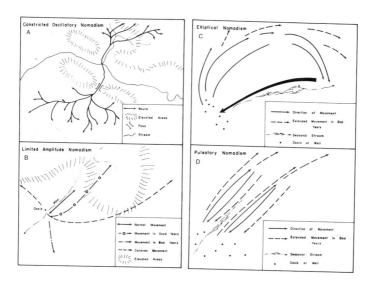

Fig. 1.--Generalized models of pastoral, nomadic spatial behavior. After Johnson, Nature of Nomadism, 1969 [see note 6].

Where environmental conditions are more extreme, this regular pattern of spatial organization loses its coherence. Livelihood activities become more diversified, the number of animal species herded increases, and the family, the basic production unit, scatters its labor across greater distances and more numerous activities. In most cases the entire family unit is only infrequently located in the same place. Oddly enough in a setting of ecologically limited opportunity, the basic subsistence unit moves over only short distances, usually within the confines of one valley system (Figure 1B). Altitudinal and seasonal variations still govern such migrations, but movement seldom exceeds forty kilometers. Milk producing herds (usually composed of the tough and resilient goat) remain close to the family tent, but the diet, except during the wetter parts of the year, remains heavily weighted toward grain and dates. These are obtained from neighboring oases where slaves traditionally labored to keep their mobile and noble masters in a nutritionally adequate state.

Superimposed on the limited movements of the subsistence herd are much longer range movements of the investment capital stock, often camels. Frequently these animals are kept far from the domestic herds and moved to highland pastures only during years with good precipitation. When conditions are bad such upslope movements are abandoned altogether[8] and the herds are shifted to more auspicious locales outside the normal tribal range. Reluctance to venture into the unknown under adverse conditions, and a predilection for concentrating on local resources, probably accounts for the heavy animal losses experienced under extreme drought conditions such as the recent Sahelian Drought.[9]

Extension of group activity into commercial ventures or, more recently, wage labor, is also an integral aspect of limited amplitude nomadism. Before the advent of modern transportation, guiding and protecting caravans, providing camels for them, and in some cases, such as the Tuareg salt trade, directly engaging in commercial ventures, were important to the economic structure of local adaptation. In the last several decades, work in the modern economy of developing countries as laborers has to some degree replaced the more manly machismo-building activities of trading and raiding. This predilection for a multiplicity of activities gives numerous options for increasing group stability, a sine qua non when local resources are limited.

Horizontal Nomadism

The absence of sharply contrasting topographic variation gives rise to different ecological conditions and lends itself to the development of a second set of characteristic pastoral adaptations. More flexible in their spatial arrangements than most vertical nomads, horizontal pastoralists move in diffuse and broad-scale patterns across the seasonal grasslands that form their rainy season pastures. Despite considerable dispersion a network of travelers and visitors dispenses information on kin, [10] custom, habit, and hereditary claim to

---

[8]Johannes Nicolaisen: Ecology and Culture of the Pastoral Tuareg, with Particular Reference to the Tuareg of Ahaggar and Ayr, Nationalmuseets Skrifter, Ethnografisk Roekke, No. 9 (National Museum, Copenhagen, 1963) and Kim Kramer: Valleys without Rain, Paper presented at the Geographical Conference, University of Benghazi, Faculty of Arts, 15-25 March 1975.

[9]For a more complete discussion of this issue, consult Douglas L. Johnson: The Response of Pastoral Nomads to Drought in the Absence of Outside Intervention (United Nations Special Sahelian Office, New York, 19 December 1973).

[10]The importance of this type of social linkage, and the thirst of desert deni-

resources that bring herders to familiar territories, if not precisely to the same pasture, year after year. Knowledge of resource availability and potential is widespread and aggressively acted upon. The scattered nature of precipitation, whether monsoonal[11] or cyclonic[12] in character, encourages a mobile regime stressing opportunistic behavior finely tuned to the vagaries of locally available pasture and water. A dearth of rainfall during much of the remainder of the year necessitates concentration around permanent water sources. Alternation between extreme concentration during the dry season, with attendant excessive grazing pressure on the local environment, and great dispersion during much of the rainy period gives horizontal nomadism a somewhat schizophrenic character.

Two variants on this theme, elliptical (Figure 1C) and pulsatory (Figure 1D), can be distinguished. The elliptical type occurs in special circumstances where the return to dry season grazing generally follows a well-defined route, often a seasonal stream bed, along which secure water supplies can be found in an otherwise rapidly desiccating environment. In both patterns migration is more a direction than a sharply defined route and great interannual variation occurs in length of displacement and the specific pastures being grazed. In general, the worse the grazing conditions in a given year, the more likely it is that the herder will move outside traditional pasture zones. Despite the existence of considerable flexibility in the basic pattern, regularity is found in broad terms and certain fixed points, especially dry season wells, constitute regular points of call for herders navigating the vaguely delimited spaces of their terrestrial seas.

---

izens for information about friends, foes and relations, not to mention stock market quotations from the tribal market town, is graphically portrayed by Cole, op. cit. [note 3], pp. 45 ff.

[11]The complexity and rationality of movements of this type (under monsoonal conditions) engaged in by one large group of Sudanese pastoralists is well illustrated in Talal Asad: Seasonal Movements of the Kababish Arabs of Northern Kordofan, Sudan Notes and Records, Vol. 45, 1964, pp. 48-58.

[12]Carl Raswan: Tribal Areas and Migration Lines of the North Arabian Bedouins, Geographical Review, Vol. 20 (1930), pp. 494-502, gives a clear picture of this type of interlocking tribal areas and migration patterns.

Complex Nomadism

Inevitably some pastoral adjustments exist that cannot be squeezed conveniently into these topographical categories. Either because they represent aberrent adjustments or because they interweave elements of several livelihoods, such groups offer problems for the classifier. These groups often place great reliance on agricultural activities as a major focus of their livelihood system. The Beni Mguild of Morocco's Middle Atlas constitute one example of this pattern. Here two constricted oscillatory movements are combined into one basic pattern of movement (Figure 2). In autumn herds are moved across the Middle Atlas to winter pastures on the Atlantic slopes. Their return to the Moulouya Valley in spring as soon as the snow melts from the mountain passes represents one constricted-oscillatory cycle. Agricultural holdings in the Moulouya provide the rationale for this movement, but because available water is devoted to agricultural crops there is insufficient pasture to support existing herds. This provides the impetus for a second constricted-oscillatory movement into the high alpine pastures of the Atlas each summer with a return in the early autumn to participate in the harvest and to graze stock on field stubble. Whether such mixed agro-pastoral modes, with their complicated mobility patterns and complex, spatially-diffuse employment of available labor resources, constitute a stable adjustment or a transitory halfway house on the road to a more conventional sedentary existence, is perhaps open to debate. Nonetheless, recent scholarship[13] indicates that such adaptations may be more permanent and widespread than generally supposed and may be eminently rational solutions to the need for reduced vulnerability in hazardous environments.

---

[13]Rada Dyson-Hudson: Pastoralism: Self Image and Behavioral Reality, in Perspectives on Nomadism (edited by Neville Dyson-Hudson and William Irons; E. J. Brill, Leiden, 1972), pp. 30-37, and Philip C. Salzman: Multi-Resource Nomadism in Iranian Baluchistan, ibid., pp. 60-68, present convincing evidence arguing for the long-term stability of mixed livelihood systems in which pastoral values predominate despite the importance of other activities. An instructive instance in which the bulk of the diet is provided by agriculture, but where the paramount symbol of value is cattle (the basic insurance against the omnipresent risk of drought), is provided by Peter Rigby: Cattle and Kinship among the Gogo, a Semi-pastoral Society of Central Tanzania (Cornell University Press, Ithaca and London, 1969).

33

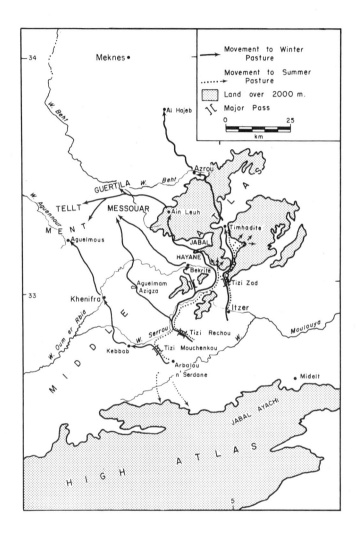

Fig. 2.--Migration cycle of the Beni Mguild, Middle Atlas,
Morocco. After Johnson, Nature of Nomadism, 1969 [see note 6].

Analogies in Other Livelihoods

Analogous spatial patterns can be observed in other livelihood systems. Spencer[14] notes several distinct patterns in the spatial behavior of shifting agriculturalists. One of these, circular migration, is shown in Figure 3. In this type of shifting agriculture movement takes place within a bounded territory and, as is suggested in the figure, the second sequence of clearing may often be located close to the previous set of clearings. As in all shifting agricultural systems, maintenance of viable production requires lengthy fallow periods but residence need not be shifted. Indeed, in this variant house clusters often retain residential preeminence and permanence while the fields move around the village. Nomadic behavior is then restricted to seasonal oscillation to the fields during growth and harvest periods, although the pattern bears a close resemblance to that of elliptical nomadism.

Hunters and gatherers also frequently move in a regular pattern. The Kung Bushmen studied by Lee[15] show a remarkable oscillatory pattern (Figure 4). This involves wet season movements to temporary water holes, establishment of camps near these regular seasonal supplies, and then a return to the permanent water site when seasonal drought takes effect. Occasional long distance forays in pursuit of wild game are engaged in by the men, but most activity is concentrated within a six mile walk from the waterhole. This limited territory is both conceptually and functionally bound, for longer distance collecting expeditions require overnight stays away from base camp, involve difficulties in acquiring adequate water supplies, and result in increased expenditures of energy to food input acquired. At some point mobility becomes undesirable because the rewards no longer justify the effort. Just as in the constricted-oscillatory nomadism of pastoralists, movement to wet-season waterholes increases the range of resources exploited and reduces pressure on resources that are essential to survival during moisture deficient periods.

Further analogs exist in other livelihoods. Peddlars and merchants frequenting periodic markets follow a regular round, visiting a fixed array of sites arranged in a regular spatial pattern. Gypsies revisit particular places at pre-

---

[14] Joseph E. Spencer: Shifting Cultivation in Southeastern Asia, University of California, Publications in Geography, No. 19, 1966, p. 144.

[15] Richard B. Lee: !Kung Bushman Subsistence: An Input-output Analysis, in Environment and Cultural Behavior (edited by Andrew P. Vayda; The Natural History Press, Garden City, N.Y., 1969), pp. 47-79.

35

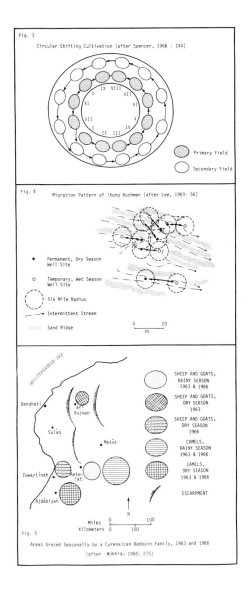

Fig. 3.--Circular shifting cultivation. Modified after
Spencer, Shifting Cultivation in Southeastern Asia, 1966
⌈see note 14⌉. Fig. 4.--Migration pattern of !Kung Bushmen. Modified after Lee, !Kung Bushman Subsistence,
1969 ⌈see note 15⌉. Fig. 5.--Areas grazed seasonally by a
Cyrenaican Bedouin family, 1963 and 1966. Modified after
Kikhia, Le nomadisme pastorale en Cyrenaique septentrionale, 1968 ⌈see note 22⌉.

dictable intervals, merchant seamen generally oscillate between ports of call along fixed sea lanes, migrant agricultural workers follow harvests northward through America's rural districts, and, somewhat facetiously, junior executives engage in a lifelong migratory existence that may differ more in timing and scale than in fundamental substance from the patterns of their pastoral cousins.

Process in Pastoral Spatial Organization

The five pastoral nomadic types (and their analogies in other livelihoods), as developed on the basis of their cartographic pattern, are ecological in a strict and limited environmental sense. They represent a generalized pattern of spatial behavior that reflects seasonal variation in the distribution of surface and accessible groundwater, available annual and perennial vegetation, topographic features, temperature considerations, the grazing or browsing potential of domesticated livestock, and mechanisms for acquiring needed agricultural foodstuffs. They do not begin to suggest the wider and more social and economic context of a pastoral community, issues that often are the focus of inquiry in anthropology[16] and that are essential components in any complete understanding of pastoral life and nomadic spatial behavior.[17]

---

[16] For a succinct and perceptive review of these features of nomadic life consult Brian Spooner: The Cultural Ecology of Pastoral Nomads, Addison-Wesley Module in Anthropology No. 45, 1973.

[17] Moreover, as gross generalizations such patterns obscure the distinction between average patterns under presumed normal conditions and the marked departures in spatial behavior that accompany sudden environmental fluctuations or the shorter-cycle movement patterns of herds that take place around dry season well sites. They offer no insight into the resource-use decision-making process engaged in by pastoralists, a topic only remotely understood in many pastoral societies for whom we have much more detailed analyses of kinship ties and marriage patterns than we do of basic energetics and resource-use efficiency. Even the rationale behind herd management practices is only beginning to be elucidated by the seminal studies of Gudren Dahl and Anders Hjort: Having Herds: Pastoral Herd Growth and Household Economy, Stockholm Studies in Social Anthropology No. 2, 1976; Anthony C. Picardi and Willaim W. Seifert: A Tragedy of the Commons in the Sahel, Technology Review, Vol. 78, No. 6, 1976, pp. 1-10. Moreover as is pointed out by Randall Baker: The Sahel: An Information Crisis, Disasters, Vol. 1, No. 1, 1977, pp. 13-22, we lack basic understandings of both the pathways along which energy flows occur and the efficiency with which pastoral nomads utilize the energy present in their environment. Despite recent indications that pastoralists may be willing to shift to agricultural pursuits, an observation highlighted in a recent baseline survey of settlement patterns and sedentarization by Ahmed A. Shamekh: Spatial Patterns of Bedouin Settlement in al-Qasim Region Saudi Arabia (Univer-

Fundamental Principles Underlying
Pattern and Governing Process

It is possible to identify several fundamental principles that underlie the patterns of nomadic spatial organization and suggest the direction of potential change and adaptation in nomadic societies. These principles are mobility, flexibility, diversity, centrality, and adaptability. Taken together they constitute a framework that enables the nomad to utilize resources that are too marginal to be exploited by other livelihood modes.

Mobility is perhaps the fundamental characteristic of nomadic societies. To this overwhelming necessity all other aspects of nomadic culture are subordinated. Mobility is ecologically conditioned, since it is the need to balance spatially-variable supplies of water and grass that are at the root of the pastoral nomadic adaptation. This feature of nomadic life is best represented by the generalized topology described in the previous sections, but some of the features of nomadic society that flow from this principle are not hinted at in a cartographic pattern.

The fact of mobility and a specialized concentration on animal production means that most pastoral communities are unable by themselves to produce the agricultural products that are the major year-long components of their diet. For the grain and dates, the rice and noodles, as well as the essential material objects and luxury foods (tea, sugar, coffee), the nomad is dependent on others. Thus an element of fundamental instability is a perpetual part of the pastoral adaptation. In situations where pastoralists have been able to dominate agriculturalists, for instance date cultivators in isolated oases, agricultural products are easily obtained. Although many nomadic groups may engage in agricultural activities, and these farming practices may determine much of the specifics of individual family movement, [18] concern for pastoral pursuits is always predominant. Only animals represent a secure investment for the exploiter of agriculturally marginal lands, and only by mobility can these resources be successfully utilized. Any shift in the balance of power between nomad and sedentary

sity of Kentucky, Lexington, Department of Geography, 1975), we still operate with a model that assumes all pastoralists everywhere are opposed to engaging directly in agriculture.

[18]See, for example, Salzman, op. cit. [note 13], pp. 60-68, and Douglas L. Johnson: Jabal al-Akhdar, Cyrenaica: An Historical Geography of Settlement and Livelihood, University of Chicago, Department of Geography, Research Paper No. 148, 1973, pp. 47-66.

in favor of the settled community invariably places the nomad in a precarious position for it both reduces the pastoralist's competitive advantage and constricts the mobility essential to survival.

Ideological values reinforce the importance of mobility in nomadic livelihood. In the nomad's self-conception, mobility is the equivalent of freedom, of austere but satisfying living, and of physical superiority over sedentary populations. Spooner[19] argues that in addition other values prominent in nomadic ideology--hospitality, realism and pragmatism, oral communicativeness, and an absence of religious ritual--can be traced to the cultural implications of mobility.

Moreover, the nomad, despite returning periodically to the same dry season well sites, is far less place specific and locale conscious than a farmer or village dweller. Animals, rather than land, are the nomadic pastoralist's central interest; if home is where the heart is, then for the nomad home is a mobile space located wherever tent and herd are. This symbolically boundless territory is, of course, circumscribed by a network of political and power relationships that sets the variable outer limits within which the nomad circulates. Further constraints are established whenever clan or individual invests capital in land, wells, cisterns, and similar infrastructure. But the "rootless" image of the nomad is more than idle fancy. It accurately describes a lack of attachment to terrestrial space.

The implications of this lack of identity with place are considerable. To some it results in environmental deterioration. In this view, the nomadic propensity to graze fully the available vegetation of an area before moving on to fresh pastures builds in a mechanism for overexploitation.[20] In contrast, other observers report examples of restraint in resources use as an integral part of pastoral systems. Kramer[21] reports that among the Tibu of Tibesti "valley

---

[19]Spooner, op. cit. ⌐note 16⌐, pp. 35ff.

[20]Spooner, op. cit. ⌐note 16⌐, p. 37. This tendency causes few long-term problems until, as Lee Talbot demonstrates in : Ecological Consequences of Rangeland Management in Masailand, East Africa, in The Careless Technology: Ecology and International Development (edited by M. Taghi Farvar and John P. Milton; Natural History Press, New York, 1972), pp. 694-711, disease and water constraints that operate in the traditional system to restrain excessive herd size are removed and new technological and managerial systems are only partially, and in many cases catastrophically, integrated into the traditional system.

[21]Kim Kramer: Valleys without Rain, Paper presented at the Geography of Libya Conference, University of Benghazi, Faculty of Arts, March 15-21, 1975.

guardians" restrict the frequency with which acacia trees are cut for forage during drought periods in order to prevent overuse, thus establishing upper limits on herd size. While the environmental implications of the nomad's lack of concern for land remain controversial, the subject of fruitful future research, there seems little doubt that it is the product of mobility engendered by a focus on animals as a device for converting otherwise marginal and unexploitable resources.

The fine tuning of a pastoral system is provided by the flexibility embedded in, and hidden by, observed average conditions. Maintenance of flexibility is an essential prerequisite in all pastoral systems since only in this way can the herding unit respond efficiently to departures from average conditions. It is a fundamental feature of dry land ecosystems that departures from the "normal" are more frequent than are the statistical normal or average conditions themselves. Interannual variations in rainfall and grazing conditions can only be coped with effectively if the herding unit retains sufficient flexibility to react to and exploit the new circumstances successfully.

Figure 5 suggests that the most common mechanism for coping with fluctuations in the environment is to change location. Most often it is the basic family unit with its subsistence herd that reacts to the deterioration of conditions by moving to dependable water resources. More rugged animals, such as camels, are invaluable in such situations. They permit the nomad to retain some stock in impoverished districts and to reduce grazing pressure around dry season wells. The network of kinship, marriage, and political relationships maintained by an individual herder or clan are crucial in this regard. These social linkages provide access to resources as well as labor supplies that ensure survival during hard times. Even in Kikhia's data, [22] where hired shepherds frequently are used to care for herds left outside the normal dry season pastures, every effort is made to secure assistance from individuals who can be comprehended within the kinship system. The combination of non-related individuals

---

Similar features are noted by Cole, loc. cit. [note 3], p. 35, who describes a finely tuned pastoral system in the Empty Quarter of Saudi Arabia that consciously avoids overstocking, and Omar Draz: Range Management and Fodder Development: Report to the Government of the Syrian Arab Republic, TA 34-92, Food and Agricultural Organization of the United Nations, Rome, 1974, who argues that traditional Hima (protection) areas can form the basis for successful cooperative development in the rangelands of Syria and much of the Middle East.

[22] Mansour M. Kikhia: Le nomadisme pastorale en Cyrenaique septentrionale (La Pensée Universitaire, Aix-en-Provence, 1968), pp. 268ff.

in a camping unit is also a reflection of the need to provide adequate labor to fulfill livelihood needs. Fissioning of such groups permits labor recombinations whenever social conditions change or conflict and disagreement becomes too extreme. Placing animals with stock-friends[23] is another device for supporting other nomads and for making sure that reserves are available in different districts that can be called on in case of need.

These ties also are essential if nomads are to have access to resources in secure, above-average conditions or are to be able to utilize abundant resources that normally fall outside a group's range. Political power relationships traditionally have governed access to pasture and water under such conditions. Boundaries seldom are firmly fixed, although the social and military pecking order is well defined. Permission asked is usually permission granted except in conditions of extreme scarcity, but failure to observe the niceties of polite discourse in such matters is frequently the basis of violent conflict and prolonged feud.

In these circumstances the precise location of a pastoral group in space, and determination of the territorial range occupied in a given year, is an ambiguous enterprise. The more variable the environment, the less rigid the spatial constraints placed on individual and group behavior. Even in relatively secure habitats, such as the Jabal al-Akhḍar upland of eastern Libya, where tribal and clan boundaries are rather precisely defined, the southern end of each tribal territory is devoid of boundary; controlled space can be extended as far as the group concerned has either inclination, ability, or need.[24]

If the flexibility inherent in pastoral nomadism encourages the development of a territorial space with vague outer limits, the diversity principle embedded in pastoral systems stimulates the fragmenting of that space into a se-

---

[23] Anders Hjört: Constraints on Pastoralism in Drylands, in Can Desert Encroachment Be Stopped? A Study with Emphasis on Africa (edited by A. Rapp, H. N. Le Houérou and B. Lundholm), Ecological Bulletins No. 24 (Stockholm, 1976), p. 72.

[24] Johnson, op. cit. (1973) [note 18], pp. 29-39. The intricately divided Zagros Mountains of western Iran provide another instance of this territorial fuzziness. Here tribes do not control solid blocks of territory linking summer and winter pastures, for substantial zones are occupied by sedentary agriculturalists whose activities and space interpenetrate the realm of the nomad. Barth (op. cit. [note 7], p. 5) points out that in these settings nomads claim rights of passage through space in an orderly sequence in tandem with other mobile groups rather than uphold an exclusive ownership of territory. Except for the claim to summer pastures, territory accompanies the moving band. This moveable territory is a mental construct surrounding the nomad during seasonal migrations rather than a rigidly defined segment of terrestrial space.

ries of discrete segments. Engaging in a multiplicity of activities is a device
whereby nomads cope with the risk present in the environmental and political
context in which they must operate. Vulnerability to sudden reductions in
environmental productivity is countered by maintaining mixed species herds.
The nomad herding goats for subsistence, sheep for capital accumulation and
eventual sale, and camels as a hedge against drought is attempting to strike a
balance between security and speculative return. The much maligned reluctance of sub-Saharan nomads to sell or consume cattle, utilizing sheep and goats
for this purpose instead, is rational in this context; few individuals are willing
to sell the family jewels unless under extreme duress.

Similarly, direct involvement in agricultural production is a common feature of many nomadic societies. In many pastoral communities one part of the
family is involved in nomadic activities, while another "shepherds" the fields
or date palms. Such activities, and particularly the exchange of products between the two economic components, are unlikely to appear in generalized cartographic patterns of group movement. [25] Beneath the facade of group stability,
component personnel are likely to be widely scattered in space, pursuing a variety of different activities that contribute to the well-being of the group. Some
of these activities, such as harvesting grain or watering animals at dry season
wells, are very place-specific. Others, for example late rainy-season camel
herding in the desert fringes, are likely to be governed by the vagaries of available resources and are quite imprecise in both time and space. This emphasis
on exploitation of a diverse array of resources introduces complexity into the
livelihood form and multi-dimensional ordering of space.

The existence of a multi-faceted, flexible spatial organization does not
imply random, aimless behavior. Not only does the ecological basis of the
nomadic lifestyle encourage a regularized and repetitive mobility, but it also
places a premium upon preservation of an identity with certain points that are
fixed in space. This insistence on a centralizing element is the fourth principle
of the nomadic ordering of space.

Numerous examples of this centrality principle could be cited. Concentration of herds and herders around dry season wells is, perhaps, centrality's
most obvious expression. Periodic return from a wider range of seasonal activ-

---

[25]The caravan activities and salt trading engaged in by Tuareg and other
desert pastoralists are an additional instance. An incidental benefit of such
long-term male absences may well be reduction in the nomadic birth rate vis-à-
vis that of settled farmers.

ities helps to affirm group identity. Even more important in this regard are the tombs of holy men that serve as an identity focus for clan and tribe. Sanctified by their association with especially holy individuals, whose spirituality and superior access to divine blessing conferred authority during life, such sacred spots serve as celestial beacons brought to earth in the cosmology of the nomadic pastoralist.[26] Market towns fulfill similar albeit less metaphysical roles. Because such sites represent a set of linkages defining relationships between nomad and farmer, they serve as essential contact points while the livelihood is mobile, and as loci for settlement when changing conditions promote sedentarization.[27]

The Dynamics of Change

The principles that undergird the nomadic ordering of space are subtle, sophisticated, and astute, albeit seldom appreciated. The patterns developed from these principles are not immutable, frozen in time and space. Rather they are capable of sudden and drastic transformation as well as slower paced evolutionary development. Nomadic livelihoods not only survive by coping successfully with a wide range of physical environmental fluctuations, but they also are forced to respond to major changes in their social, economic, and political milieu. These pressures have increased in the middle decades of the twentieth century and nomads have exhibited a remarkable, although generally poorly understood and underresearched, ability to adapt positively to the new opportunities available. Often the result is an abandonment of activities that are labor-demanding and arduous, and a shift of family resources to exploit new niches.[28]

---

[26]These sacred sites often serve as the focus of a clan pilgrimage once each year, during which group identity is reaffirmed. In a very influential statement, Emrys Peters: The Proliferation of Segments in the Lineage of the Bedouin of Cyrenaica, Journal of the Royal Anthropological Institute, Vol. 90, 1960, pp. 29-53, demonstrates that failure to perform this obligatory obeisance to communal values and identity symbolizes the division of a lineage into potentially hostile units. Divisions in territory are inextricably tied up in such fissioning, and space is reordered to take account of the new set of social and political relationships.

[27]Daniel G. Bates: Shepherd Becomes Farmer: A Study of Sedentarization and Social Change in Southeastern Turkey, in Turkey: Geographic and Social Perspectives (edited by Peter Benedict, Erol Turnertekin and Fatma Mansur; E. J. Brill, Leiden, 1974), pp. 92-123.

[28]Douglas L. Johnson and Farron Vogel Roboff: Alternative Futures for Pastoral Peoples. Wingspread Conference Background Paper, Racine, Wisconsin, 19-22 October 1975.

Several aspects of the pre-adapted willingness to change merit attention because they both affect and are themselves conditioned by the principles of nomadic spatial behavior.

Perhaps the most universal trend characterizing change in nomadic populations is increased sedentarization. Government encouragement of settlement is a major factor but such developments often occur spontaneously. These spatial changes are associated with rapid movement into new occupations made available by expanding economic opportunities in many developing countries.[29]

The dimensions of this shift in livelihood support are indicated by the genealogy of a family that once was engaged exclusively in nomadic pastoralism (Figure 6). Formerly herding a mixture of camels, sheep and goats, the family engaged in a variety of herding and agricultural activities. Their pattern of movement was quite complex, with different species being herded in different parts of the family's range at the same time during the year. Dispersion was particularly widespread during the rainy season, changes in anticipated grazing areas were common on an interannual basis, depending on local grazing conditions, while agricultural activities played an important, although supplementary, role in the family economy and migration pattern. Emphasis on the diversity and flexibility principles in the traditional system prepared the way for a rapid alteration in the extended family's livelihood system when Libya experienced its oil boom in the 1960's.

Labor that formerly would have been invested in camel-herding was rapidly withdrawn and applied to urban-based activities. This change was widespread in the pastoral community and reduced the number of camels herded by one-half.[30] Other family members found administrative jobs in the university and the department of agriculture, while two family members went abroad to study for doctoral degrees. Those males uninterested in or unsuccessful in the educational system found less spectacular employment in the military, police,

---

[29]This adaptive process is best observed in the oil rich states of the Middle East. In a provocative recent study, Cole, loc. cit. [note 3], pp. 108, 112ff., indicates that the al-Murrah bedouin of southern Saudi Arabia, in common with many other Saudi tribes, provide personnel for a unit in the National Guard. Not only does this regularize, control, and legitimize the traditional bedouin predilection for military activities, but it also provides a secure income to participating individuals and families. Since animals are usually maintained in the care of relatives, the result is probably a net increase in income.

[30]United Nations, Economic Commission for Africa: Summaries of Economic Data, Libya, Sixth Year, No. 21, 1975, pp. 5-6.

or less-skilled urban work force. For women, the changes were less rapid since tradition assigns a limited role outside domestic affairs. But even in this area movement of younger girls into the educational system indicates that change is operating, albeit at a slower pace. Few males remained in traditionally pastoral pursuits or districts, but those who did continued to maintain an active interest in the animal economy. In this case the main activity is supervising hired shepherds and monitoring the animal market to determine the most advantageous moment for sales. Because it is exceedingly difficult to monitor the flow of capital between the traditional livestock sector and the modern economy and vice versa, it is hard to evaluate the total effect of this transformation process on social well-being. Measured in visible material terms the signs of prosperity seem obvious. Social solidarity continues to be maintained in large part because the traditional principles of resource use are being applied successfully in altered circumstances, but whether the system can withstand the stress of population growth and socioeconomic change awaits further study.

In other respects the adaptive changes taking place may be less positive, although evidence is as yet too limited for firm conclusions. Households remaining in rangeland have become increasingly sedentary, generally around dry-season sites, with resulting increases in pressure year-round on pasture within a limited radius of the well. Changes in residence from tent to house reflect the increasing importance of the centrality principle to the exclusion of mobility and foreshadow the environmental effects of decreased mobility noted in other parts of the Middle East.[31] The diminution of movement inevitably culminates in increased deterioration in the productivity of local environments.

Paralleling the decline in camel numbers has been an increase in the Libyan sheep population from 1,678,000 in 1967 to 2,400,000 in 1973.[32] Production has been concentrated on species that are vulnerable to drought and that can only use semiarid grassland environments. Browse utilized by camels, and to a lesser extent goats, is underexploited. Deterioration in range quality is a potential threat under such circumstances, a degradational process that is referred to in current parlance as desertification. This process is enhanced by traditional pastoral values that place primary emphasis on animals as expressions

---

[31]F. Fraser Darling and Mary A. Farvar: Ecological Consequences of Sedentarization of Nomads, in The Careless Technology: Ecology and International Development (edited by M. Taghi Farvar and John P. Milton; Natural History Press, New York, 1972), pp. 671-682.

[32]United Nations, op. cit. [note 30], pp. 4-6.

45

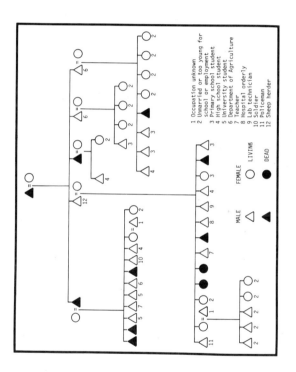

Fig. 6. --Changing occupation in a former Bedouin family.

of productivity, as symbols of wealth, as a guarantee of survival during adverse environmental conditions, and as the medium through which venture capital is invested and multiplied. The traditional nomadic willingness to seize short term opportunity and to vary spatial behavior to suit the constraints and potentials of both internal and external milieu support increasing commercialization of animal production. Technological solutions (such as aerial reseeding) to the problem of declining range quality may solve the problem in the short term, although with presently unforeseeable long-term consequences.[33]

Changes in pastoral spatial arrangements can have positive results as well. This is particularly true where traditional nomadic concepts of space and resource use have been utilized as the building blocks for pastoral cooperatives that attempt to meet changing economic and social needs.[34] In Mongolia these take traditional pastoral ethnoscience and develop it in ways that support the new socialist order. Traditional patterns of mobility within a bounded group space remain the bedrock of the system. Rapid movement of a number of animal species across pasture was a feature of the traditional regime that prevented excessive concentrations of animals and the overgrazing that frequently results. Diverse herds of sheep, goats, horses, cattle, and camels moving to distant pastures were maintained to fully exploit available vegetation, although herds were organized in larger units and on a more specialized basis. Great efforts were made to remove constraints in the traditional system by providing fodder reserves for the winter months, developing supplemental agriculture, and providing shelters in order to reduce herd losses due to winter cold. The result was a more productive pastoral economic sector, and a set of flexible spatial arrangements that combined better provision of social services at central points with seasonal exploitation of distant pastures.[35]

---

[33]Certainly removal of traditional constraints to animal numbers by the introduction of technological inputs has, in the absence of effective control, resulted in serious problems elsewhere (e.g. Talbot, loc. cit. [note 20], p. 8).

[34]Caroline Humphrey: Pastoral Nomadism in Mongolia: The Role of Herdsmen's Cooperatives in the National Economy, MS presented at the United Nations Graduate Study Program, Geneva, 26 July-6 August 1976.

[35]Similar attempts to use traditional pastoral principles as the basis of development undergird rangeland development in Syria. Here nomadic concepts of hima (protection) have been reapplied to pastoral cooperatives. Traditionally tribes protected grazing areas and restricted access to these rangelands in such a way that overstocking was prevented and pasture deterioration was avoided. Coupled with the use of seasonal patterns of mobility, this system has been extended successfully to some 1.5 million hectares of rangeland

These efforts to utilize traditional ethnoscience and spatial organization to establish viable production systems have been successful because they apply traditional nomadic principles and processes, but not patterns, to development needs. Sensitivity to the processes embedded in and producing pastoral patterns is a key ingredient. Yet many fundamental aspects of process and change within pastoral communities remain either relative or absolute mysteries. Little is known about the physical health and well-being of traditional pastoral groups, the terms of trade governing their exchanges with sedentarists, the labor requirements of nomadic systems, their productivity and efficiency relative to other exploitive systems, or the degree of resilience and adaptability that they contain. These, and related topics, seem essential to a full understanding of the process of change within pastoral and other mobile livelihoods. However, it would appear that a flexible and pragmatic organization of space that is more mental construct than bounded reality seems to assist nomadic communities to organize a structured spatial universe and to cope with rapid change.

---

with very promising results. For a full account of the project, consult Omar Draz: The Role of Range Management in the Campaign against Desertification: The Syrian Experience as an Applicable Example for the Arabian Peninsula, UNCOD/MICS/13, Paper prepared for the Regional Preparatory Meeting for the Mediterranean Area, International Cooperation to Combat Desertification, Algarve, Portugal, 28 March-1 April 1977.

CHAPTER 4

LANDSCAPE IN ART

Ronald Rees
University of Saskatchewan

In "The Stones of Venice" Ruskin[1] distinguishes between the domains of science and art. To art belongs the immeasurable, the intangible, and the indivisible--whatever is of the spirit. Science, by contrast, embraces whatever can be measured, handled, or demonstrated--whatever is of the body only. Few geographers would quibble with this distinction. The core of geography lies well within the scientific domain. But as the range of geographical inquiry extends to include the nature of man as well as his works, increasing numbers of geographers are being drawn away from the solid center of the discipline into J. K. Wright's[2] peripheral zone of "informal geography." Here they scan non-scientific sources for information and ideas that might elucidate the human relationship with environment. One such source is landscape painting. What follows is an examination of ways in which landscape painting mediates between us and our surroundings, affecting our views of the world and the nature of our relationship with it.

In the discussion leading up to his definition of art and science, Ruskin[3] defines the role of the artist. His whole function in the world, he asserts, is to be a seeing and a feeling creature, intimating that those of us who are not artists do not see or feel enough. At other times[4] he was more direct, saying

---

[1]John Ruskin: The Stones of Venice (3 vols.; George Allen, London, 1903), Vol. 3, pp. 61-62.

[2]J. K. Wright: Human Nature in Geography (Harvard University Press, Cambridge, Mass., 1966), p. 81.

[3]Ruskin, op. cit. [see note 1 above], p. 49.

[4]John Ruskin: Modern Painters (5 vols.; George Allen, London, 1900-1904), Vol. 4, p. 76.

unequivocally that we never see anything clearly. Ruskin's misgivings about
the capacity of ordinary vision were later reinforced by artists, critics and
experimental scientists. In one of the better known statements, art critic Roger Fry[5] maintained that we normally see by means of a visual shorthand, reading only the labels, or identifying features on the objects around us and trou-
bling no further. Eyes, as Fry put it, were designed to see with not to look at
things, adding that "biologically speaking art is a blasphemy." Yet pictures,
being unusual, belong to the small class of objects that we do look at and, ironically, they clarify our vision and extend its range.

Painting and the Sense of Sight

New Eyes. What is, appears. Go out to walk with a painter, and you shall
see for the first time groups, colors, clouds and keepings, and shall have
the pleasure of discovering resources in a hitherto barren ground, of finding
as good as a new sense in such skill to use an old one.[6] (Ralph Waldo Emerson)

Paintings elucidate first by temporarily isolating us from the flux of life
and by addressing themselves to our sight alone. Pictorial space is not the
space in which we live and act; it is virtual, not experiential space. As a semblance, or an illusion, it has power over our perceptions. Undistracted by the
claims of life, we look at it with a concentration that we rarely bestow on the
landscape. In paintings, thanks to what Bernard Berenson[7] called the ex-
quisitely naive device of making objects visible no matter how diminished in
size, our eyes traverse space without strain and with no loss of visual clarity.
Paintings give the feeling, said Berenson, that at last one has got into the right
kind of world. More sharply defined than the actual world, it is also, being
smaller, more easily understood. Losses in sensible dimension bring gains in
intelligibility, quantitative reduction suggesting qualitative simplification.[8]
Thus Wordsworth's[9] pleasure in Rubens' "Landscape with Steen Castle":

---

[5]Roger Fry: Vision and Design [1920] (Penguin Books, Harmondsworth,
Middlesex, 1961), p. 29.

[6]E. W. Emerson and W. E. Forbes: Journals of Ralph Waldo Emerson
(10 vols.; Houghton and Mifflin, New York, 1909-1914), Vol. 4, p. 321.

[7]Bernard Berenson: Seeing and Knowing (Chapman and Hall, London, 1953),
p. 4.

[8]See Claude Levi-Strauss: The Savage Mind (University of Chicago Press,
Chicago, 1962), p. 63.

[9]Quoted in Martha Hale Shackford: Wordsworth's Interest in Painters and

He has brought, as it were, a whole County into one Landscape, and made the most [of] formal partitions of cultivation; hedgerows of pollard willows conduct the eye into the depths and distances of his picture; and thus, more than by any other means, has given it that appearance of immensity which is so striking.

In a landscape painting, as in most representational models, reduction of scale requires selection of detail. Selection is a simplifying process that heightens perception. Truman Capote[10] explains how it works:

Reflected reality is the essence of reality, the truer truth. When I was a child I played a pictorial game. I would, for example, observe a landscape: trees and clouds and horses wandering in the grass; then select a detail from the overall vision--say grass bending in the breeze--and frame it with my hands. Now this detail became the essence of the landscape and caught, in prismatic miniature, the true atmosphere of a panorama too sizeable to encompass otherwise. . . . All art is composed of selected detail.

In a painting the selected details are arranged over a given space within an arbitrary frame. A painting is a pattern of relationships, and a successful painting is one in which the parts are so related that they create a convincing whole. Constable[11] said that art must remind, or suggest; it cannot imitate. Since a painter can rarely hope to reproduce detail with accuracy, the truth of landscape painting is relative; so long as a painting looks natural, said Herbert Read,[12] it is natural. As a guide to the nature of the objective world paintings are obviously unreliable, even in those cases where the artists have aimed at literal truth. Yet despite errors of fact, paintings can look more natural than photographs. C. Day Lewis[13] tells that when looking at a book of colored photographs he found the subjects to be flat and unreal and the colors crude and exaggerated even though he was assured that they were dead accurate. Dead accurate, said Lewis is just what they were, adding that precision isn't everything. In reality nothing is isolated; reality involves relationships. Thus Whistler,[14] supremely confident of his command of relationships, could make his celebrated

---

Pictures (Shackford, Wellesley, Mass., 1945), p. 30.

[10]Truman Capote: Truman Capote reports on the filming of In Cold Blood, Saturday Evening Post, No. 241, 1968, pp. 62-65; reference on p. 63.

[11]Quoted in E. H. Gombrich: Art and Illusion (Pantheon Books, New York, 1960), p. 38.

[12]Herbert Read: Art and Alienation (Thames and Hudson, London, 1967), p. 87.

[13]C. Day Lewis: The Poetic Image (Jonathan Cape, London, 1947), p. 24.

[14]Quoted in D. C. Seitz: Whistler Stories (Harper, New York, 1913), p. 27.

response to a woman who said that a landscape reminded her of his work: "Yes madam, Nature is creeping up." Paul Nash[15] made a similar point, less tartly, when he averred that nature is "simply that which the artists of the day before yesterday made people believe in."

Painting and Sensibility

Landscape has been evocative rather than literal. . . . Landscape, like music, liberates feelings and dreams rather than stimulates observation.[16] (Bernard Berenson)

As a seeing creature the painter clarifies, and as Whistler and Nash intimate, organizes our vision. As a feeling creature he heightens sensibilities. Since our pleasure in landscape is primarily visual and aesthetic, painting might reasonably be regarded as the chief arbiter of feeling and attitude toward nature. Although tempting, this is too simple a view. Art historian Otto Pacht[17] reminds us that the discovery of aesthetic values in landscape was the final outcome of a complex ripening process involving every form of the imagination and which concerned "the entire attitude of man toward his physical environment." The development of affection for landscape owed as much to science, which dispelled fear, and to technology and the rule of law, which made travel comfortable and safe, as it did to art. Yet even allowing for a shared, as opposed to a leading role, art has strongly influenced perceptions of landscape.

The extreme positions taken toward landscape in painting are expressed in a line from "The Winter's Tale":[18] "An art which does mend nature . . . change it rather, but the art itself, is nature." The "mending" art is the ideal painting, based on Platonic conceptions of ideal form, of Italian and Italianate painters. In it, phenomena are re-arranged to suit human ends: facts, said Fry[19] of Florentine Renaissance painting which began the tradition, had to be

---

[15]Quoted in Anthony Bertram: Paul Nash: The Portrait of an Artist (Faber and Faber, London, 1955), p. 130.

[16]Bernard Berenson: Aesthetics and History (Doubleday and Co., Garden City, New York, 1954), p. 100.

[17]Otto Pacht: Early Italian Nature Studies and the Early Calendar Landscape, Journ. Warburg and Courtauld Insts., Vol. 13, 1950, pp. 13-47; reference on p. 46.

[18]William Shakespeare: The Winter's Tale (Cambridge University Press, London, 1931), Act 4, Scene 4, p. 63.

[19]Fry, op. cit. [see note 5 above], p. 147.

digested into form before they could be allowed into the system. Ideal art is patently anthropocentric, and although designed to elevate or improve nature, ended by converting it into prospects and views--into scenery. Eighteenth century English travellers were so enamored of Claude Lorraine's paintings of the Roman Campagna (Fig. 1) that they carried a "Claude glass, " a rectangular, tinted mirror which by deadening local color allowed them to see their own landscapes in the muted tones of the paintings.[20] Some, not satisfied with a mere reflection, re-designed their estates to look like the landscapes of the paintings. By the end of the eighteenth century, the idea that paintings set the standards for natural beauty was so well established that William Gilpin, an apostle of picturesque taste, could advise landowners to place in their meadows five cows, not four, since four will not compose.

The antithesis of the ideal landscape is the naturalistic landscape, Kenneth Clark's[21] "landscape of fact." Instead of mending nature, naturalistic painting attempts a correspondence with it. To learn to paint landscape, said Asher Durand,[22] "go first to nature." Although a painting is a creative organization of selected forms, never an inventory, naturalistic painting ostensibly is passive, the devotee regarding himself as a humble recording instrument in the presence of Shakespeare's "great creating Nature."[23] Andrew Wyeth[24] has said that when outdoors he likes to lose all sense of self so that he is like an animal stalking nature.

In European art the naturalistic tradition is associated with the North rather than the South. Flemish painters, who painted "patches, masonries, plants in the fields . . . which they call landscapes, " were rebuked by the lofty Michelangelo[25] for not dignifying their paintings with "reason or art . . . sym-

---

[20]The reduction of landscape to scenery is evinced by an extension of the application of "picturesque." At the beginning of the eighteenth century "picturesque" described landscapes that looked like those in paintings by Claude and Nicolas Poussin. Gradually the meaning shifted to refer to all landscapes worthy of being painted.

[21]Kenneth Clark: Landscape into Art [1949] (Penguin Books, Harmondsworth, Middlesex, 1966), pp. 31-49.

[22]Quoted in Allan Gussow: A Sense of Place: The Artist and the American Land (Friends of the Earth, New York, 1971), p. 147.

[23]Shakespeare, op. cit. [see note 18 above], p. 62.

[24]Wanda M. Corn: The Art of Andrew Wyeth (New York Graphic Society Ltd., Greenwich, Connecticut, 1973), p. 55.

[25]Quoted in Robert J. Clements: Michelangelo's Theory of Art (New York

53

Fig. 1.--"The marriage of Isaac and Rebekah," Claude Lorraine, ca. 1648. With permission of the National Gallery, London.

metry or proportion." The high point of naturalism was the nineteenth century which saw, in the Romantic Movement, the conjunction of intense interest in natural science and emotional engagement with the landscape (Fig. 2). Art and science shared similar goals and until mid-century artists and scientists frequently worked together. Von Humboldt,[26] whose own interest in tropical landscapes had been quickened by William Hodges' paintings of the Ganges, urged painters to travel extensively, using their "almost magical command over masses and forms" to convey the true image of the varied forms of nature. Many did,[27] thus popularizing the idea of both the natural and the typical landscape. The first typical landscapes were painted by artists who accompanied Cook on his voyages of exploration. Humboldt's wish was to see landscape panoramas displayed in the galleries and museums of major cities. Like Goethe, he hoped that the marriage of art and science would enlarge our understanding of nature.

By encouraging an integrated, ecological view of landscape, nineteenth century art stimulated the modern movement for the protection of nature. A contemporary ecologist[28] claims that by revering the exotic and by presupposing "a divine fullness in kinds of things" Romantic art laid the groundwork for natural history and modern ecology. Clarence Glacken[29] also reminds us that in certain phases of its development Romanticism rebelled against the dichotomy between man and nature by making us conscious of our attitudes toward the natural world and encouraging the notion of man in, as opposed to man against, nature. In doing so painters and poets complemented the writings of Darwin and others in natural science.

In America, an expression of concern for the spectacular in nature was the designation of Yosemite and Yellowstone as national parks. Both regions

University Press, New York, 1961), p. 208.

[26]Alexander von Humboldt: Cosmos (5 vols.; London, 1848-1858), Vol. 2, p. 99.

[27]For example, the American landscape painter Frederick Erwin Church who painted in South America. While in Quito, Church sought out the family who had housed von Humboldt.

[28]D. McKinley: The New Mythology of "Man in Nature," in D. McKinley and P. Shepard: The Subversive Science (Houghton Mifflin Co., Boston, 1969), pp. 351-362; reference on p. 354.

[29]C. J. Glacken: Man against Nature: An Outmoded Concept, in H. W. Helfrich: The Environmental Crisis (Yale University Press, New Haven, 1970), pp. 127-142; reference on p. 132.

Fig. 2. --"Water-meadows near Salisbury," John Constable, 1823. Constable is the acknowledged master of the "natural vision." With permission of the Victoria and Albert Museum, London.

were espoused by painters, notably Thomas Moran and Albert Bierstadt, whose
works became widely known through reproduction in calendars and such popular
magazines as "Scribner's" and "Harper's Weekly." In addition, engravings of
Bierstadt's paintings are said to have adorned nearly every American parlor
(Fig. 3).[30] Moran's "Grand Canyon of the Yellowstone"--a giant-sized canvas
(7½ ft. x 9½ ft.) bought by Congress for $10,000--and his "Chasm of the Colo-
rado" are said to have so fired legislative imaginations that they are considered
to be partly responsible for America's system of national parks. But, as in-
struments for shaping attitudes to environment, far more instructive than paintings of distant, spectacular landscapes are those of artists who stay close to
home. "I should paint my own places best," wrote Constable,[31] and it is our
own places rather than the "museumized" nature of the parks that need our
attention.

Painting and Place

Always in my life it has been place. My work as a painter, my most personal concerns, my obsessions and interests and involvements, all these
have their origins and substance in the spirit of place.[32] (Reuben Tam)

Landscape painting influences the way we think and feel about the whole
environment; particular paintings, or painters, on the other hand, affect our
perceptions of particular places. Occasionally, the association of place and
painter, or group of painters, is so strong that paintings determine the popular
definitions of regions and countries. Cezanne and Provence, Constable and
East Anglia, the Group of Seven and the Canadian Shield are well-known associations. The painter's gift for evoking the essence, or spirit, of place is demonstrated by London critic Bernard Levin's[33] response to the Constable bicente-
nary exhibition in the Tate Gallery:

I quite astonished myself with the feeling of rootedness I had by the time I
left the Tate, and I think I rarely feel any such thing while looking out of the
train window at the kind of scene he painted, or even when actually standing

---

[30]Hans Huth: The American and Nature, Journ. Warburg and Courtauld
Insts., Vol. 13, 1950, pp. 101-149; reference on p. 131.

[31]C. R. Leslie: Memoirs of John Constable [1845] (Phaidon Press, London, 1951), p. 86.

[32]Quoted in Gussow, op. cit. [see note 21 above], p. 63.

[33]Bernard Levin: Gently, Gently through the Constable Country, The
Times, London, March 5, 1976, p. 14.

57

Fig. 3.--"Yosemite Valley, Glacier Point Trail," Albert Bierstadt, ca. 1872. With permission of the Yale University Art Gallery; gift of Mrs. Vincenzo Ardenghi.

in the middle of it and walking past the fields. . . . He takes us gently by the hand and leads us before the scenes he loved to paint, and leaves us there to see what he saw.

Although Levin's identification with Constable's landscapes is particularly intense, it nevertheless characterizes the response generally elicited by regional art. At the simplest level, the appeal of regional art is nostalgic. In both art and literature the regional world is essentially the world of childhood recaptured through memory. For uprooted adults living in an alien present, a familiar, congenial past with a definite geographic location has siren-like qualities. When it beckons few resist and we succumb to David Lowenthal's[34] "deadly disease of nostalgia." Lowenthal points out that another attraction of the past is that it is more comprehensible than the complex, shifting present. He quotes Susanne Langer:[35] "Memory is the great organizer of consciousness. Scenes, events, persons and things that were ambiguous or inconsistent become coherent, straightforward, clear. . . . Memory simplifies and composes our perceptions."

Although alluring, dreams of a lost Eden in themselves hardly account for the profound feeling for place paintings sometimes evoke. In regional art it is not so much the world of childhood that appeals as the child-like nature of the artist's vision.[36] Edith Cobb[37] makes the distinction:

Adult memories of childhood, even when nostalgic and romantic, seldom suggest the need to be a child but refer to a deep desire to renew the ability to perceive as a child and to participate with the whole bodily self in the forms, colors, and motions, the sights and sounds of the external world of nature and artifact.

Cobb's observations are based in part on the autobiographical recollections of gifted people. These indicate that there is, in Cobb's phrase, a "prepubertal, halcyon middle age of childhood," from the ages of about six to twelve, when the world is experienced in a most intense way. In his state of heightened perception, the child has a sense of profound continuity with natural processes.

---

[34]D. Lowenthal: Past Time, Present Place, Geogr. Rev., Vol. 65, 1975, pp. 1-36; reference on p. 1.

[35]Susanne Langer: Feeling and Form (Charles Scribner, New York), 1953, p. 263.

[36]Andrew Wyeth has said that for him the supreme compliment is not that a painting reminds a viewer of a place he, or she, has known, but that it revives childhood perceptions. Corn, op. cit. [see note 23 above], p. 152.

[37]Edith Cobb: The Ecology of Imagination in Childhood, in D. McKinley and P. Shepard, op. cit. [see note 27 above], pp. 122-132; reference on p. 130.

Bernard Berenson[38] described his own childhood sensations as a feeling of "oneness with the landscape," which he later labelled IT. IT, or the intimation of it that we get from landscape painting, makes us feel, as Karl Kroeber[39] said of Constable's paintings "that we are at home on earth." In Cobb's terminology, Constable organized his world into the good gestalt, into environmental shapes that hold and are rich in perceptual meaning.

The child's or artist's vision is unitary or holistic. The child does not separate the environment perceived by the senses (the perceptual environment) from the one he is learning about (the conceptual environment). In Gestalt terms, his behavioral and geographical environments are one. Wallace Stegner[40] elucidates: "He [the child] sees only what he can see Only later does he learn to link what he sees with what he already knows, or has imagined, or heard, or read, and so comes to make perception serve inference." Canadian painter Lawren Harris[41] put the matter more bluntly: "The child," he remarked, "is pure perception." Such unencumbered vision, complemented by adult levels of experience and skill, is the condition of success in art. Only those artists endowed with it, said Ruskin,[42] can see "to the heart" and create landscapes that are convincing wholes. Mere assemblages he dismissed as the products of "composing legalism."

The difference between an assemblage and an holistic image is clarified by an incident in the career of Scottish painter P. G. Hamerton.[43] Hamerton spent a year studying Loch Awe and Ben Cruachan and painting a topographically accurate picture of them. The scene had earlier been painted by Turner. Some of Turner's details were wrong but the landscape as a whole, fused and heightened by the power of Turner's imagination was, Hamerton generously admitted, "in reality more truthful."

---

[38]Bernard Berenson: Sketch for a Self Portrait (Pantheon Books, New York, 1949), p. 175.

[39]Karl Kroeber: Romantic Landscape Vision (University of Wisconsin Press, Madison, 1975), p. 25.

[40]Wallace Stegner: Wolf Willow (Viking Press, New York, 1966), p. 12.

[41]Bess Harris and R. G. P. Colgrave: Lawren Harris (Macmillan and Co., Toronto, 1969), p. 133.

[42]Ruskin, op. cit. [see note 4 above], Vol. 3, pp 109-114.

[43]E. B. Greenshields: The Subjective View of Landscape Painting (Desbarats and Co., Montreal, 1904), ,p. 10.

Like Ruskin and Hamerton, Wordsworth[44] also championed unitary vision. He said to Hazlitt, on the subject of Poussin's paintings, that he would not give a rush for any landscape that did not have "this character of wholeness in it." In the same vein, he[45] deplored Walter Scott's mechanical fashion of jotting down in a notebook items that struck him when he took a walk:

> He went home and wove the whole together into a poetical description. But nature does not permit an inventory to be made of her charms. He should have left his pencil and notebook at home, fixed his eye as he walked with reverent attention and . . . after several days had passed by . . . that which remained--the picture surviving in his mind--would have presented the ideal and essential truth of the scene, and done so in large part by discarding much which, though in itself striking, was not characteristic. In every scene many of the most brilliant details are but accidental; a true eye for nature does not note them, or at least does not dwell upon them.

The same sentiment was repeated about a century later by the president of the British Geographical Society.[46] In his annual address, he urged budding geographers to develop "a seeing eye; an eye that can see into the very heart and, through all the thronging details, single out the one essential quality." Geographers, he concluded, should have in them "something of the poet and the painter." Artistic synthesis may be the highest achievement of humanistic geography, but as Yi-Fu Tuan[47] has pointed out it is not a program that can be advocated for all modern geographers. Most of us, he concludes, must be content with the role of intellectual middleman, taking the nuggets of experience provided by art and turning them into themes that can be systematically ordered. As journeymen, we must follow Ruskin's[48] sensible advice to the landscape painter of modest talents. "Be a plain topographer if you possibly can; if Nature meant you to be anything else, she will force you to it." But as plain topographers we need not feel despondent. Pure topography and pure history Ruskin considered "most precious things, [sometimes] of more value to mankind than high imaginative work."

---

[44]Quoted in Shackford, op. cit. [see note 9 above], p. 51.

[45]Ibid., p. 32.

[46]Francis Younghusband: Natural Beauty and Geographical Science, Geogr. Journ., Vol. 56, 1920, pp. 1-13; reference on p. 8.

[47]Yi-Fu Tuan: Humanistic Geography, Annals Assn. of Amer. Geogrs., Vol. 66, 1976, pp. 266-276; reference on p. 274.

[48]Ruskin, op. cit. [see note 39 above], Vol. 4, p. 29.

Painting, Place and Identity

In bird, fish, beast, or man the need to make a world is intricately related to the sense of identity.[49] (Edith Cobb)

A contemporary American painter and conservationist[50] recently remarked on the critical difference between environment and place. Environment is physical space whereas place is "a piece of the whole environment that has been claimed by feelings." Environment sustains the body but place nourishes the spirit. By endowing pieces of the environment with feelings painters convert space, which has neither cultural nor personal associations, into familiar place. Since painting is also an organizing process that confers order on the environment, art helps to satisfy the need for both comfort and coherence in our surroundings. Through images, as Gyorgy Kepes[51] puts it, we "domesticate" the world and make it home:

It is not only with tools that we domesticate our world. Sensed forms, images and symbols are as essential to us as palpable reality in exploring nature for human ends. Distilled from our experience and made our permanent possessions, they provide a nexus between man and man and between man and nature. We make a map of our experience patterns, an inner model of the outer world, and we use this to organize our lives. Our natural "environment"--whatever impinges on us from outside--becomes our human "landscape"--a segment of nature fathomed by us and made our home.

The domesticating impulse is most evident in unfamiliar territory. At the most basic level, image-making takes the form of giving names and making maps. As symbolic organizations of landscape, maps help to establish an emotionally safe relationship with environment by making the world smaller, less intimidating, and more comprehensible. But unless they are descriptive and evocative, maps are an objective ordering of environment that, alone, do not make a new land home. The sense of intimacy and state of intensified perception associated with the home place are the bequests of time, experience, and the heightened images of art.[52] Australia, America and Canada provide convincing examples.

---

[49] Cobb, op. cit. [see note 34 above], p. 128.

[50] Gussow, op. cit. [see note 21 above], p. 27.

[51] Georgy Kepes: The New Landscape (Paul Theobald and Co., Chicago, 1956), p. 18.

[52] Conventional maps and landscape paintings, respectively, are examples of Martin Buber's two basic relationships--"orientation" and "realization"-- with environment. "Orientation" orders the environment for knowledge and use; "realization" brings out the inner meaning of life through intensified perception

In each country the historical process is instructive. The first paintings were inevitably European in both sentiment and style; familiar objects were rendered in the known fashion, and without artistic formulae to guide them, painters tended to ignore the unfamiliar. As a result new world landscapes acquired an old world aura, and, occasionally, old world phenomena. In America, for example, desperate painters sometimes added European tree species to the landscape. [53] Although blatant, these subterfuges were overlooked by homesick viewers who were understandably eager to maintain cultural links with the homeland and sustain the illusion that the new landscape was comparable with the old. By shielding settlers from the harsh realities of their new lives, pioneer art served as a soporific. More lifelike images became possible only after the new land had been imaginatively absorbed and with the development of new techniques in art. In Australia and Canada, for example, problems associated with painting the harsh light and the unfamiliar tones and colors of both heat-drenched and snow-covered landscapes--features which had defeated the first European painters--required the broken-color techniques of Impressionism for their solution.

In each of the new countries the development of native images in art was associated with the loosening of European ties and the search for both regional and national identities. Since an area as large as a country can seldo.n be experienced directly by most of its inhabitants, the artist's gift for creating place from space proved invaluable. Alive to the persuasive powers of art, painters set about the creation of images that would symbolize the spirit of the nation. Given the commanding physical presence of the three countries, the significance of pioneering to each, and the sanctity of the notion of a place and a people, painters chose the land itself as the most appropriate symbol of national identity. Canada, through the ardent nationalism of the Group of Seven, provides the most striking example.

The Group of Seven were Toronto-based painters who decided, just after the First World War, that Canada needed an art which would define the Canadian identity in native rather than European terms. In the catalog to their first exhibition, in 1920, they declared that "an Art must grow and flower in the land

---

and existence. See Martin Buber: Daniel (Holt, Rinehart and Winston, New York, 1964), pp. 61-81.

[53] See Paul Shepard: They Painted What They Saw, Landscape, Vol. 3, 1953, pp. 6-11; reference on p. 8.

before the country will be a real home for its people."[54] Until 1920, Canadian
art, for the most part, had been European art transplanted (Fig. 4). Except
for its pastoral corners, the Canadian landscape was thought to be aesthetically
unsuitable, and until the advent of Impressionism, unpaintable. An elderly
woman is reported to have said to A. Y. Jackson, a prominent member of the
Group, that it was bad enough having to live in the country without hanging pictures of it on your walls.[55] The embargo was not confined to individuals; the
Canadian government banned winter scenes from its publicity posters on the
grounds that they might discourage immigration.

To break the European hegemony in art, the Group chose a previously
unpainted, defiantly Canadian landscape--the Laurentian Shield--and painted it
in a suitably rebellious manner. Bright, glowing colors, hard outlines, vigor-
ous, "chopped out" brush strokes and abstracted, isolated forms were used to
convey a dramatic impression of a powerful, empty land (Fig. 5). To a public
anxiously seeking national symbols, these northern landscapes were irresist-
ible. They gave Canada, as A. Y. Jackson[56] put it, "a new world, the north
country." That the new world was not the one actually inhabited by most Canadians was unimportant. What mattered was that the paintings of the Shield gave
Canadians something of their own with which they could identify. Although most
Canadians cling to cities in the south, Canada's northern image is no myth.
The Shield, never distant, dominates the whole eastern section of the country
and winter, as much as a shared culture, is the common bond. The sentiment
is expressed in a popular French-Canadian song: "Mon pays, ce n'est pas un
pays, c'est l'hiver."

Similar nationalistic trends are discernible in American art of the twen-
ties and thirties. Painters of the American Wave or American Scene Movement
were just as anxious to throw off foreign influences and to express, as one observer put it, "the spirit of the land."[57] In 1931, the year of the opening of the

---

[54]Quoted in Peter Mellen: The Group of Seven (McLelland and Stewart,
Toronto, 1970), p. 111.

[55]Ibid., p. 5.

[56]Quoted in Ottelyn Addison and Elizabeth Harwood: Tom Thomson: The
Algonquin Years (Ryerson Press McGraw Hill Co. of Canada, Toronto, 1969),
p. 75.

[57]The editor of Art Digest. Quoted in Matthew Baigell: The American
Scene (Praeger, New York, 1974), p. 18.

64

Fig. 4. -- "Evening after rain," Homer Watson, 1913. Oscar Wilde dubbed Watson "the Constable of the New World." With permission of the Art Gallery of Ontario; gift of the Canadian National Exhibition Association, 1965.

Fig. 5. -- "The west wind," Tom Thomson, 1917. With permission of the Art Gallery of Ontario; gift of the Canadian Club of Toronto, 1926.

66

Whitney Museum of American art, the art critic of the New York Times[58] advised American painters to sing in their own voices or not sing at all. As in Canada the objective was to raise both national and regional consciousness by presenting the public with familiar images of the land. Two general themes were pursued; first, that the struggle with the land was the basic American experience; second, that worthwhile art could grow only out of the locale in which the artist lived. The regionalist movement came to be identified with the heartland, the middle west, and with middle western painters: Thomas Hart Benton (Fig. 6), Grant Wood, and John Steuart Curry. Wood's "American Gothic" is probably the best-known painting of the period.

The distress which absence of native images of environment can cause is the subject of an autobiographical essay by the Canadian historian W. L. Morton.[59] Morton grew up on a farm in rural Manitoba at the beginning of this century, and as a boy was disoriented by the conflict between the landscape he saw daily and the landscape in his mind's eye formed by reading Victorian English literature. "My actual landscape, the one the neighbours had made and worked in . . . and my literary landscape . . . were in conflict. I had no single vision for both, but had to re-focus like one passing from dark to light." Although the experience was not an existensialist trauma, Morton, nevertheless, had a strong desire to see his workaday surroundings transformed through art into a "humane landscape of heightened tone and enriched association." In other words, he wanted his space converted into place.

In the absence of a homegrown art and literature, Morton's only recourse was to create his own images, which he eventually did not through the arts but through historical writing. To be good, he asserts, a historian's work must not only be true to fact but must possess its own integrity, the truth of total vision. In writing about the West, Morton admits that he was participating in the ancient human game of possessing by naming and describing. But his naming was no mere taxonomy: "No country," he writes, "can be really owned except under familiar name or satisfying phrase. To be apprehended by the mind and [made] personal, it requires not only the worn comfort of a used tool or a broken-in shoe; it requires also assimilation to the mind, ear, eye, and tongue by accepted, or acceptable description in word, or line, or colour." For Morton, reconciling the actual with the mind's landscape was "a rite of

[58]Ibid., p 19.

[59]W. L. Morton: Seeing an Unliterary Landscape, Mosaic, Vol. 3, 1970, pp. 1-10.

Fig. 6.--"Cradling wheat," Thomas Hart Benton, 1938. Like Frederick Jackson Turner, Benton believed that opening the land was the "primary reality of American life." With permission of the St. Louis Art Museum.

reassurance . . . which fuses the thing seen and the person seeing." The recon-
ciliation of the inner with the outer vision, he concludes, is part of the magic of
art and also of the historian's craft.

Morton's single, or "total" vision, fusing objective and imaginative views
of environment, is as important to geographical as to historical writing and
study. In North America the sense of place has seldom been strong and it can
be argued that geographers bear a special responsibility in the work of strengthening it. For most localities there is now a pool of art and literature that we
can draw upon to balance our own usually objective and analytical views of our
surroundings. Distressed by the imbalance of our current approach, and its
inappropriateness to environmental needs, D. W. Meinig[60] has suggested that
geographers create a special education in the art of environmental appreciation.
The education, to take the form of field observation and study of regional literature and art, would be designed to make us more sensitive to our surroundings
so that we would, in Meinig's phrase, be enriched by the good and appalled by
the bad. A keener awareness of locality Meinig sees as a necessary first step
toward a cure for our environmental problems which he regards as fundamentally psychosomatic, the consequence of indifference and improper attitudes and
values.

As well as adopting the perceptions of artists, imaginative geographers
might also follow Morton's example and create their own images of place that
could be shared with others. Used carefully, the imagination is an effective
instrument that can be employed not only to enliven writing and teaching, but,
more important, to interpret experience and endow it with meaning. Arguing
for the freer use of imagination in geography, J. K. Wright[61] quotes Sir Douglas Newbold: "No one can get to love a country without seeing it properly: all
true affection rests upon vision. . . . Knowledge must pass into vision, that
state of mind and heart which does not merely swallow evidence, but changes
that evidence into a judgement, an appreciation, a living picture of a country."

---

[60]D. W. Meinig: Environmental Appreciation: Localities as a Humane Art,
Western Humanities Review, Vol. 25, 1977, pp. 1-11. See also S. Robert
Aitken: Towards Landscape Sensibility, Landscape, Vol. 20, 1976, pp. 20-28.

[61]Wright, op. cit. [see note 2 above], p. 73. The passage is taken from
Newbold's inaugural lecture delivered at the Sudan Cultural Centre. Quoted in
R. A. Hodkin: Sudan Geography (Education Dept. of the Sudan Govt., 1946), p.
147; see also Geogr. Rev., Vol. 37, 1947, p. 340.

CHAPTER 5

SIGNATURES AND SETTINGS: ONE APROACH TO LANDSCAPE IN LITERATURE

Christopher L. Salter

University of California, Los Angeles

The story was gradually taking shape. Pilon liked it this way. It ruined a story to have it all come out quickly. The good story lay in half-told things which must be filled in out of the hearer's own experience. [1]

What sources of information does the reader (or the hearer) turn to in order to complete the half-told story? Steinbeck suggests experience in the quote above from Tortilla Flat. Geographers would add the resource of objective knowledge provided by scholarly literature, perhaps statistical abstracts, or depictions offered by respected observers. Some would exhort the person who is attempting to fill in the picture to use imagination, common sense and even fantasy in order to fully interact with the reality being pursued. No matter the inventory drawn up, it is clear that the acquisition of understanding is the product of a process of selective acceptance of scattered information from distinct sources. And, as Pilon notes above, the process of sorting out the data and putting the vision together is probably as valuable as having the final knowledge itself. That evaluative process is the mechanics of intellectual, educational growth. We would do well as a profession to further stimulate such a course of inquiry. Literature as a source--but not the only source--of evidence is one corpus of material which generates such stimulation.

Creative literature is inherently evocative. As a source of evidence it possesses the chronicle of mankind's ambitions and creative efforts at transforming geographical space, as well as individual and culture group attempts at ordering life itself. If we as a profession approach this chronicle with care, an

---

[1] John Steinbeck: Tortilla Flat (The Modern Library, New York, 1935), p. 74. Steinbeck exercises this delight in prolonging the telling of a story perhaps most effectively in "Of Mice and Men" (Viking Press, New York, 1937).

69

admission of willing speculation, and a desire to ourselves engage in some of the creative spirit of good writing, we will find that we have established an additional humanistic facet of geography. This is a goal which I would like to pursue through landscape signatures and the consideration of landscape in literature.[2]

The majority of the verities which we claim as geographic can be expressed in creative as well as scholarly terms. A well-chosen excerpt from The Grapes of Wrath or Hawaii can serve to enhance any number of theories relating to migration.[3] The only danger in such an augmentation to formal text material is that the employment of fiction might expand to overshadow the hard facts. The responsibility for proper balance and productive interplay of these dissimilar bodies of knowledge falls to the geographers who choose to explore literature as a source of evidence in their teaching and research. This paper

---

[2]This method of utilizing fiction in the tasks of geography, and in instruction in landscape in particular, is offered as one among many. Others considered might have different emphases, including a diminished interest in setting, but all of the sources below advocate a critical use of literature. See, for example, Gary T. Moore and Reginald G. Golledge, edits.: Environmental Knowing (Dowden, Hutchinson & Ross, Stroudsburg, PA., 1976), with papers by Yifu Tuan, Myongsup Shin, David Seamon, William J. Lloyd and David Lowenthal contained within a section entitled "Literary and Phenomenological Perspective," pp. 260-293; H. C. Darby: The Regional Geography of Thomas Hardy's Wessex, Geographical Review, Vol. 38, 1948, pp. 426-443; David A. Lanegran: The Pioneers' View of the Frontier as Presented in the Regional Novel "Giants in the Earth," International Geography, Vol. 1, 1972, pp. 350-352; Colin D. Gunn: The Non-Western Novel as a Geography Text, Journal of Geography, Vol. 73, 1973, pp. 27-34; William J. Lloyd: Images of Late Nineteenth Century Urban Landscapes, Unpublished Doctoral Dissertation, University of California, Los Angeles; and Yi-fu Tuan: Topophilia (Prentice-Hall, Englewood Cliffs, N.J., 1974). This list is only suggestive. Any reader with adequate interest can create his or her own methods.

[3]I experimented with a blending of fiction and scholarly writing in "The Cultural Landscape" (Wadsworth, Belmont, CA., 1971) with the inclusion of excerpts from Mark Twain (Following the Equator, 1898), John Steinbeck (The Grapes of Wrath, 1939), Khushwant Singh (I Shall Not Hear the Nightingale, 1959) and Paul Ehrlich (Eco-Catastrophe!, 1969) among others. In working with that anthology it has often been the case that a provocative piece of fiction provides a most effective lead-in to a more substantial consideration of the geographic themes being studied. It may not even be the excerpt itself which triggers the expanded discussion, but rather the atmosphere of speculation and willingness to participate engendered by the subjectivity of fiction. This pedagogical use of fiction is treated briefly by A. J. Lamme: The Use of Novels in Geography Classrooms, Journal of Geography, Vol. 76, 1977 pp. 66-68. See also Michael Eliot Hurst: I Came to the City (Houghton Mifflin, Boston, 1975).

is intended to facilitate, even encourage such a choice. Perhaps the structuring of an approach to this window on geographical space afforded by fiction will provoke you to make creative demands on yourselves for fuller utilization of this resource.

The Definition of Landscape

Landscape is a frequently used term, but the chore of denotative, let alone connotative, definition is a tricky one. In another paper in progress, I am attempting to illustrate the broadly disparate ways in which geographers have used the term, but for the use of the term in conjunction with literature, I have employed the following broadly inclusive meaning.

Landscape is that segment of earth space which lies between the viewer's eye and his or her horizon. In the miniature, it encompasses the appointments of a room, a suite of rooms, a single house facade. In its inclusiveness, it embraces the natural elements of the eyefull vista such as hills and woodlands, rivers and clouds in combination with the artificial adornments which mankind has added such as settlements, roads, billboards, or deserted buildings.

The scale of the landscape prospect changes with the visual intent and physical location of the viewer. Peering into a room through a crack in a slightly-opened door, environmental knowledge is gained as the eye falls on furniture, wall-hangings, or people. Turning from the door, a gaze out of a window into a dawn sun would change scale and bring brightness, as the sunlight might be reflected from a pond, a parking lot, a building's steely surface or an entire city skyline. In these examples, and in the infinite additional ones available to the imagination or reality, it is landscape which is being viewed. It is these apparently random artificial and natural elements of geographical space which stand ready to communicate meaning and significance to the viewer. Like the monuments of a departed people, this landscape can be read, interpreted, learned from, confused by, and interacted with if the viewer possesses even modest powers of observation, fundamental interest in the prospect before him, and a willingness to evaluate inferential information. The information thus gained is far from perfect. but the process of its interpretation is a stimulating one, and the knowledge acquired does enhance the understanding of the landscape's parent people.

To the reader of literature who is innocent of our particular interest in landscape, these same scenes will probably be defined as the setting, the accommodating space for the more dynamic and personal unfolding of the drama being anticipated. For this reader it is the characters in their overt as well as subtle interaction who are being most closely watched through the crack in the door or the dawning window. To the geographer, however, these same fields of vision possess their own independent dynamics. Even before people are focused upon, the drama is already underway. The messages given by the partially viewed room or the windowed panorama are an integral element of the total expression communicated by what is seen and what is to be seen. This is true for literature. This is true for the objective landscape as well.

This added significance given to the landscape by the geographer is one aspect of what we as professionals may bring to our consideration of selected fiction. And reciprocally, pensive regard of the nature of the characters' interaction with this specific spatial construct will communicate to us information about these people as well as the setting. The potential for this heightened sense of the influence and the importance of landscape on the dramatis personae is what we as geographers are able to bring to the reading of fiction. Our benefit comes from this expanded awareness of the significance of the role of landscape in literature.

Obviously and intentionally this expansive definition of landscape will not please those of you who seek a very explicit delimitation of the term. But little good is served by placing overly restrictive constraints on the geographical space in which the characters of fiction play out their roles. These people are alive to the presence of a garden as well as the awesomeness of a metropolitan skyline. Moods are created by the lighting in a stairwell just as they are by the flames of a desert campfire. All of these images are engendered by the manipulation of, as well as perception of, geographical space. I see them all as facets of landscape. As such they are open to our professional analysis.

Our professional analysis. Just the term sounds foreboding. The layering, perhaps encrusting, of common sense patterns of spatial and cultural interaction with obtuse jargon is one of the hallmarks of our discipline's quest for scientific acceptability. We have grown proud because of the successes we have had in explaining that people move for other than economic reasons. But such victories may well turn Pyrrhic unless we improve in our abilities to communicate the resultant verities in an evocative and humane manner. Let us acknowledge a continuum of analysis and expression within our discipline. At the one extreme we have the hard and apparently objective scientific commentaries of, for an example, energy balance climatology. George Stewart's Storm would be of little use to that domain. But, just as fully within the parameters of our profession are the significant ambiguities of perception studies. Literature may serve as a comfortable and extremely valuable source of evidence for that shadowy realm of behavioral and humanistic analysis. Moreover, that mythic range of the continuum may turn out to be as valuable to the growth of our discipline as the more objective, hard science realm.

It is this tandem interest then, in evocative and humane sources, processes of analysis, and laws of the profession which brings literature to the fore as a supplemental tool in the researching and depiction of culture and geographical space.

In the main, a geographer is concerned with the comprehension of the nature of place and the potentials for the spatial and cultural interaction between a multiplicity of places. Through the use of literature the underlying realities of such descriptive and interactive characteristics emerge as the patterns of real people dealing with real space. The validity, for example, of the gravity model in migration theory remains the same whether it is described as a mathematical formula or as a fictional character's mental map of potential goal areas in a migration decision. The additional explanation of the theory's significance through use of literature is simply likely to make this academic speculation meaningful to a larger proportion of the intended listening or reading population. Fiction possesses the quality of stimulating the listener or the reader to a greater sense of individual concern in the information being presented. This expansion of interest generates a more forceful intellectual involvement in the learning process. This is a goal common both to teaching and the authoring of geographic research.

To evoke, to elicit a response, to stimulate the imagining of parallel phenomena to those being presented--these are responsive states of awareness which are productive for academic intercourse. The objective presentation of solely factual material may also stimulate reaction, but relative to the evocative power of strong literature, the listener withholds more of himself from the learning experience. Explanation is enhanced by the use of properly chosen literature.

One Approach to Landscape in Literature

Literature is highly personal both in its creation and in its perception. There is no canon by which we--either as academics or even as interested readers--can objectively define the meaning of a work of fiction. One reader's excitement with Frank Norris' description of wheatfields may be another's bore-

dom with seemingly endless description in The Octopus. This very subjectivity,
however, is to be seen as a shortcoming only in that it invalidates literature as
a necessarily reliable source for explicit knowledge of the objective landscape,
or that segment of geographical space which may be defined in exact and unambiguous terms. We are not turning to literature for that information. What we
should be searching for in belles-lettres is the range and variations in different
characters' views of the same landscape. We should be attempting to understand the dissimilarity of depiction of the same landscape by different authors.
We should read this fiction in an attempt to better understand our own interaction with geographical space, with the landscape. A whole world of learning
falls outside the realm of objectivity. Much of it is spatial. Much of it is cultural and psychological. Geographers should have some better means of dealing with this subjective reality. The basis for such analysis in literature which
I want to outline is the use of landscape signatures.

Landscape Signatures and Literature

> As a poet of the historic consciousness I suppose I am bound to see land-
> scape as a field dominated by the human wish--tortured into farms and ham-
> lets, ploughed into cities. A landscape scribbled with the signatures of men
> and epochs. [4]

These signatures of men and epochs; these idiosyncratic and specific landscapes standing as representations of the human wish are the basis of the approach I would like to suggest for the study of landscape in literature. If we
are able to segment our study of the landscapes which catch our eye in fiction
then we can begin to form an enhanced sense of how people have used the earth
and, at the same time, we gain a new sense of how authors have used the landscape. The landscape signatures utilized below fall into two categories: structural and behavioral. The structural signatures are those which are the product of cultures working on a large scale to transform either natural or an ear-
lier-modified geographical space into a new shape. This new environment is a
reflection of not only landscape preferences but cultural preferences. These

---

[4]Lawrence Durrell: Justine (E. P. Dutton and Co., Inc., New York, 1961),
p. 112. Durrell is an author who frequently captures landscape images to advantage. The entire Alexandria Quartet, of which "Justine" is the first volume,
is graphically illustrated with his discussions of landscape. Earlier in "Justine,"
he asserts an even closer bond between the characters of his novel and their setting: "We are the children of our landscape; it dictates behaviour and even
thought in the measure to which we are responsive to it. I can think of no better identification" (p. 41).

structural signatures may include: patterns of settlement, agriculture, and transportation as well as landscapes of livelihood and sacred space.

The behavioral signatures are those landscape features which more generally reflect individual decisions, either for landscape creation or landscape use. Such signatures could include: house types, gardens, and entertainment, language and costume. While neither of these sets is necessarily complete, their discussion may well stimulate one into his or her own personal speculation on an author's use of landscape. Given the subjectivity of creative literature, it is better to have a motivated geographer make his own demands on such materials than to create such a rigid methodological construct that the fiction suddenly becomes as inflexible as objective environmental evidence. Let me offer examples of this signature approach.

Structural Signatures

Settlement Signatures

> It is only a few miles drive to the ocean, but before reaching it I shall be nowhere. Hard to describe the impression of unreality because it is intangible; almost supernatural; something in the air. (The air . . . Last night on the weather telecast the commentator, mentioning electric storms near Palm Springs and heavy smog in Los Angeles, described the behavior of the air as "neurotic". Of course. Like everything else the air must be imported and displaced, like the water driven along huge aqueducts from distant reservoirs, like the palm trees tilting above mortuary signs and laundromats along Sunset Boulevard.) Nothing belongs. Nothing belongs except the desert soil and the gruff eroded-looking mountains to the north. . . . The houses are imitation "French Provincial" or "new" Regency or Tudor or Spanish hacienda or Cape Cod, and except for a few crazy mansions, seem to have sprung up overnight. The first settlers will be arriving tomorrow from parts unknown. [5]

In this passage from Gavin Lambert's The Slide Area we are given an overview of one person's reaction to the settlement of Los Angeles. While we are not shown the geometries of the city outlines, we are given a more significant evaluation of the exotic nature of this particular urban area. In the novel, as Lambert's scriptwriter continues his drive toward the ocean, he utilizes the

---

[5]Gavin Lambert: The Slide Area (Hamish Hamilton, London, 1959), pp. 14-15. The settlement patterns of Los Angeles have been the focus of a number of interesting novels. Evelyn Waugh gave special attention to the cities of the dead (pets as well as people) in "The Loved One" (Penguin, Harmondsworth, 1951) and Alison Lurie describes some of the same places and social landscapes as Lambert in her book, "The Nowhere City" (Heinemann, London, 1965). Two additional authors who explore the settings in the Los Angeles area in detail are Raymond Chandler and Ross MacDonald, both of whom place much importance on their characters' perception of various neighborhoods in Los Angeles.

landscape of southern California as a metonymy for the whole of American culture. The sense of illusion, of artificiality, of rapid change and infatuation
with an American dream all speak to him from the street scenes he winds
through while going from Hollywood to the Pacific Palisades.

The beauty of this passage and the associated consideration of the structural landscape signature of settlement is that it becomes essential to read the
associated landscape as one reads Lambert's work. The eye must be focused
not only upon the theme of artificiality which the author is overtly alarmed with,
but the senses are forced to turn again and again to the landscape description
which is the vehicle for this philosophic view articulated in The Slide Area. It
is this dual reading of sentiment and setting which this signature and this particular work of fiction provokes. The reader as geographer senses the hodge-
podge settlement of Los Angeles. The geographer as reader more completely
appreciates the use of landscape to focus a philosophical tirade.

In another example of the landscapes which are the product of large-scale,
collective modification decisions, Paul Theroux lets his eye drift along a Japanese farming scene while on a train in Honshu. He describes an agricultural
scene in these terms:

> A glimpse of two acres of farmland made me hopeful of more fields, but it
> was a novelty, no more than that: the tiny plow, the narrow furrows, the
> winter crops sown inches apart, the hay not stacked but collected in small
> swatches--a farm in miniature. In the distance, the pattern was repeated on
> several hills, but there the furrows were filled with snow, giving the land-
> scape the look of seersucker.[6]

The images in this passage remind us of our interest in the evocative nature of
literature, in this case travel literature. The idea of seersucker with its flat
and puckered fabric surface suggesting the terraces and ridges; the diminutive
farming vista with tiny plow and hay in small swatches . . . these word pictures have a more gripping image of Japanese farming than would an excerpt
from a Statistical Abstract. The picture they provide, however, is not an adequate replacement for facts which outline farm parcel size and degree of agri-

---

[6]Paul Theroux: The Great Railway Bazaar (Houghton Mifflin, Boston,
1975), p. 290. While travel literature as a genre falls outside fiction narrowly
defined, it is included in this paper because of its eminently geographical qualities. Theroux gives considerable space to landscape and landscape comparison
in this volume, as well as drawing provocative inferences from the relationships between peoples and their settings. Three quarters of a century earlier
Mark Twain covered some of the same territory and his literature serves well
as a comparative corpus, especially for South Asia. See particularly "The
Innocents Abroad" (New American Library, New York, 1966).

cultural mechanization in Japan, but the seersucker landscape image combined with the knowledge that nearly 50% of Japan's farmland is terraced becomes a reliable example of environmental knowledge.

The use of these signatures is not limited to explicit examples in isolation. An effective employment of highly graphic passages is to compare landscapes of a similar use, but of a very distinct configuration. Theroux's description of the Japanese farming scene above, contrasts effectively with Frank Norris' overview of an agricultural scene across the Pacific from the Japanese seersucker landscape. In both cases wheat is being raised and agriculture dominates the view of the pensive observer.

> As he had planned, Presley reached the hills by the head waters of Broderson's Creek late in the afternoon. Toilfully he climbed them, reached the highest crest, and turning about, looked long and for the last time at all the reach of the valley unrolled beneath him. The land of the ranches opened out forever and forever under the stimulus of that measureless range of vision. The whole gigantic sweep of the San Joaquin expanded Titanic before the eye of the mind, flagellated with heat, quivering and shimmering under the sun's red eye. [7]

Farm size, degree of landscape modification, means of transformation and the explanation of the cultural context within which this scene was created are all a part of the drama of The Octopus. The book serves well as a handbook for the analysis of creation of an agricultural region or mono-crop landscape if it is utilized in conjunction with other, less-impassioned accounts of the development of California in the last third of the nineteenth century. The geographer who incorporates the Norris view in his commentary on that particular era, landscape, or developmental process has a broader footing upon which to base his assessment. And at a broader level, for the student of comparative Japanese and American landscapes, the contrasting images of agricultural activity

---

[7] Frank Norris: The Octopus (Doubleday Page & Co., Garden City, N.J., 1922), p. 633. This passage continues with a philosophic consideration of the sheer force that can be associated with the raising, marketing and management of an agricultural crop. Norris intended to write a trilogy about wheat, of which "The Octopus" was the first volume. The second volume (The Pit) changed the setting from California wheat fields to Chicago where this grain became the prize of competing speculators. It was published in 1903. The third tome was never written. It was to be entitled "The Wolf" and to show the role of this crop in a famine-stricken European village. Norris is an excellent author to study in pursuit of the ways in which commitment to a single crop can have ramifications through all aspects of culture and landscape. Leslie Byrd Simpson does this for maize in his volume "Many Mexicos" (University of California Press, Berkeley and Los Angeles, 1967), pp. 12-21. Effective comparisons about the landscape impact of diet and cropping preferences can be made between fiction and non-fiction in the reading of these works.

may well serve as a prod to additional, objective research into modes of farming and land use.

Sacred Space

Another example of a structural landscape signature and its capacity to
represent a culture group is drawn from Edna Ferber's Giant. Leslie has just
been brought from the genteel farmlands of Virginia to her new home in southwestern Texas. As she first arrives in the small town of Benedict, as the wife
of Jordon Benedict, she is agape at virtually all that she sees in this foreign
landscape. It is, however, the particularly sacred space of the Courthouse
Square which most captures her attention.

"I can't believe it. A--cow stuffed and put into a glass case on the street."
He touched her flushed cheek tenderly and laughed a little.
"You're in Texas, honey. Anyway, they have lions outside the New York
Public Library, don't they?"
"But this is real."
"Everything's real in Texas."
"What's it for? Do they worship it, or something?"[8]

This sacred signature of the cattleman's corner of Texas serves not only
to give the reader environmental and cultural information, but it is an ideal
theme point for the introduction of Leslie to a world she had not adequately
anticipated. The landscape catches all of her attention in this first trip through
town and author Edna Ferber continues to skillfully use setting with dramatic
power in this novel of a family's changing influence over a whole region.

Such a treatment of the flavor of a locale should be capitalized upon by a
geographer. Music, local art motifs, folklore, drama and literature all provide similar regional and environmental perspective. Used in conjunction with
more objective information on the locale being studied, these sources serve the
discipline well.

These structural landscape signatures are only several of what one might
turn to in order to illustrate the means by which landscape has been utilized by
authors to give enhanced shaping to the development of their artistic work. The
scale of these particular facets of the built environment is relatively large.

---

[8]Edna Ferber: Giant (Doubleday and Co., Inc., Garden City, N.J., 1952),
p. 115. Another curious perception of sacred space is given in Erskine Cald-
well's "God's Little Acre" (The Modern Library, New York, 1933) where Ty Ty
cloaks an acre of his unproductive farmland with a sacred quality, agreeing to
give the church all the produce of that piece of land. He generally leaves God's
acre unfarmed.

The architects of such modifications have been culture groups, generally working within the boundaries of a system of values which is identifiable and frequently uniquely associated with a particular population. Literature, then,
records the flavor and spirit of the elaboration of these culture monuments by a
people. Simultaneously, it serves as a vehicle for the literary task of identifying order in the apparent chaos of so much of life.

As people organize their geographic space in the course of a novel, the
author may well be attempting to illustrate a parallel structuring of inner, psychological space. The geographer is very possibly in the best position to interpret the resultant geographical space. The employment of specific landscape
signatures affords the geographer a linkage between specific culture groups and
associated built environments. Viewing this relationship may well provide the
reader with knowledge about the author, the author's style, the characters and
even the objective landscape of the passage or work. This composite is an
intriguing return on a geographer's efforts in the use of fiction.

Behavioral Signatures

House types and gardens are orthodox tools of the geographer in the attempt to explain the shape of the human environment. To these personal signatures of taste add the observations one may make about people by noting their
recreational landscapes; their food preferences; their costumes and their languages. All of these culture phenomena have an individual expression. All
have a visual, environmental manifestation. In this behavioral category, I
include three elements to cite as examples of this scale change in the landscape
signature approach. They are examples evoked by personal tastes in house,
garden, and entertainment.

House Types

I didn't know a house could be designed for a woman, like a dress. You
can't see yourself here as I do, you can't see how completely this house is
yours. Every angle, every part of every room is a setting for you. It's
scaled to your height, to your body. Even the texture of the walls goes with
the texture of your skin in an odd way. [9]

---

[9]Ayn Rand: The Fountainhead (Bobbs-Merrill Co., Inc., Indianapolis,
1952), p. 634. Although this paragraph is particularly direct in its statement
of the relationship between building design and human characteristics, this
theme is dominant throughout the novel. In her other major work, "Atlas
Shrugged" (Random House, New York, 1957), Ayn Rand uses other landscape
signatures, particularly the railroad and transportation networks, to manifest

In this passage from Ayn Rand's The Fountainhead the ultimate meaning
of Howard Roark's existence is suggested by the allusion to architectural bonding between person and structure. The novel's continual need for Rand's positive characters to image themselves in clear and concise forms is set in counterpoint to the way in which her weak and negative characters fail to commit
themselves to any coherent landscape expression. Obviously there is much
room here for subjectivity in a reader's assessments of motivations on the part
of the author as well as her characters. But, in the main, the environmental
expression of the world of The Fountainhead is structured to provide a profile
of the personalities in the novel. The quote given above paralleling the house
and a woman's dress is one example of this literary ploy operating at the individual, behavioral level.

The Garden

The garden of flowers and herbs which lay on the gentle south slope between
the farmhouse and the brook was, next to the grandchildren, Maria Fergu-
son's great delight in life. For her it was what theater and parties were to
most women. It was her great amusement, and working in it, even when she
was a bent old lady, after a day of hard work, seemed not to tire her, but to
refresh her spirit and charge her frail body with new strength.[10]

The garden as a signature gives a student of landscape information about
care of the earth, interest in plants, time or money allocated to the shaping of
personal environment as well as facts on climate, and plant diffusion. It may
occasionally suggest data on the ethnic composition of the household as well.
An author, however, can use a garden in the way that Louis Bromfield does in
The Farm where he has this pastime embrace an entire suite of needs for Maria. Activities ranging from entertainment to clothes-buying were subordinated
to the care of this personal space from which Maria gained so much identification and satisfaction. In this case we see how a small scale landscape can be
utilized by an author to embody virtually the whole cosmography of an individual

---

the strength or weakness of her characters. Both of these long novels serve
geography well in the display of individual personalities in the configuration of
the cultural landscape.

[10]Louis Bromfield: The Farm (Signet Books, New York, 1955), p. 82. A
short story which is particularly effective in depicting a woman's bond with her
garden is John Steinbeck's "The Chrysanthemums" in The Long Valley (The Viking Press, New York, 1938). In this story a rigid woman is made soft and pli-
able by an observant stranger who shows a false interest in her garden. Helen
Worthen relates garden types to individual personalities in a most convincing
manner in "How Does a Garden Grow?" in Landscape, Vol. 19, 1975, pp. 14-27.

character. Like the house-dress association of Rand's character above, Bromfield creates a strong case for the reflection of an individual's personality in a dooryard garden. Landscape thus becomes an additional source of not only environmental communication, but of the casting of a character's personal profile as well.

The Landscape Signature of Entertainment

As a final example of the use of the signature concept to make demands on literature as a geographer, entertainment is considered. In the act of recreation, mankind has created some of the most artificial of all environments. In that context, one may thus infer that such landscapes created in the name of entertainment are intended to be the most ideal modes of space modification. One might be uneasy arguing that either Coney Island or Disneyland represent America's highest landscape design goals, but there is a reality to the observation that landscapes of recreation are designed specifically to be environmentally exciting, pleasing, or both. And the design of such space is a very major component in the creation of an atmosphere which is felt to be conducive to entertainment or recreation. Very seldom, for example, is a design firm which specializes in junior high schools called to do an amusement complex or a resort.

This landscape, then, is one which provides messages to the viewer about the builders and the users of such geographical space. In terms of our interest here, however, we must see still the additional significance which is invested in such geographical space by authors. We are looking not only at the structures themselves, but at the ways in which fictional characters perceive them, utilize them, and react to them.

Author Ray Bradbury has given focus to the importance of landscape in a feature he created in The Illustrated Man. This imaginative novel has a home with a room which might be described as the ultimate in a home entertainment center. It is a variable step-in diorama. Described below it serves well to show the reader the fantastic aspects of the use of landscape in literature.

> He unlocked the door and opened it. Just before he stepped inside, he heard a faraway scream. And then another roar from the lions, which subsided quickly.

> He stepped into Africa. How many times in the last year had he opened this door and found Wonderland, Alice, the Mock Turtle, or Aladdin and his Magical Lamp, or Jack Pumpkinhead of Oz, or Dr. Dolittle, or the cow jumping over a very real-appearing moon--all the delightful contraptions of a make-believe world . . .

George Hadley stood on the African grasslands alone. The lions looked up
from their feeding, watching him. The only flaw to the illusion was the open
door through which he could see his wife, far down the dark hall, like a
framed picture, eating her dinner abstractedly.[11]

The entertainment medium itself--and it does play a role in the development of Bradbury's story--is that of the flexible environment; environment on
demand. It is part of the author's intention to use space in this way. It is part
of the geographer's burden to relate such a contrivance to real geographical
space (what landscapes are chosen in this fantasy?) and to establish how distinct settings might have differential impact on the course of a story. There
are demands in this disciplinary border jumping, but there are also exciting
and stimulating rewards.

Conclusions

Landscape signatures may serve as one arbitrary means of exploring the
role of landscape in literature. Patterns as vast as agricultural and settlement
geometries may be studied in creative writing. Personal expressions of spatial and design preferences as small as gardens and cafes are also available to
the student of landscape who wishes to make inferences for authors and characters regarding culture, personality and geographical space. There is no guarantee that such inferences are bringing the reader or viewer objective truth,
but the evocative power of such an exercise, and frequently such chosen literature, is a certain source of increased environmental sensitivity. The exploration heightens our concern for, interest in, and awareness of the shaping of geographical space.[12]

---

[11]Ray Bradbury: The Illustrated Man (Doubleday and Co., Inc., Garden
City, N.J., 1951), p. 20. Ernest Hemingway made environment and entertainment conjoin in a critical way in one of his most well-known short stories, "A
Clean, Well-Lighted Place " It is the distinct and contrasting choices the characters make for a nighttime setting that give this story much of its impact.
The entire genre of science fiction with its anticipated landscapes also builds on
exotic settings for entertainment as well as daily life. The use of landscape as
an explicit tool for entertainment in the years to come is the dominant theme of,
for example, "Future World" by John R. Hall (Ballantine, New York, 1976).

[12]It should be pointed out that it is not literature alone that can be evocative.
Certain authors are gifted with the ability to make objective, scientific writing
generate clear and unambiguous images. A good example of the way in which a
single landscape can be seen in a variety of different, equally objective ways is
D. W. Meinig's "The Beholding Eye: Ten Versions of the Same Scene" in Landscape Architecture, January 1976, pp. 47-54. Cultural and human geographers
should be rather more concerned with authoring works which induce readers to

In this intense and creative process of geographic speculation it is not only geographical space and the characters that become more vital, but geographers themselves have been known to come alive in company with rich landscape imagery. That is a goal we should all find some pleasure in.

---

complete and contemplate their articles instead of losing interest in a morass of flat and unimaginative prose. Truths, whether allegedly objective or subjective, are not communicated if no one chooses to follow a work through to its conclusion.

CHAPTER 6

SACRED SPACE: EXPLORATIONS OF AN IDEA

Yi-Fu Tuan
University of Minnesota

What does the word "sacred" mean? For many of us it brings to mind certain images such as a temple, a shrine, or the consecration of a bishop, but if we are to understand the true meaning of "sacred" we must go beyond these traditional, culture-bound images to their common experiential ground. At the level of experience, sacred phenomena are those that stand out from the commonplace and interrupt routine. Of course, not everything that is set aside spatially is sacred space, nor is every interruption of routine a hierophany. The word "sacred" signifies apartness and definition; it also suggests order, wholeness, and power. Its meaning is often ambiguous and paradoxical. This enlarged sense of the sacred reminds us that the attempt to understand it is more than an arcane exercise of little relevance to contemporary problems. Planners recognize that a major barrier to their work based on the twin gods of rationality and efficiency is that the distinction between the sacred and the secular is often fuzzy. We normally take parks, neighborhoods, and national territories to be secular entities; yet, given the force of our sentiment toward them, are they not also types of sacred space? To answer this question we need to clarify the meaning of the sacred by exploring its major attributes.

Apartness and Definition

The Latin word sacer carries the sense of restriction: an area stands apart and has limited access because it pertains to the gods. The Hebrew root of k-d-sh, which is usually translated as holy, is based on the idea of separation. A peculiar feeling of dread marks off the holy from the ordinary. Ronald Knox, in his version of the Old Testament, chooses to emphasize this idea of separation in the meaning of k-d-sh. Thus the stirring lines "Be ye Holy, Because I am Holy" turn into the rather pallid "I am set apart and you must be set

84

85

apart like me" (Leviticus xi, 46).[1] That inexpressible sense of dread which is
the religious awareness of the holy is objectified into something "out there" and
spatially distinct. As a thing becomes "holy" it is cut off from surrounding
space. A temple is a sacred templet. The Latin "templum" is derived from
the Greek "templos, " and the root "tem" means "to cut out." Carl Hamburg
says:

> What is cut out, delimited, is at first the space devoted to a God, later any
> section of space (soil, garden or forest) belonging to a king, hero or chief.
> This act of "delimitation" also extends to the heaven whose constellations
> and divisions are related to the "templa" (divisions) of divine effectiveness;
> it establishes "property" as that around which boundaries may be drawn, [an
> idea that] eventually penetrates the realms of social, political and legal
> relations.[2]

Among the most ancient of the known forms of the manmade sanctuary
was the enclosure--a circle of stones or a wall. The enclosure might delimit
an area of concentrated divine power; it then served to warn profane man of the
danger to which he would be exposed if he were to enter without purifactory
rites. City walls, on the other hand, enclosed space that exhibited divine and
human order, or cosmicized space in which people and presiding divinities
could dwell. Mircea Eliade believes that long before walls had military functions they were a magical defense against demons and other forces of chaos
beyond. In times of crisis like a siege or an epidemic, the whole population
might gather and parade around the city walls for the purpose of strengthening
their magico-religious potency.[3]

The literal meaning of "profane" is the ground before and outside the temple. The walls and roof of a temple physically delimit sacred space. Where
physical boundaries are inconspicuous or absent, processions serve to establish apartness. In ancient Roman times the head of a household marked the borders of his domain by circumambulating his fields, singing hymns, and driving
sacrificial animals before him. With such ritual means he hoped to waken the
gods and direct their power to satisfy his needs.[4] In Britain the custom of

---

[1]Mary Douglas: Purity and Danger (Penguin Books, Harmondsworth, 1970),
p. 18.

[2]Carl H. Hamburg: Symbol and Reality (Martinus Nijhoff, The Hague,
1970), p. 100. His authority is Heinrich Nissen: Das Templum: Antiquarische
Untersuchungen (Weidmann, Berlin, 1869).

[3]Mircea Eliade: Patterns in Comparative Religion (World Publishing Co.,
Cleveland, 1963), pp. 370-371.

[4]N. D. Fustel de Coulanges: The Ancient City (Doubleday Anchor Books,
Garden City, n.d.), p. 67.

"beating the bounds" required the parish priest to walk around his parish and strike certain markers with a stick. In traditional China a religious procession through a ring of villages defined the domain of the temple god housed in the central marketplace.[5]

Delimitation, definition, and keeping the categories apart, these intellectual procedures are primordially religious. The Lord said to Moses: "You shall not allow two different kinds of beast to mate together. You shall not plant your field with two kinds of seed. You shall not put on a garment woven with two kinds of yarn" (Leviticus xix, 19). "Holiness," Mary Douglas writes, "requires that different classes of things shall not be confused. [It] means keeping distinct the categories of creation. It therefore involves correct definition, discrimination and order."[6]

Order and Wholeness

In the beginning of creation, Genesis tells us, the earth was without form and void, darkness hovered over the face of the abyss and a mighty wind swept over the surface of the waters. In the end was perfect order. St. John saw a new heaven and a new earth on which there no longer existed any sea or darkness for the glory of God gave light. In the beginning was confusion. In the end St. John beheld the holy city of Jerusalem, which had the crystalline structure and radiance of some priceless jewel (Revelation xxi).

The city symbolized heavenly order. Within its walls one found just rules and discriminations; beyond them lay chaos and arbitrariness. The most heartfelt eschatological longings drew on city imagery in utterance. Thus St. Bernard cried: "O Sion, thou city sole and single, mystic mansion hidden away in the heavens, now I rejoice in thee, now I mourn and yearn for thee . . . None can disclose or utter in speech what plenary radiance fills thy walls and citadels."[7] William Blake denounced the dark Satanic mills but what he yearned for was not just England's green and pleasant land; he wanted the New Jerusalem to be built on it. Of course we realize that the city has long lost its power to symbolize order and justice. Indeed it now stands for chaos and oppression.

---

[5]G. William Skinner: Marketing and Social Structure in Rural China, Journal of Asian Studies, Vol. 24, 1964, p. 38.

[6]Douglas, op. cit. [see note 1 above], p. 67.

[7]Quoted in Rudolf Otto: The Idea of the Holy (Oxford University Press, London, 1958), pp. 34-35.

The modern metropolis is perceived to be a sprawl with no discernible edge, polluted, and dangerous. In religious language the city is profane--a wilderness, whereas what was once wilderness has acquired the aura and the esteem of sacred space. Nature areas are set aside. They have well defined boundaries. Profane commerce is forbidden within. Motorized man must be unshod, that is, abandon his wheels at the gate. Raw nature, far from being chaotic, is now perceived to be a model of ecological harmony. Wild life, far from being red in tooth and claw, is a lesson in symbiotic cooperation. Order remains a characteristic of sacred space but the environments in which we discern order are reversed.

A root meaning of "holy, " we have noted, is separateness. In addition the word connotes the idea of the whole and the complete. Things presented at the temple, including persons, must show physical perfection. Sacrificial animals should be without blemish. A priest, according to Leviticus, cannot be a mutilated being; he must be a whole or holy man. In the field of work and action, wholeness implies that any task, once begun, must not be left unfinished. "What man is there that has built a new house and has not dedicated it? Let him go back to his house, lest he die in the battle and another man dedicate it" (Deuteronomy xx). Several passages in the Bible strongly suggest that a man should not put his hand to the plow and then turn back. [8]

These ideas can be applied to the city and to wilderness as types of sacred space. Significantly, when the city symbolized cosmic order it also projected an image of wholeness and completion. An ancient city--its walls, streets, and major buildings--might take only a year or so to construct. By building rapidly with an army of workmen, a ruler was able to create the impression that his capital had descended from heaven. [9] In contrast, wild nature beyond the walls looked unfinished and chaotic. Our age has witnessed a reversal of perceptions. To us it is the city that looks raw and protean. Buildings are constantly being torn down and raised again, suburbs grow and decay, so that it is hard for anyone to associate the ideas of wholeness and completion

---

[8] Douglas, op. cit. [see note 1 above], pp. 65-66.

[9] I have noted the rapidity of construction of Chinese cities in A Preface to Chinese Cities in Urbanization and Its Problems (edited by R. P. Beckinsale and J. M. Houston; Blackwell, Oxford, 1968), pp. 247-259. Construction of Medinat-as-Salam, the round capital of the Abbasid Caliphs, began in A.D. 762. One hundred thousand workers built with such speed that the caliph al-Mansur was able to move in the following year. See Guy Le Strange: Baghdad during the Abbasid Caliphate (Clarendon Press Oxford, 1924).

with the modern metropolis. On the other hand, people appear to sense stability and permanence in wilderness areas.[10] Ecologists contribute to this feeling when they describe the tropical rain forest and desert life forms as "climax" communities. Having achieved "climax," such communities will resist change. More and more people are learning to see nature, not as something raw but rather as an achieved work--complete, whole, and even holy.

Power

Power is an attribute of the sacred. How is power manifest? It is manifest in two contradictory ways: order and violence. Order, whether we see it in the procession of the stars or in the smooth running of a vast bureaucracy, signifies functioning power. On the other hand, violence is the most dramatic display of power. In Genesis, we see God's might revealed in the orderly processes of creation. He made the world by a series of steps, bringing light into darkness, separating day from night and land from water. There was confusion, there is now order; thus God created and thus human beings create. But once an orderly system comes into being power is no longer a dramatic presence; it is merely that which maintains the system. Living in a perfect cosmos, without even an occasional meteor or rebellion to disrupt the ritual round, induces boredom. Such a world seems sterile. Rather than the mineralized city, darkness and the sea appear to be more suitable emblems of potency. Power therefore has another meaning in religious discourse: it signifies urgent, compelling, and unpredictable energy. In nature power is manifest as thunder, lightning, and the whirlwind. In the Old Testament it is the wrath of God. Rudolf Otto says that such divine might has no concern whatever with moral qualities. It acts like "a hidden force of nature, like stored-up electricity, discharging itself upon anyone who comes too near. It is 'incalculable' and 'arbitrary.'"[11]

This image of power suggests destruction, but also renewal and freedom. One must undo to redo, and break the bounds of order to feel free. Power is the capacity to begin anew, open up and venture forth. Power thus conceived is compatible with the idea of boundary but not boundary as limit or separation, rather boundary as starting line or threshold. Growth is the successive attainment and transcendence of limits. For a child to grow and assume the full

---

[10] Linda Graber: Wilderness as Sacred Space, Monograph Series No. 8 (Assoc. of Amer. Geogrs., Washington, D.C., 1976).

[11] Otto, op. cit. [see note 7 above], p. 18.

potency of manhood he must cross a threshold marked by the disorienting rites of initiation. For the pilgrim to reach sacred place, he must abandon the safe borders of home and traverse unfamiliar space. [12]

Ambiguity and Paradox

The concept "sacred" is ambiguous. It cannot be described at length without a deepening sense of paradox. On the one hand, the sacred is a gentle tide of life, inducing in the worshiper a feeling of serenity and well-being; on the other, it is a force, violent and unpredictable, causing terror. The sacred can be both terrible and fascinating: people both fear it and feel irresistibly drawn to it. The sacred can mean a plenitude of being, yet mystics have described it as the void and nothingness. Whereas life and abundance are the fruits of creative power, the sacred also signifies the "wholly other." It cannot therefore be anything that is obviously made; it is not this, not that. From one viewpoint the golden calf, the tabernacle, and the righteous city are all sacred. However, because these are defined essences and restricted modes of being they cannot be the "wholly other." Thus, from another viewpoint the sacred cannot manifest itself in the fruitful garden or bustling city; rather the desert-- bare and silent--is its proper stage.

Light and Darkness

The sacred exhibits polarized characteristics. Consider three such pairs: light and darkness, structure and anti-structure, power and purity. Light is a prime symbol of the sacred. Day and night are common experiences. In the dark we are like blind men, disoriented and fearful. Our world has shrunk and lost shape. Dreams and nightmares haunt us. As the sun rises over the horizon and we wake up, our world expands, gains shape and precision. Fields and houses emerge out of darkness. What was invisible and nonexistent is now thrown into sharp relief by the levitating sun. It is as though God is recreating the world before our eyes. Light means life; night brings oblivion and sleep seems a little death. Can anything wholesome thrive in the dark? Starless nights feel oppressive in contrast to pellucid days which invigorate. Awareness of light and darkness is fundamental to the distinction between sacred and profane space. In Near Eastern and gnostic traditions, illuminated

---

[12]Victor Turner: The Center Out There: Pilgrim's Goal, History of Religions, Vol. 12, 1973, pp. 213-214.

space is sacred space.[13] In the Upper Nile region, the Dinka cattle herders associate darkness with unseen and sudden dangers. Darkness is in opposition to daylight, yet for the Dinka a sign of respect is to shade an object or person from the sun.[14]

This "yet"--this detail from an African culture--reminds us that the human experience of light is sufficiently ambivalent for light to carry negative meanings. Thus not darkness but light may signify death. Seeds must be buried in the ground before they can grow. Nothing that is unremittingly exposed to strong light will live. Even ideas require darkness to germinate.[15] A public man, always under the limelight, is shallow and can have no new thoughts. In sleep we recuperate. Night refreshes, day exhausts. Black connotes potency, whereas white suggests sterility and languor. Darkness, moreover, evokes mystery and awe which are essential to the idea of the holy. The walls of a temple keep out the sun and thereby create a pool of darkness. When the worshiper steps into the temple he moves from the sunlit but profane public square into the dark and numinous world of the sacred.

Structure and Anti-structure

Structure and anti-structure constitute another polarized pair in religious experience. I have stressed earlier that sacred space is demarcated and differentiated space; it shows order, its antithesis being formlessness and chaos. However, the opposite of structure need not be formlessness; it can be freedom. Religious experience is able to lift one to a transcendental plane where the structure and distinctions necessary to the ordering of life in this world do not apply.

Mystical, universalist, and apocalyptic religions have little use for particularized sacred space. From the mystical and apocalyptic viewpoint, the

---

[13]On the symbolism of light and darkness in ancient Israel, see J. Pedersen: Israel: Its Life and Culture (Oxford University Press, London, 1926), pp. 464-466.

[14]Godfrey Lienhardt: Divinity and Experience: The Religion of the Dinka (Clarendon Press, Oxford, 1961), p. 159.

[15]"Darkness" here is of course used in a more metaphorical sense. It suggests privacy and withdrawal. On the Dark Age of Greece as the gestation period of Greek culture and the incubation of the Mediterranean way of life, see Dan Stanislawski: Dark Age Contributions to the Mediterranean Way of Life, Annals Assn. of Amer. Geogrs., Vol. 63, 1973, pp. 397-410.

world is a threshold to eternity; in the light of the eternal the hierarchies and boundaries of social life and space seem unimportant. "It is useless to offer your spirit a garden--even a garden inhabited by saints and angels--and pretend that it has been made free of the universe, " wrote Evelyn Underhill. "You will not have peace until you do away with all banks and hedges, and exchange the garden for the wilderness that is unwalled."[16] The apostle Peter completely misunderstood the meaning of Christ's transfiguration on the mountain when he offered to make three shelters there, one for Christ, one for Moses, and one for Elijah (Matthew xvii, 1-9). The Kingdom of God is not a locality. A religion that emphasizes the universal fatherhood of God and his role as creator also tends to minimize the significance of those earthly categories to which mortals are bound. The burden of rules and taboos is lifted from a child of God. The apostle Paul could write: "You may eat anything sold in the meat-market without raising questions of conscience; for the earth is the Lord's and everything in it" (I Corinthians x, 25-26).

Pilgrimage, according to Victor Turner, may be seen as a movement from structure to anti-structure. A pilgrim is a person who abandons his assigned roles and status in a structured community for the hazardous journey to a sacred place. At the sacred place the pilgrim becomes one individual among a multitude of like-minded seekers after truth. His particular loyalties and obligations are there transcended by the overarching value of universal brotherhood and love.[17] The pilgrim feels disencumbered at the sacred place, which is peripheral to his workaday life but central to his religious life.

Sacred space or place varies greatly in character. Both the cathedral in the heart of a city and a remote shrine are instances of it. Consider Rome. All roads lead to Rome--the center of Christendom and the goal of major pilgrimages. Rome may well be a larger and more hierarchically structured community than the one the pilgrim has left. The journey, then, is from one structure to another even more highly organized. This would seem to contradict what we have noted earlier. Yet even Rome is not the Christian's final destination; in a sense, it is merely the gate to the eternal. Viewed as gate rather than as everlasting city, Rome becomes a place for "people of the way, " which was a common label for early Christians. At Rome the pilgrims feel less

---

[16]Evelyn Underhill: Practical Mysticism (Dutton & Co., New York, 1961), p. 109. "Practical Mysticism" was first published in 1915.

[17]Turner, op. cit. [see note 12 above].

bound to rules and social constraints than they do in their own hometowns. In fact, as Turner observed, although many European sacred places are great cathedral cities, many others--like the shrines of the Virgin at Lourdes, Fatima, La Salette, and Oostacker--occupy marginal locations. The placing of the holiest shrines at circumferential sites is not confined to Christian pilgrimage systems. For example, Mount Kailas and Lake Masas, two of the holiest places for Hindus, are located on the further side of the Himalayas in Tibet. Peripheral location is a geographical emblem of anti-structure.[18]

This interplay between center and periphery, structure and anti-structure, is a well known theme in the settlement of the United States. As Daniel Boorstin puts it, "There is a hidden precision in the reverent cliché which describes the earliest New England settlers as Pilgrims." The first Puritans and Separatists saw themselves going on a pilgrimage. They abandoned the structured communities of the Old World for the freedom of the New; they left the center for the periphery. New England was a wilderness, and yet it was the goal of their pilgrimage and the sacred place upon which they would rebuild Jerusalem.[19]

Power and Purity

Power and purity form an antinomic pair in religious experience. When both are viewed as attributes of the sacred, their contradiction becomes evident. Power can take care of itself, purity cannot. The holy person is endowed with power; people are drawn to him and yet keep their distance. The holy ground emanates power, and a fence encircles it for the same reason that a station generating electricity is fenced in--to warn and shield unwary man. Raw might cannot be polluted: we can pollute a lake but not a whirlwind, we can contaminate the earth but not the sun. The sacred as awesome energy does not need protection; mortal beings like us need to be shielded from it. On the other hand, the sacred as purity does require protection. Fences must be built and guards hired to keep the sacred areas pure.

Feelings concerning power and purity, dirt and the limits of being arise out of common human experiences and dilemmas. Edmund Leach puts it this way. Every child, as he develops a consciousness of identity, will pose the questions, "What am I? Where is the boundary of myself?" The exuviae of the

---

[18]Ibid., pp. 212-213.

[19]Daniel J. Boorstin: The Exploring Spirit (Random House, New York, 1976), pp. 20-21.

93

body present a special problem. "Are my faeces, urine, semen, and sweat a part of me or not?" Skin forms a tangible boundary and the orifices of the body are gateways. Human exuviae are the prototype of dirt: they are very much matter out of place. In most societies they are a focus of taboo. Dirt at the boundary is threatening and portends desecration. But such formulations lead to paradox. Individuals are not self-sufficient beings with closed boundaries; they are connected with each other in relations of interdependence and of power. The paradox is that I can only be sure of my own integrity if I am clean, but a completely clean "I" with no boundary dirt can have no traffic with other individuals and the outside world.[20] Note the way we use polite language to keep acquaintances at arm's length. With intimate friends we may exchange good-natured abuse and off-color jokes. In some societies (Mali, for example) best friends literally throw excrement at each other.[21] What are we to infer from this curious behavior? One inference is that communication--particularly at an intimate level--is inherently polluting. Another is that to be clean and pure is to be impotent and that power resides in dirt. This paradox, Leach claims, is responsible for a vast variety of religious practices, including the tendency for holiness to be attributed both to ascetic and to ecstatic behavior.[22]

Sacred Space in the Modern World

I have noted certain characteristics associated with the idea of the sacred. How are they manifest in the modern world which is commonly described as secular? The landscapes of today still contain many church buildings and these we tend to label "sacred," unreflectively. In an equally unreflective manner we think of the modern nation-state, suburb, and neighborhood as secular spaces and institutions. But if we look at these spaces more closely, we may find that their claim to the epithet "sacred" is not inferior to that of most churches and church buildings of our time.

---

[20]Edmund Leach: Culture and Communication (Cambridge Univ. Press, Cambridge, 1976), pp. 62-63.

[21]Robert Brain: Friends and Lovers (Basic Books, New York, 1976), p. 10.

[22]Leach, op. cit. [see note 20 above].

Secular Church?

Consider, first, the church. In the medieval period the sacred affected
social life on every level. It had potency because it was taken to be radically
different from the world it penetrated. "The sacred," Peter Brown observed,
"was all that the human community was not."[23] Here are two illustrations of
the power and sanctity of the House of God in medieval times. William of
Malmesbury attributed such might to the church building at Glastonbury that, as
he put it, "if any person erected a building in its vicinity, which by its shade
obstructed the light of the church, it forthwith became a ruin."[24] A sacred edi-
fice radiated power. All consecrated church buildings and lands possessed in
some degree the privilege of affording sanctuary to the fugitive, but a few privi-
leged churches such as Durham cathedral, the abbeys of Westminster, and Glastonbury offered the fugitive an immunity from pursuit of up to a mile from the
building sites.[25]

In the Middle Ages the reality of the sacred was everywhere evident; its
power and otherness were not in doubt. Because of this fact the sacred could
mix with the secular with seeming abandon. Houses of God, for example, took
on a wide range of secular functions. Carolly Erickson noted that in Italy,
"nobles and civic officials commonly held banquets in cathedrals, and oaths of
all sorts--including political conspiracies--were solemnized on holy ground."[26]
In our time, as the church and its buildings accommodate more and more secular functions we seem to be returning to a practice common in the Age of Faith.
However, because the sacred has lost its aura of transcendental otherness and
because it no longer plays a vital role in group life, the current trend does not
indicate--as churchmen would like to believe--an expansion of the divine into
the secular sphere; rather it augurs the total capitulation of the divine. The difference between a medieval and contemporary church is this. A medieval

---

[23]Peter Brown: Society and the Supernatural: A Medieval Change, Daeda-
lus, Vol. 104, 1975, p. 141.

[24]Carolly Erickson: The Medieval Vision (Oxford Univ. Press, New York,
1976), p. 19. Skyscrapers dwarf and overshadow St. Patrick's Cathedral on
Fifth Avenue, New York. Their builders clearly felt no qualms over infringing
the Cathedral's sacred space.

[25]John Bellamy: Crime and Public Order in England in the Later Middle
Ages (University of Toronto Press, Toronto, 1973), p. 106.

[26]Erickson, op. cit. [see note 24] p. 75.

95

church, however much it catered to secular activities, was primarily sacred space: it radiated power. A modern church, notwithstanding its remaining religious functions, is increasingly a social and service center.

Sacred State

In 1964 the then Archbishop of Canterbury, Arthur Michael Ramsey, wrote: "The State--not only the Christian State but the State as such--has a divine role."[27] He was expounding a doctrine that goes back to Saint Paul (Romans xiii, 5-6). Order is an attribute of the sacred. The state imposes and maintains order. When an atheistic government declares that in Moscow or Leningrad one may drive only on one side of the street, it is fulfilling a divine role. Power is an attribute of the sacred. The state has great power over its people. We even personalize modern nations and call them sovereign powers as though they constitute an order of angels. The state's power can be oppressive, but to its influential citizens it is normally nurturing. A nation feeds its people and supports their way of life. It seems natural to address the nation as motherland or fatherland. From time immemorial political leaders have periodically sounded the alarm. "Our sacred soil (motherland or fatherland) has been violated." To this rhetorical cry, citizens are expected to--and do--respond by offering their lives.[28] The ultimate sacrifice is appropriate to the defense of the sacred. Completeness is an attribute of the sacred. The modern nation-state has at various times sought for self-sufficiency, for a shape and a size that can provide it with an illusion of completeness.[29] The modern

---

[27]Arthur Michael Ramsey: Sacred and Secular (Harper & Row, New York, 1965), p. 61.

[28]Much of the modern rhetoric of patriotism, which substituted the state for God as that which commanded a people's ultimate allegiance, originated in France after the Revolution. See H. F. Stewart and P. Desjardins: French Patriotism in the Nineteenth Century 1814-1833 (Cambridge Univ. Press, Cambridge, 1923). One example of the rhetoric: In Turkey's Republican People's Party program, adopted in 1935, are the words: "The fatherland is the sacred country within our present political boundaries, where the Turkish nation lives with its ancient and illustrious history, and with its past glories still living in the depths of its soil." Bernard Lewis: History Remembered, Recovered, Invented (Princeton Univ. Press, Princeton, 1975), p. 39.

[29]Norman J. G. Pounds: France and "Les Limites Naturelles" from the Seventeenth to the Twentieth Centuries, Annals Assn. of Amer. Geogrs., Vol. 44, 1954, pp. 51-62.

nation-state has been described as "organic," a term that suggests complete-ness--an integral whole which must not be violated or contaminated. Boundary or limit is a characteristic of sacred space: the temple is a precisely circum-scribed area. The modern nation-state, unlike an ancient empire or a medieval fief, has well defined boundaries. People who cross them are required to per-form the appropriate rites, which can be stringent or lax depending on the trav-eler's degree of purity.

Pure Suburb and Neighborhood

We see, then, that the sharply bounded political state is a type of sacred space for our time. Another example (at a smaller scale) is the segregated social space within a city. The pure neighborhood that deliberately excludes poor people and enterprises of low status is a relatively modern phenomenon. In England, even in the seventeenth century, social and economic areas within the city were not yet clearly demarcated and labeled. Great houses, slums, and stables, merchant residences and warehouses, market stalls and inns stood side by side. A person of rank could and did spend the greater part of his waking life in the presence of people of all conditions. He was confident of his status in society. His rank and wealth were manifest in his speech and gesture, and in the clothes and accouterments he carried on his person. These personal emblems rather than residential address proclaimed his social standing.[30] By the nineteenth century, as the rigidities of rank weakened and membership in the middle class swelled, people of new affluence could not be sure of their sta-tus; clothes and deportment might fail to command the expected degree of defer-ence. To a person rising up the ranks of the middle class it was a risk to be seen with workmen and laborers. Safety lay in geographical segregation--in having the right kind of house in the right area. Social distance was translated progressively into spatial distance.

Crowding, social disorientation, and the soiling of the environment by new industries made it imperative for people who could move out to do so. In the suburbs, members of the striving middle class sought to create not only a pleasant physical setting but also a moral ambience of purity and innocence antipodal to the begrimed city and to the ruthless world of business. The sub-urb was a modest Eden to be protected from pollution by factories and the great

---

[30]Elizabeth Burns: Theatricality· A Study of Convention in the Theatre and Its Social Life (Harper Torchbooks, New York, 1973), p. 77.

unwashed. It was a type of sacred space in which only women and children were refined or innocent enough to dwell. Cigar-chomping men were tolerated. Profanity and business talk had a place in a middle-class Victorian household only under special conditions--after the ladies had withdrawn. [31]

In our time, and especially in the period after the Second World War, the suburbs as a whole have been shedding their collective image of purity and exclusiveness. One factor that contributed to this trend was the mass construction of inexpensive, amorphous, and often crudely finished housing estates. Another factor was the willingness of even well-to-do suburbs to accept shopping centers in their midst for the services they provide, and to encourage the presence of clean industries for their share of the tax burden. In the United States the civil rights movement of the 1960s dealt one more severe blow to the ideal of residential purity. People living in exclusive enclaves find it more and more difficult to defend their neighborhood as inviolate space. They can still keep out commerce and industry but--except under the newest pretext of "no growth"--they can no longer exclude other human beings with an air of virtue. In protecting nature, however, well-educated members of the middle class remain free to articulate their indignation. As one type of sacred space loses its exclusiveness, another may gain. It is not surprising that the passion for pure water and air, for pure environments unspoilt by powerlines and reservoirs, blazed high when that for civil rights began to cool. [32]

Secular: Loss of Fear and Splendor

The modern world has its sacred spaces. Nevertheless the feeling may persist that when we apply the term "sacred" to the wilderness and even to the suburb we are stretching--though I believe legitimately--its meaning. What is largely absent in the modern world is a sense of awe as before a numinous pow-

---

[31] Lewis Mumford: The City in History (Harcourt, Brace & World, New York, 1961), pp. 492-493; Christopher Lasch: The Emotions of Family Life, New York Review of Books, Vol. 22, No. 19, 1975, pp. 37-42; Richard Sennett: The Fall of Public Man (Cambridge University Press, Cambridge, 1976), pp. 178-180. For a sensitive portrayal of the development of an American suburb and of the American suburban ideal, see Suzannah Lessard: The Suburban Landscape: Oyster Bay, Long Island, The New Yorker, October 11, 1976, pp. 44-49.

[32] Calvin W. Stillman: This Fair Land, in Landscape Assessment: Value, Perceptions, and Resources (edited by Ervin H. Zube, Robert O. Brush, and Julius Gy Fabos; Dowden, Hutchinson, & Ross, Stroudsburg, 1975), pp. 18-30.

er that both attracts and repels. From a secular viewpoint purity almost seems the antithesis of power. We tend to think of a good fellow as an ineffectual fellow, a pure being as a vulnerable being. From a religious viewpoint purity's import is more ambiguous. Saints, it is true, suffer; on the other hand the Lamb--that symbol of innocence--ruled in New Jerusalem, and when Christ died the death of a common criminal on the cross the event had immediate and cosmic repercussions: the apostle Matthew reported that the moment Christ breathed his last the earth quaked, the rocks split and the graves opened.

In times past trespassing on a sacred grove brought dire consequences on the culprit. He suffered automatically, as we would when we touch a high-tension wire. Of course the guardians of the sacred grove might apprehend the trespasser and punish him, as we would be fined for intruding on the property of a power company, but it is not the human and legal power that can inspire awe. People approached a cave or mountain in fear and trembling because they believed it to be the habitation of a supernatural power that far exceeds human grasp. Today the gods no longer dwell in forests and streams. If we abuse nature we shall pay for our wantonness in the long run, and ecologists can tell us just how this will happen with the help of systems analysis and computers. But such rational and longwinded argument cannot chill our spine as can the belief that if we polluted a sacred spring our limbs will at once wither.

The sacred landscape was, in an important sense, a landscape of fear. Progressive knowledge of how nature works has removed much of the fear. We are now likely to encounter it only in tales of the supernatural such as those of Algernon Blackwood. In his short stories--and particularly in "The Willows"-- Blackwood can still waken in us that sense of uncanny dread before an alien and malevolent nature which our distant forebears knew through personal experience.[33] The diminishment of superstitious fear is good. On the other hand,

---

[33]"Great revelations of nature, of course, never fail to impress in one way or another, and I was no stranger to moods of the kind. Mountains overawe and oceans terrify . . . But all these at one point or another, somewhere link on intimately with human life and human experience. They stir comprehensible, even if alarming, emotions . . . With this multitude of willows, however, it was something far different, I felt. Some essence emanated from them that besieged the heart. A sense of awe awakened, true, but of awe touched somewhere by a vague terror. Their serried ranks, growing everywhere darker about me as the shadows deepened, moving furiously yet softly in the wind, woke in me the curious and unwelcome suggestion that we had trespassed here upon the borders of an alien world, a world where we were intruders . . ." In Algernon Blackwood: Best Ghost Stories of Algernon Blackwood, selected with an introduction by E. F. Bleiler (Dover Publications, New York, 1973), p. 8.

our pretense to scientific understanding and power has also corroded our feeling for profound mysteries. The world seems transparent. Contemporary space, however colorful and varied, lacks polarized tension as between the numinous and the quotidian. Contemporary life, however pleasant and exciting, moves on one plane--the plane encompassed by rational and humanist vision. Ecstasy and dread, the heights and the depths, the awesome and the transcendent rarely intrude on our lives and on our landscapes except under the influence of chemical stimulus. Along certain dimensions our world has contracted. At the United Nations, for example, fellowship reaches out to the whole of humanity; it is a noble ideal, but at a communion service humanity is called to join with angels and archangels and the whole company of heaven--far outnumbering the people now living on earth--in the worship of God. A sense of holiness and of otherwordly splendor has dimmed in modern times, and some people feel the loss.

CHAPTER 7

RELIGION AND LANDSCAPE IN THE MORMON CULTURAL REGION

Richard H. Jackson

Brigham Young University

Mormonland: The word itself evokes an image of some type in the mind of the listener. For some, Mormon Country represents an enclave of religious zealots, for others that strip of territory which breaks the monotony of the landscape between the Rockies and the Sierra Nevadas. Whatever their mental image, all who have heard of the Mormons also have some stereotype of the land occupied by Brigham Young and his followers. Vignettes of burning deserts, miraculous seagulls, temples and angels, abandoned barns and irrigation systems combine to provide an image of the West: Mormonland.

The area occupied by the Mormons is a special example of the impact of culture on the natural landscape. The worldview of the Mormon belief system contains values which have directly affected the landscape of the region. Paramount among these views is the doctrine that the Rocky Mountain area is a sacred site reserved for occupation by the Mormons. This view affected Mormon doctrine from the time of Mormon settlement in the Salt Lake Valley in 1847. Converts to the church were taught that it was their duty to migrate to Zion to assist in transforming the "wilderness." Biblical statements concerning the desert blossoming as a rose and establishment of Zion in the mountain tops were interpreted by the Mormons as reference to their settlement activities.

From church doctrine and biblical references the Mormon culture region emerged as sacred space to adherents of the religion. Until the post-World War II era Mormons residing outside of the intermountain area viewed themselves as temporary residents in profane space. The goal of those in the diaspora was to return to their Zion in the west. Although the center of this sacred region was Salt Lake City, varying levels of sanctity were, and are, ascribed to the entire region occupied by the Mormons in the intermontane west.

The areas settled and occupied by Mormons are dotted in a discontinuous pattern across three countries and more than ten states. Several studies have attempted to delimit the areal extent of the Mormon culture and although there are minor variations among authors as to the precise boundaries, the general extent of the region is fairly uniform (Figure 1). The basis for this regional distribution is the dominance of membership in the Church of Jesus Christ of Latter-day Saints (Mormon) among residents of the region. Since membership in the Mormon church does not require adoption of unique styles of dress nor markedly different food types, there is no readily discernible characteristic of the residents of the region which defines them as Mormon. Some casual observers have maintained that while the Mormon people are not necessarily recognizable outside of the region, there are features common to the Mormon cultural region which allows categorization of a unique, readily recognizable, Mormon landscape.

Inherent in the statement "Mormon Landscape" is the idea that there is such a unique setting. A number of factors complicate an answer to the question of "is there a unique Mormon landscape?" First, the people themselves have always tended to be isolationist and to maintain their culture as being unique, whether it is or not. Second, their settlements were based on religion, so that non-Mormons were not involved and the result initially was a homogeneous culture occupying the land. Third, their geographic location in Utah has been one of isolation, with the mountains and sparsely settled areas of semiarid Wyoming and Colorado to the east, arid Arizona and New Mexico to the south, and the deserts of the Great Basin to the west. Fourth, the geographic setting is unique in that the Rocky Mountains provide a relative (to the West as a whole) abundance of moisture and the resultant agricultural economy is based on irrigated farms producing crops rather than the grazing economy typical of most of the land in the West. Thus to the traveller or casual viewer there appears a unique Mormon landscape in the West. This landscape can generally be described as one of small rural communities with the seemingly unique characteristics of extraordinarily wide streets, irrigation ditches, cardinal orientation of streets, agricultural related activities in the town, and relic architectural features of unpainted barns and simple central hall houses.[1] The fact that the

[1] Richard V. Francaviglia: The Mormon Landscape: Definition of an Image in the West, Proceedings, Association of American Geographers, Vol. 2, 1970, pp. 59-61. See also: Donald Meining: The Mormon Culture Region: Strategies and Patterns in the Geography of the American West, 1847-1964,

Selected Definitions of the Mormon Culture Region

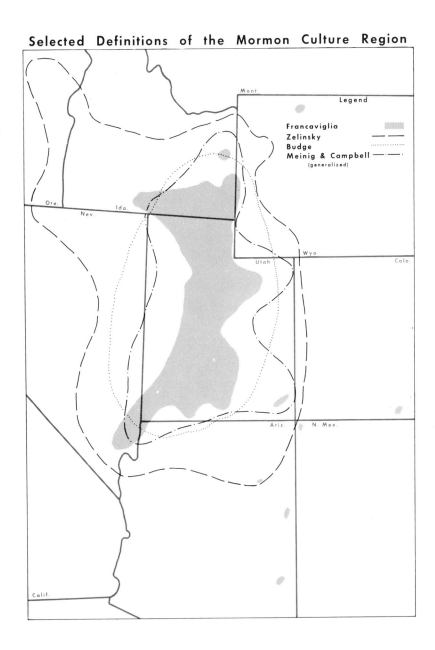

Fig. 1. --Selected definitions of the Mormon Cultural Region

small towns are primarily populated by Mormons who steadfastly maintain their uniqueness results in classifying the landscape as unique to the Mormons.

Did the distinct Mormon Culture develop a unique landscape or has the landscape been classified as unique because it is occupied by a unique cultural group? In considering the cultural landscapes of the United States does the landscape occupied by the Mormons stand out as unique because of its distinctive components, or does it reflect the American rural landscape in general, only in an isolated geographical setting occupied by a unique culture? The fundamental question becomes one of whether or not the area settled by the Mormons would have a markedly different appearance today if it had been colonized by typical American settlers having a heterogeneous religious commitment. An examination of the specific features normally associated with the Mormon Cultural Landscape provides insight into this question.

Elements of the Mormon Cultural Landscape

Four major categories of elements are normally recognized by works describing the Mormon landscape.

1) The nucleated Mormon Village with its wide streets.

2) Architectural styles and construction materials.

3) Agricultural related phenomena (barns, fences, irrigation, field patterns).

4) Mormon chapels and other religious edifices.

The Mormon Village

The Mormon village has been described by observers as a uniform, nucleated settlement with a regular grid pattern characterized by extreme street

Annals, Association of American Geographers, Vol. 58, 1965, pp. 191-220; Seth Budge: Perception of the Boundaries of the Mormon Cultural Region, Great Plains--Rocky Mountain Geographical Journal, Vol. 3, 1974, pp. 1-9; Lester D. Campbell: Perception and Land Use: The Use of the Mormon Culture Region (Thesis, Brigham Young University, 1974); Peter L. Goss: Architectural History of Utah, Utah Historical Quarterly, Vol. 43, 1975, pp. 286-300; Leon Sidney Pitman: A Survey of Nineteenth Century Folk Housing in the Mormon Culture Region (Thesis, Louisiana State University, Baton Rouge, 1973); Cindy Rice: Spring City: A Look at a Nineteenth Century Mormon Village, Utah Historical Quarterly, Vol. 43, 1975, pp. 261-277; Barry M. Roth: A Geographic Study of Stone Houses in Selected Utah Communities (Thesis, Brigham Young University, Provo, Utah, 1973); J. E. Spencer: House Types of Southern Utah, Geographical Review, Vol. 35, 1945, pp. 444-457.

width. The basis for the Mormon Village is supposedly the "City of Zion" city plan developed in Ohio by the founder of the Mormon church, Joseph Smith, in 1833[2] (Figure 2). This plan specified streets 132 feet wide, ten and fifteen acre blocks, half-acre lots, uniform spacing and setbacks for buildings, and required that all houses be built of brick and stone, and all agriculturally related activities to be carried out on small farms outside of the community.

These characteristics of the City of Zion plan are found to be less than unique when compared to communities established in the Ohio-Mississippi lowland during the same period. Philadelphia, the example for most communities in the Trans-Appalachian area, had a regular gridiron pattern, uniform spacing and setbacks for all buildings, and major streets of 100-feet width. Since wide streets are so often viewed as synonymous with Mormon settlement, it is interesting to compare the City of Zion street width with those of other Ohio settlements of the early 1800s. Waverly, Ohio (1831) was platted with a main street 215 feet wide; Sandusky, Ohio (1830) had streets 125 feet wide; Fremont, Ohio

[2]The widespread acceptance that the Mormon settlements were all the same is found in most works Representative examples include: Lowry Nelson: The Mormon Village: A Pattern and Technique of Land Settlement (University of Utah Press, Salt Lake City, 1952), p. 38, states that all the villages of Utah were based on the plan presented by Joseph Smith; Jan O. M. Broek and John W. Webb: A Geography of Mankind (McGraw-Hill, New York, 1968), p. 354, state that all Mormon villages are alike, having square blocks with four lots per block; Leland H. Creer: The Founding of an Empire (Bookcraft, Salt Lake City, 1947), p. 362, states that they were all laid out following the pattern of Salt Lake City; Milton R. Hunter: Utah in Her Western Setting (Deseret News Press, Salt Lake City, 1959), p. 346, states that all of the cities were built on the same plan with ten acre blocks in all; John W. Reps: Making of Urban America (Princeton University Press, Princeton, 1965), p. 48, says that while the villages may have varied slightly from one another, they are essentially uniform; P. A. M. Taylor: Expectations Westward (Oliver and Boyd, London, 1965), p. 111, maintains that all of the Mormon communities were planned on the basis of the plan of Joseph Smith.

Nearly any book which mentions the Mormon villages in Utah states that they were based on the City of Zion plat. As an example, Nelson, op. cit., p. 38, states that the plan for the City of Zion was the guide for all the villages of Utah, and Reps, op. cit., p. 472, states that "While not all of them [Mormon villages] adhered to the strict prescriptions of Joseph Smith, they were all planned in the spirit of his original conceptions." Others inform the reader that all Mormon communities were laid out exactly like Salt Lake City. "Located in Millard County, Utah, the town of Fillmore was laid out in 1851 according to the plat universally followed in building Mormon communities. The land was first divided into blocks of ten acres each, which in turn were sub-divided into eight equal lots, in R. Baily, ed.: Lt. Sylvester Mowry's Report on His March in 1855 from Salt Lake City to Fort Tejon, Arizona and the West, Vol. 7, 1965, p. 333, italics added.

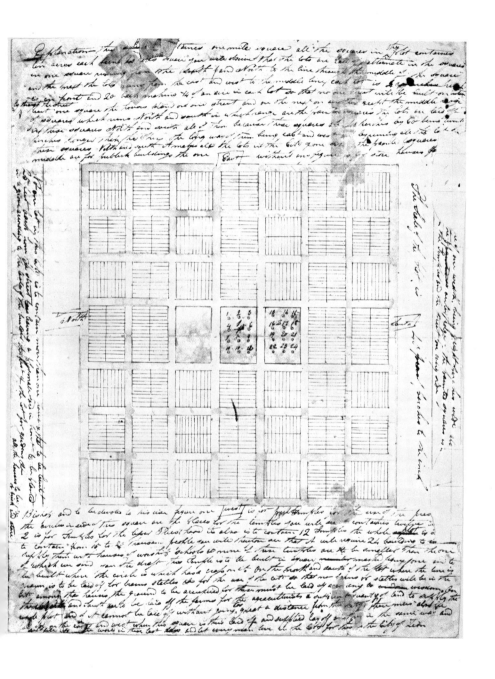

Fig. 2.--City of Zion plat of 1833

(1816) had main streets 132 feet wide, as did Cleveland; and Bellevue, Clyde, and Woodville, Ohio, all had streets 120 feet wide.[3]

The City of Zion requirement for locating barns outside of town reflects a basic concern in trans-Appalachian communities for livestock in town with their attendant odor and waste. The concept of small farms outside the town was found in New England and in many trans-Appalachian settlements. When Cincinnati was established in 1789 for example, lands around the town were divided into four-acre farms while at Lexington, Kentucky (1781) they were divided into five- and ten-acre plots.[4] The only factor which was unique to the City of Zion plan of Joseph Smith was the uniform width of the streets. Other communities established during the era had wide main streets, but the side streets were normally much narrower. Aside from the uniformly wide streets, the City of Zion plan is similar to other communities founded or proposed in the period.

The villages founded by the Mormons in the western United States are superficially like the City of Zion plan, but are certainly not uniform. No existing Mormon Village follows the City of Zion plan exactly, although some, including Salt Lake City, do have ten-acres blocks and 132 foot streets,[5] and Mormons typically believe towns in "Zion" are all modelled after the sacred city of Zion plan. The existing Mormon Villages can be recognized by wide streets approximating orientation to the cardinal directions, but there is great diversity in the actual morphology of the communities. Street widths in Mormon towns range from 50 to 172 feet, and there is no common denominator although one-half of all Mormon towns have streets either 90 or 99 feet (6 rods) in width.[6] Wide streets are not unique to the Mormons in the West, as evidenced by 27 percent of non-Mormon towns in the West having streets 90 feet or wider. They are more common in Mormon towns as 73 percent of all Mormon towns have streets 90 feet or greater in width.[7] Non-Mormon towns are few within the core of the Mormon culture region, but are very different from Mormon towns

---

[3]Richard H. Jackson: The Mormon Village: Genesis and Antecedents of the City of Zion Plan, Brigham Young University Studies, Vol. 17, 1977, p. 3.

[4]Richard C. Wade: The Urban Frontier (University of Chicago Press, Chicago, 1964), pp. 20, 24.

[5]Richard H. Jackson and Robert Layton: The Mormon Village: Analysis of a Settlement Type, The Professional Geographer, Vol. 23, 1976, p. 136.

[6]Ibid., p. 138.   [7]Ibid., p. 139.

since they are mining towns with narrow streets and a linear pattern.

Lot and block sizes found in Mormon villages are much more distinctive as evidence of Mormon influence than street width. Although the City of Zion plan specified half-acre lots, only 9 percent of Mormon towns in the west have lots this small. Eighty percent of the towns platted by the Mormons had lots one acre or larger, a size rarely found in non-Mormon settlements of the West. Block size in Mormon communities is also much larger. Although only 5 percent of non-Mormon towns in the west have blocks of four acres or larger, all Mormon communities have such large blocks. [8] The combination of large blocks and lots grew out of the Mormon leaders' background in the milieu of the Jeffersonian era. The Mormon leaders adopted the thesis that the self-sufficient farmer was the embodiment of virtue when compared to citizens of urban areas, and hence coupled the rural ethic with their New England communitarian heritage to develop the Mormon Village, which was actually a clustering of micro-farms.

The independent yeoman farmer in control of his own land, growing his own food, and subservient to none, of the Jeffersonian model had one difficulty: the paucity of his educational and cultural opportunities. These could best be met by residing in villages where according to Smith:[9]

> The farmer and his family, therefore, will enjoy all the advantages of schools, public lectures, and other meetings. His home will no longer be isolated, and his family denied the benefits of society, which has been and always will be, the great educator of the human race; but they will enjoy the same privileges of society, and can surround their home with the same intellectual life, the same social refinement as will be found in the home of the merchant or banker or professional man.

The large lots of the Mormon villages allowed the rural ethic to be combined with the cultural and intellectual advantages of community life.

Mormon Village Agriculture

The large lots in the Mormon village of the West allowed each family to keep its own cow, pigs, chickens, and large garden for subsistence while maintaining proximity to neighbors for education and other social benefits.[10] Addi-

---

[8]Ibid.

[9]Brigham H. Roberts: A Comprehensive History of the Church of Jesus Christ of Latter-day Saints (Brigham Young University Press, Provo, 1957), Vol. 1, p. 312.

[10]Richard H. Jackson: Meadow, Millard County Utah: The Geography of a

tionally, the cooperative effort necessary to provide irrigation for the garden and field crops with which the Mormon colonists were familiar was facilitated by compact settlements. Until governmental intervention in irrigation schemes replaced the need for such cooperative effort, it was difficult to develop a dispersed settlement pattern based on irrigation. Until federal reclamation projects with their attendant capital and technological characteristics were applied to irrigation, it was necessary for the farmer to immediately irrigate a small area to provide food while the larger project was engineered and completed. The Mormon village with its large lots and blocks was the vehicle whereby this was accomplished.

In Mormon villages outside the rapidly urbanizing Wasatch Front region, the early Mormon emphasis on agriculture and community has created a unique village landscape. Older homes still occupy the large lots, but the subsistence agriculture for which the lots were used has been abandoned. As a result, the Mormon village presents an "open" appearance, and the majority of the land within the village is vacant. Occasional barns, corrals, and other related agricultural phenomena occupy the weed-infested lots in uneasy conjunction with a garden, lawn, and home (Figure 3). The irrigation water delivery system to the town lots has been abandoned in many Mormon towns as the pressurized culinary water system is more convenient for lawns and gardens than the old rotation irrigation system with its night, weekend, and holiday "turns." In such towns only the main irrigation lateral taking water to the surrounding fields remains to remind residents of the once-ubiquitous irrigation culture. Some towns do retain the delivery system which brought water to the individual lots, but it is impossible to generalize about them. The ditch systems range from the narrow slit ditches of Mt. Pleasant, Utah, which are one foot deep and six inches wide with grassy banks and wooden headgates to divert water, to the typical cement gutters of Payson, Utah, which double as irrigation ditches carrying water to the lots but are outwardly identical to other gutters. Only metal guides in the cement for a metal gate at the corner of each lot to force the water to flow from gutter to lot reveals dual function of the gutters. Between these two extremes are a variety of ditch systems, but all consist of small ditches between road and sidewalk and most have been cemented. Few are larger than one square foot in size. The contention that "functional irrigation ditches rather than the deep gutters in non-Mormon towns" is a characteristic

---

Small Mormon Agricultural Community (Thesis, Brigham Young University, 1966), p. 40.

Fig. 3. --Mormon Village showing the open nature of the blocks

of Mormon villages[11] is questionable at best since they are found today in a minority of Mormon villages.

The barns and other outbuildings associated with the subsistence agriculture of the Mormon village are distinctive elements of the relic landscape found outside of the urbanized Mormon core. These buildings and associated corrals and fences are rarely in good repair as the agricultural economy which used them is gone, and their continued existence is not a function of Mormon culture, but of economics. If used at all, the use is peripheral and does not justify any capital improvement; if abandoned, there is no incentive to raze them. They remain until urbanites purchase and disassemble them to use their silvery wood for paneling. As a result, the presence of the unpainted Mormon barn in villages today is directly related to distance from urban areas. Other than their lacking paint, the relic barns found in areas occupied by Mormons are not unique (Figure 4). Modern transportation has made the subsistence micro-farms of the original village obsolete and many full-time farmers have relocated on their farm outside of the village, thus breaking down the initial nucleated village pattern. In the farmlands around the villages the functional farm structures consist of pre-fabricated steel barns, standard silos, and simple hay shelters of poles with a nearly flat steel roof. The relic unpainted wood barns at one time were distinctive, and can still be found in marginal farming areas, but they are rapidly disappearing and represent cultural relics.

Two other farm-related features have been described as part of the Mormon Landscape: the so-called "Mormon Fence" and the hay derrick. The Mormon fence is described as "a paling fence of sorts which is made out of a tremendous variety of picket styles--all in one fence, " and all unpainted.[12] These fences are common in the rural areas in the margins of the Mormon cultural region where the agricultural economy is marginal. Such fences are not unique to the Mormon landscape, but to all marginal farming areas of the arid and semi-arid west. The Mormon aspect of the fences is that they are found within the Mormon village with its large lots used for subsistence agriculture. As with much of the rural Mormon landscape, the capital investment required to construct any type of fence dictates its maintenance. The Mormon fence was functional, if untidy, and there is no economically rational reason or ability to replace it.

The hay derricks are concentrated in the Mormon culture region and ex-

---

[11]Francaviglia, op. cit. [note 1], p. 59.

[12]Ibid., p. 60.

Fig. 4. --Mormon barn typical of rural Utah communities

amples can be found in any rural Mormon community in the intermountain west (Figure 5). Although actual construction is highly varied by sub-regions in the west the basic technology of the derrick is that of fulcrum comprised of four poles forming a pyramid with a boom across it which can be pivoted on the center support of the fulcrum. By means of a cable and a large fork, hay can be easily moved from wagon to stack. With the introduction of alfalfa to Utah in 1853, [13] and resultant expansion of hay production, the derrick provided a rapid way to build large stacks of hay which adequately resisted limited precipitation without covering. The derrick represented a technological change which made one of the main functions of the barn obsolete, and it in turn has been made obsolete by subsequent changes in hay handling technology. Where the derrick remains, it is used by farmers still using nineteenth-century technology or as a multipurpose support for such varied items as children's swings or newly butchered animals. More often it is simply abandoned and the dry climate and initial care in construction ensures its permanence as a landmark of "Mormonland."

Perhaps more characteristic of the landscape of rural Mormon towns than mere barns, derricks, and Mormon fences is the general variety of obsolete structures and equipment. Mormon country is largely marginal country, unsuited for the intensive small farm crop agriculture of the Ohio area upon which it is based. As a result, the Mormon farmer tried almost every type of agricultural activity in his attempts to maintain the small farm system as an economically viable activity. The resultant relic features include the barn and derrick, but also a host of others including chicken coops from the egg flurry in the 1930's-1960's, the small milking parlor from the dairy boom of the late nineteenth and twentieth centuries, small concrete silos of the early twentieth century for corn silage for animals, potato cellars from the pre-1940 era, and obsolete equipment. Abandoned horse-drawn hay mowers, hay rakes, and wagons rust away beside grain threshers, corn binders, and 1930 Case tractors. But again these are not confined to Mormon farming areas. The unique aspect is their concentration in town on the large lots and their high visibility because there is no vegetation to camouflage them since the land they occupy is un-irrigated. It should be noted that even junk equipment, old barns, and derricks are part of a dual Mormon landscape. On the large, profitable farms in Mormon

---

[13]Robert C. Brough: The Diffusion and Adoption of Alfalfa in Utah (Thesis, Brigham Young University, 1975), pp. 34-35.

Fig. 5.--Hay derrick utilized
in stacking hay in intermountain West.

country, most of these characteristics are not found. Only in the marginal villages with their uneconomic, often part-time, farming operations do they exist.

Mormon Village Architecture

Mormon architectural styles have been widely characterized as distinctive, and can be divided into three categories. The first consists of folk housing constructed during the first decades of occupation of the West (1847-1860)
by the Mormons. Homes constructed during this period are simple folk housing;
small single-story, rectangular, low, with little or no roof overhang and no dec-
oration. The vast majority of these homes were constructed of adobe bricks
roughly twice the size of conventional bricks, and some towns maintained a pub-

lic clay pit where individuals could make their own adobes (Figure 6). The rationale for use of adobe was two-fold: first, soil suitable for adobes could be found in or near most settlements; and second, there was little timber available. Immediately after their arrival in the Salt Lake Valley in July 1847, the Mormons decided in a public meeting that adobe was both cheaper and faster than log housing.

> Colonel A. P. Rockwood remarked that a log house, 16 x 18 feet, would cost $40, and one of adobe half as much. Captain Brown was in favor of setting men to work building both log and adobe houses, in order to hasten the work. Captain Lewis, Lieutenant Willis and Samuel Brannan spoke in favor of erecting adobe houses. The latter remarked that he had a man in California, who, with three men, would agree to make adobes for a 30 foot house, build the house and put a family in it in a week. . . . After some remarks by Willard Richards, it was voted to put up a stockade of adobe houses. Samuel Gould and James Dunn reported themselves as lime burners, and Sylvester H. Earl, Joel J. Terrill, Ralph Douglas and Joseph Hancock as brick makers. (Journal History of the Church, August 1, 1847)

Initially the Mormons attempted construction of flat-roofed adobe buildings patterned after those of the Spanish, but after the first winter's precipitation they changed to the gabled roofs with which they were already familiar.

The second period of Mormon architecture developed during the 1860-1890 period when the Mormons were expanding their colonization efforts because of an infusion of migrants from northern and western Europe and sale of agricultural products to mining communities in the West. Homes constructed during this period are characterized by their abundant use of Greek Revival detailing. The Greek Revival period extended roughly from 1820 to 1860 in the eastern United States and was brought to Utah by the Mormons in 1847 where Mormon settlers relied almost exclusively on it until their self-imposed isolation began to break down in the late 1800's. Adobe remained the common building material until the latter part of the period, but homes and public buildings were liberally embellished with pilasters, molded cornices, brackets, and other Greek Revival features.[14] Plans for public buildings were generally square or rectangular, homes were rectangular with extensions forming the common "L, " "T, " "I, " or "H" styles. Doors and windows were normally rectangular with wooden beam lintels, but cornices were boxed and returned (Fig-

---

[14] Allen D Roberts: The Greek Revival Style in Utah, Utah State Historical Society Newsletter, Vol. 26, 1976, pp. 1-4.

[15] Richard V. Francaviglia: Mormon Central Houses in the American West, Annals, Association of American Geographers, Vol. 61, 1971, pp. 65-67.

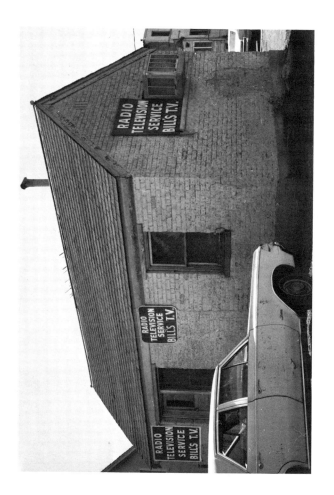

Fig. 6. --Simple adobe home of early Mormon folk housing style

ure 7). Since many of these homes were initially adobe they weathered to a greater or lesser degree and as finances permitted, their owners covered the adobe with stucco. Essentially all of the extant Greek Revival style homes are stuccoed with quions at the corners or a design in the stucco simulating stone.

The third period of recognizably Mormon architecture extended from the late 1800's until the end of World War I, a time of relative prosperity for the rural Mormon settlements. Homes constructed during this period can be described as Mormon eclectic and their only common characteristic is their large size and the use of brick or stone as a building material. Homes are typically two or three stories high, combine elements of numerous architectural styles in the same home, are commonly the most substantial homes in the community, and are readily identifiable. Mormon homes of this period reflect the general American penchant for grandeur and lavishness common around the turn of the century (Figure 8). After World War I the architectural styles found in Mormon villages are identical with those generally popular in the United States for the same period. [16] The one feature which is unique to the area is the preponderance of brick as construction material. Many of the Mormon settlers were from England where the use of brick had become dominant in 1700 and 1800 and this ethic was compounded by lack of timber in the Great Basin and resultant admonitions from church leaders to conserve it for fuel. Once established, the reliance on brick tended to perpetuate itself and today nearly all homes are constructed with brick veneer. Since the majority of homes in the core area of the Mormon cultural region are of post-World War II construction with the rambler and split-level style common to suburban America, only the use of brick is a common denominator. Other communities in the western United States are not characterized by such uniform use of brick since they were rarely settled by a group which was large enough to justify a brick yard or cooperative enough to develop one. It should be noted, however, that the use of brick is common in some areas of the United States, and many communities of the eighteenth and nineteenth centuries in the hearth area of the Mormons had regulations concerning use of brick to minimize fire danger, the greatest threat to communities in pre-industrial America. [17] In the frontier communities of the west developed in the late nineteenth and twentieth centuries, more adequate fire protection was

---

[16] John E. Rickert: House Facades of the Northeastern United States: A Tool of Geographic Analysis, Annals, Association of American Geographers, Vol. 57, 1967, pp. 211-223.

[17] Wade, op. cit. ⌈note 4⌉, p. 91.

117

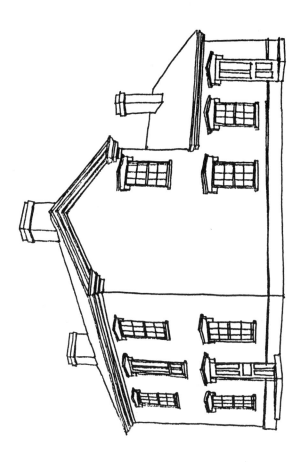

Fig. 7.--Example of Mormon architecture of 1860-1890 era with Greek Revival influence (Allen D. Roberts).

developed before formal regulations requiring use of brick were necessary.

The architectural characteristics found in the Mormon cultural region are far from unique to the Mormons and they can be found in communities in the United States east of the Mississippi which were the models for the Mormon settlements. The Mormon village and its associated architecture is unique to the West because it represents an area where the village pattern of the eastern United States was transplanted intact. Irrigation was added from necessity, and the architectural styles of the first half of the nineteenth century persisted an additional fifty years because of isolation, but otherwise the Mormon village is much less distinctive than might be expected from a group with such strong central control and direction. The Mormon village is more important as the hearth from which the landscape was modified than as an example of the unique sacred city of Zion.

Mormon Chapels and Temples

Mormon religious edifices are an integral part of the Mormon landscape and consist of temples, tabernacles, and chapels. The Mormon temples represent the most sacred portions of Mormonland. Architecturally the early ones in the core area (Salt Lake City, Manti, Logan, and St. George, Utah) are recognizable by their massive stone construction, lack of crosses, abundant (for Mormons) ornamentation, and numerous steeples and general Gothic Revival influence. The actual architectural characteristics vary, but all initially had a square or rectangular pattern with numerous angles, pilasters, and recesses along the walls in contrast to the flat undecorated walls of Mormon homes of the period. More recent temples are either abstractions of the Salt Lake Temple or have their own idiosyncratic functional style and are not restricted to the Mormon culture region.

Mormon chapels and tabernacles[18] constructed prior to 1950 were highly varied. Architecturally one can find examples of Greek Revival, Gothic Revival, Classical, Italianate, Baroque, Romanesque, Muscovite, Byzantine, and Frank Lloyd Wright's Prairie style used as the basis for a single building or

---

[18]The Mormon Tabernacle was simply a building larger than the chapel and was used when it was necessary to gather several congregations together for conferences. Construction of tabernacles ended in the early twentieth century as one chapel was designated as a regional center and built to accommodate a larger congregation.

119

Fig. 8.--Example of grandiose brick architecture in
Mormon homes of 1880's-1920 era.

mixed in the same building.[19] The only distinctive feature of Mormon religious structures of this period is the complete absence of a cross or bells and the rare use of stained glass (Figure 9).

With the rapid growth of the Mormon church into the post-World War II era, a central committee was established in Salt Lake City to supervise building in the Church. This committee developed a distinctive style of architecture referred to by the committee as "International" which combines elements of stylized colonial architecture with simple functional lines. The general form of Mormon chapels of the last three decades is a modified A-frame with adjoining wings which cover a chapel complex, a recreation complex, and a classroom complex.[20] Early variants of this standardized complex are recognizable by their brick construction, single steeple on a tower attached to the A-frame, and the lack of bells, crosses, or stained glass. More recently the standard form has been slightly modified by the use of dimension stone to replace part of the brick, and a tower with a steeple detached from the main building (Figure 10).

Architectural Styles of Public and Quasi-Public Buildings

The stores and shops of Mormon communities are no different from those in other areas of the United States. Main Street in Mormon towns is typically occupied by two- and three-story rectangular brick buildings. In areas of population growth, modern buildings of glass and steel replace the brick structures, and in urban areas the central business district is rapidly acquiring the high rise commercial buildings common to urban America. The Salt Lake Temple is dwarfed by the tall buildings around it, and only the names and people separate Salt Lake City from other urban areas. The emerging high-rise landscape is part of the Mormon landscape, and the Mormon Church Office Building in Salt Lake City is the tallest building in the cultural region. Unlike some areas, there has been no public concern evinced for the change in the visual character of Salt Lake City created by such structures. The adoption of the high rise office building as a supplement to the turn-of-the-century three-story Greek Revival style office building is symbolic of the Mormon landscape. For Mormons, the form has never been as important as the function, and resultant land-

---

[19]Allen D. Roberts: Religious Architecture of the L.D.S. Church: Influences and Changes since 1847, Utah Historical Quarterly, Vol. 43, 1975, pp. 316-236.

[20]Ibid., p. 327.

Fig. 9. --Mormon chapel of the 1930 period with Gothic Revival characteristics

scape features reflect this utilitarian view. Where population growth is slow the Mormon landscape reflects nineteenth century origins, where growth is rapid the landscape reflects twentieth century urban and suburban America.

Mormon Typonyms

To the gentile (the Mormon term for any non-Mormon) casually observing the Mormon landscape as he traverses the region, the Mormon names upon the land are the embodiment of Mormon country. Communities called Moroni, Nephi, Manti, and Deseret are uniquely Mormon, using names taken from the Book of Mormon, a book viewed as scripture by the Church. The term Deseret means honeybees in the Book of Mormon lexicon and is symbolic of hard work and industry and is synonymous with the Protestant work ethic. The term is quantitatively the most common distinctively Mormon name, and is used for towns, businesses, buildings, and organizations. Zion is the second most common Mormon name and has been given to canyons, mountains, communities, automobile dealerships, barbershops, and savings and loan institutions. Such uniquely Mormon names are the exception rather than the rule in Mormon country, however. The majority of communities take their name from historic events, prominent settlers, Church leaders, or local geographic phenomena. Salt Lake City and Utah are synonymous with Mormons to most people, yet neither name is uniquely Mormon, as Salt Lake City was named after the Great Salt Lake and Utah as the state name was chosen by Congress to replace the Mormon-named territory of Deseret. From Cardston and Raymond in Canada to Huntsville or Leeds in Utah, to Mesquite in Nevada, or Mesa in Arizona the majority of Mormon toponyms initially had no distinctive Mormon character. Cedar City, Provo, Meadow, Pleasant Grove, Spanish Fork, Lake City, and Panguitch are Mormon towns, but their names are not distinctive. Outnumbered by mundane names, the few distinctively Mormon toponyms are still an integral part of the Mormon landscape. The presence of Nephi's barbershop, Moroni's Chamber of Commerce, Brigham's restaurant, and Zarahemla Street are the embodiment of Mormonland. The presence of several such names as Deseret Book, Brigham City, Zion's Mercantile, Mormon Hill, or Mormon Peak are sufficient to categorize the land as Mormon, even though the majority of the toponyms are not unique to the Mormons.

123

Fig. 10.--Mormon chapel constructed in early 1970's
following standardized "International Style."

Patterns on the Land:
Mormon Land Distribution

The Mormon rural landscape is recognizably different from the rest of
the West. The communitarian ethic of the Mormons held that land was not to be
obtained for profit, but for subsistence.[21] The background of Joseph Smith and
other early leaders in New England resulted in an original land distribution
scheme including many of the aspects of the New England village. In Salt Lake
City for example, each family received a city lot large enough for subsistence,
a five-acre parcel in the irrigated land immediately adjacent to the platted community, and a ten-acre parcel in the "Big Field" beyond the five-acre parcels,
and if family need justified it a twenty-acre parcel farther out. In the words of
Brigham Young:[22]

> It is our intention to have the five-acre lots next to the city accomodate the
> mechanics and artisans, the ten acres next, then the twenty acres, followed
> by the forty and eighty acre lots, where farmers can build and reside. (Ital-
> ics added)

It is significant that Brigham Young's statement indicates that the Mormons intended to allow dispersed settlements on large farms similar to that of
the hearth area they had left in the mid-west. The tremendous demand for land
and the difficulty of providing irrigation water prevented wholesale adoption of
the dispersed farmstead in Salt Lake City.[23] Subsequent Indian conflicts caused
Young to counsel those Mormons residing on dispersed farmsteads in the Great
Basin to come together into defensible villages thus ending the dispersed farmsteads around the Mormon village.

The Jeffersonian ethic is apparent in Brigham Young's insistence that all
individuals were to have at least a five-acre parcel to provide the family's subsistence. The infrastructure necessary to provide irrigation and to fence these
small parcels of land required an immense investment of labor and capital, and
simply maintaining it from year to year precluded any revolutionary organizational changes. Consequently, the small field pattern of the initial settlement
era remained permanent even though land holdings were later expanded and con-
solidated. The small fenced fields with their associated ditch systems are a

---

[21] Leonard Arrington: Great Basin Kingdom (Harvard University Press,
Cambridge, 1958), pp. 50-54.

[22] Journal History of the Church, Manuscript, Latter-day Saints Church Historian's Office, Salt Lake City, Utah, July, 1847; October 9, 1848.

[23] Arrington, op. cit. [note 21], p. 52.

distinctive part of the landscape associated with the nucleated settlements of the
rural portions of the Mormon cultural region which are found in no other part of
the West in the same abundance, but again they are restricted to the marginal
areas of Mormonland. The original five-, ten-, and twenty-acre parcels of
Salt Lake City have long since been divided into 8, 000-foot square residential
lots for the single-family home of faceless American suburbia.

Beyond the lands which were easily irrigated by the simple technology
available to the Mormon pioneers, modern reclamation technology has developed large irrigated farms or dry farming patterns with large fields and farms.
Such areas are identical with any geographically similar area of the West and
defy categorization as Mormon unless the occupants are queried as to religious
preference. Even the small nucleated settlements are becoming less apparent
as the full-time farmer moves his residence to his larger holding and suburban-
ites attempt to recapture the Jeffersonian ethic embodied in the initial Mormon
settlements by dispersing onto five-acre "ranchettes." Only in the marginal
areas where the population of the Mormon villages is stable or declining is the
nucleated settlement found. The general low income levels coupled with the
large number of existing vacant houses in such marginal locations minimizes
new construction and has tended to maintain the village pattern.

Mormon Cemeteries

The Mormon cemetery is perhaps the most easily recognizable element in
the Mormon landscape. Unique aspects of the Mormon cemetery are the essentially total absence of crosses of any type on markers, and the inscriptions on
the markers. There are several uniquely Mormon inscriptions including a book
labelled "Book of Mormon," carvings of the Salt Lake Temple, and clasped
right hands. The individual family cemetery found in areas of dispersed settlement in the United States is completely lacking in Mormonland. The vegetation
of the cemeteries is unique in that coniferous trees have been liberally planted
causing the cemetery in a Mormon town to stand out as a block of evergreen
trees amidst the residences.

Conclusion

On the basis of the visual elements, there are two Mormon landscapes.
One is a relic landscape of small nucleated settlements with wide streets, unpainted barns, and houses of Greek Revival style. Communities with all of the
characteristics of this landscape are found today only in the marginal fringes of

the Mormon culture region. The other is the urbanized areas of the Mormon cultural region in which Mormons are the dominant cultural group, but whose landscape is part of the general American suburbia, recognizable as Mormon only because of toponyms and the predominance of brick. The Mormon landscape commonly described by observers is the first, relic landscape which is distinctive when compared to America in general.

The intriguing aspect of the Mormon West is that the cultural group, with its homogeneity of values, strong central leadership, obedient members, geographic isolation, occupied a land viewed as sacred, but developed a landscape only marginally different from those of New England and the Ohio Valley. Villages are somewhat more grandiose in their morphology, but that simply represents implementation on a uniform scale of urban ideas current in the early nineteenth century. The uniqueness of the Mormon landscape typically recognized, lies in the re-appearance of the New England nucleated village and the persistence of nineteenth century structures and field patterns in the twentieth century. The group's insistence on establishing the same type of agrarian economy proposed by Jefferson in an area unsuited to it is unique. The persistence of that pattern was ensured by the marginal resource base which made additional capital investment beyond the maintenance level irrational. This rural landscape is "Mormon" landscape because it was settled and occupied by Mormons, but the value system underlying it is American agrarianism.

The resurgence of interest among Americans for a return to small-town life threatens even the recognizably "Mormon" landscape of the Mormon cultural region with suburban sprawl. Additions to the Mormon communities substitute narrow curving streets for the wide, open gridiron pattern, and vegetative or scenic names for the functional first or second north, south, east, and west coordinates of the original village. Civic pride and a determination to "clean-up" leads to razing of old barns and removal of obsolete equipment. In time only the broad streets, brick houses, and toponyms of the original village will remain as a reminder of the Mormons' attempt to recreate the village life of New England in the semiarid west. The Mormon landscape is more unique because of the tenacity with which the settlers maintained and recreated the rural America they had known than because it was settled by a specific religious group. The presence of the village system creates a unique landscape in the West, but its roots are primarily Jeffersonian, not Mormon. The emerging landscape of the Mormon cultural region is not distinctive in the West, since architectural styles and urban morphology were adopted intact from other regions. It remains a sacred land to adherents, but the sacred view is related more to the function of the landscape features than to their form. Thus Mormonland exists as a unique region to observers and practitioners alike, a special example of sacred space in which the landscape features are constantly changing but whose sanctity remains.

CHAPTER 8

ANALYTICAL APPROACHES TO THE URBAN LANDSCAPE

Michael P. Conzen

University of Chicago

Perceptions of the urban crisis in the 1960s and the environmental crisis of the 1970s have done much to alter the goals and methods of the social sciences. Among geographers, urban research has gained great status, and the bulk of current geographical wisdom concerning the modern city, it could be argued, dates from this period. In North America, particularly, however, such understanding has concentrated heavily upon the functional aspects of urban structure, to the serious detriment of urban form, particularly as an inherited framework within which change must be accommodated. Yet the urban landscape is of special significance today, given the rising concern for environmental quality, physical planning, and visual symbolism in urban life. Recent neglect notwithstanding, the urban landscape, as the socially transformed physical manifestation of land division, land use, and built form, does have a long if uneven tradition in urban geography. Now that American geographers are showing a renewed concern for the urban landscape, it seems appropriate to examine the intellectual background of this approach and assess the value of its methodological advances to date.

The Decline and Rise of the Urban Landscape in Urban Geography

Most commentators place the emergence of urban geography as a distinct sub-discipline in the opening decades of this century, and note its early emphasis upon site and situation, the relationship of the city to its physical context, and landscape character—particularly as reflected in generalized ground plan features. [1] Early work by Schlüter, Fleure, and Passarge was echoed in American studies by Leighly, Trewartha, and Scofield that exploited a morphological approach to urban settlements, namely, analysis of their form, in an era when direct field observation of townscapes and study of historic city plans compensated for the lack of readily available social and economic statistics for small geographical areas. [2] While urban monographs appeared in France and Germany, relatively less work on cities emerged in Britain or America before the Second World War. [3] Thereafter, a geometric rise in geographical urban interest occurred, spurred in no small measure by Dickinson's translations of German work on towns and his broader summaries of existing European and American work on internal structure and external relations of cities. [4]

Study of the urban landscape during the 1950s proceeded with vigor, [5] but

---

[1] H. M. Mayer: Urban Geography, in American Geography: Inventory and Prospect (edited by P. E. James and C. F. Jones; Syracuse University Press for the Association of American Geographers, Syracuse, N. Y., 1954), pp. 143-145; Harold Carter: The Study of Urban Geography (2nd ed.; Edward Arnold, London, 1975), pp. 1-8.

[2] Otto Schlüter: Über den Grundriss der Städte, Zeitschrift der Gesellschaft für Erdkunde zu Berlin, Vol. 34, 1899, pp. 446-462; H. J. Fleure: Some Types of Cities in Temperate Europe, Geographical Review, Vol. 10, 1920, pp. 357-374; Siegfried Passarge: Stadtlandschaften der Erde (Friederichsen, de Gruyter and Co., Hamburg, 1930); J. B. Leighly: The Towns of Mälardalen in Sweden: A Study in Urban Morphology, University of California Publications in Geography, Vol. 3 (University of California Press, Berkeley, Calif., 1928); G. T. Trewartha: Japanese Cities: Distribution and Morphology, Geographical Review, Vol. 24, 1934, pp. 404-417; E. Scofield: The Origin of Settlement Patterns in Rural New England, Geographical Review, Vol. 28, 1938, pp. 652-663.

[3] In the American case, the early dominance of environmentalism may have diverted attention from the quintessential man-made settlement form, and the rural bias of Sauer's interest in cultural geography likewise may have dampened interest in cities. See C. O. Sauer: The Morphology of Landscape, University of California Publications in Geography, Vol. 2, No. 2, 1925, pp. 19-53. For an important exception, see C. C. Colby: Centrifugal and Centripetal Forces in Urban Geography, Annals, Association of American Geographers, Vol. 23, 1933, pp. 1-20. This relative void was undoubtedly related to the rise of geographical concepts of urban social and physical structure in neighboring social sciences, most notably the Chicago school of human ecology.

[4] R. E. Dickinson: City, Region, and Regionalism (Routledge and Kegan Paul, London, 1947) and The West European City: A Geographical Interpretation (Routledge and Kegan Paul, London, 1961).

[5] H. S. Thurston: The Urban Regions of St. Albans, Transactions, Institute of British Geographers, Vol. 19, 1953, pp. 107-122; H. Boy: Die Stadtlandschaft Oldenburg, Hamburger Geographische Studien, Vol. 5 (Institut für

it was challenged increasingly by a drift towards exclusively functional studies of urban organization, especially in English-speaking geography, fueled by new statistical approaches and standards of analytical precision. With charges that morphological study was no richer then than twenty years before, the approach was derided for its apparent lack of theory and normative orientation.[6] In retrospect, however, morphologically-inspired urban geography before the Second World War had laid important foundations upon which later work could build. In what might be termed the high era of urban field geography, advances were made, for example, in the basic differentiation of the city's spatial structure. Since form complexes often reveal function, land use districts within the city had been morphologically delimited in the 1930s, well ahead of the specialized studies of the central business district, transition zones, and other identifiable areas in the 1950s.[7]

The internal dialectic of form and function in urban geographical writing, however, became specialized and external to individual studies, so that in the heat of the technical revolution then sweeping English-speaking geography, the urban landscape along with other difficult-to-quantify geographical domains was thrown on the defensive, safe in America only in the context of a cultural geography that had rarely dealt effectively with the city.[8] Outside Anglo-America,

---

Geographie und Wirtschaftsgeographie der Universität, 1954); F. Schwiecker: Die hamburgische Stadtlandschaft und ihre Entwicklung, in Hamburg: Grossstadt und Welthafen; Festschrift z. 30 Dt. Geographentag in Hamburg 1955 (edited by W. Brünger; Ferdinand Hirt, Kiel, 1955), pp. 142-162; K. Dziewonski: Nowy dzial badan geografisznych: Fizjografia urbanistyczna [A new branch of geographic research: Urban physiography], Special number, Przeglad Geograficzny, Vol. 27, 1955, pp. 489-499 (English summary); A. E. Smailes: Some Reflections on the Geographical Description and Analysis of Townscapes, Transactions, Institute of British Geographers, Vol. 21, 1955, pp. 95-115; M. B. Stedman: The Townscape of Birmingham in 1956, Transactions, Institute of British Geographers, Vol. 25, 1958, pp. 225-238.

[6]The most notable attack on morphological approaches in urban geography was made by Garrison in 1960 (W. L Garrison: Discussion on Urban Morphology, in Proceedings of the I.G U. Symposium on Urban Geography Lund 1960, edited by K. Norborg, Lund Studies in Geography, Ser. B, Vol. 24, 1962, pp. 463-464).

[7]H. Louis: Die geographische Gliederung von Gross-Berlin, Länderkundliche Forschung, Krebs-Festschrift, Stuttgart, 1936, pp. 146-171.

[8]Indicative of the few British and American morphological studies in the 1960s are M. R. G. Conzen: Alnwick, Northumberland: A Study in Town-Plan Analysis, Publication No. 27 (Institute of British Geographers, London, 1960); H. J. Nelson: Townscapes of Mexico: An Example of the Regional Variation of

however, the urban landscape tradition proceeded without interruption, and with increasing methodological sophistication.[9] Explanation for this divergence might be sought in the intellectual history of American geography: the relative impotence of the old Berkeley cultural geography in dealing with complex industrial society, coupled with the appropriation of geographical concepts by other social sciences, left American urban geographers vulnerable to the immediate allure of "scientific" respectability that the technical revolution seemed to offer. Besides, the brevity of American urban history and the economic Darwinianism of American urban life have resulted in cities that call less immediately for cultural geographical analysis than European cities. Whatever the case, the varying consensus on the appropriate contents and goals of urban geography vis-à-vis the urban landscape is well illustrated in the topics covered by different national compendia on urban geography in recent years.[10] German, French,

Townscapes, Economic Geography, Vol. 39, 1963, pp. 74-83; E. T. Price: Viterbo: Landscape of an Italian City, Annals, Association of American Geographers, Vol. 54, 1964, pp. 242-275; and S.-D. Chang: Some Observations on the Morphology of Chinese Walled Cities, Annals, Association of American Geographers, Vol. 60, 1970, pp. 63-91.

[9]J. Bastié: La croissance de la banlieue parisienne (Presses Universitaires de France, Paris, 1964); L. Améen: Stadsbebyggelse och Domänstruktur: Svensk stadsutveckling i relation till ägoförhållanden och administrativa gränser [Urban settlement and domain structure: Urban development in Sweden in relation to proprietary rights and administrative limits], Meddelanden från Lunds Universitets Geografiska Institution, Avhandlingar 46 (C. W. K. Gleerup, Lund, 1964) (in Swedish, with English summary); H. Friedmann: Alt-Mannheim im Wandel seiner Physiognomie, Struktur und Funktionen, 1606-1965, Forschungen zur deutschen Landeskunde, Band 168 (Bundesforschungsanstalt für Landeskunde und Raumordnung, 1968); H. Schäfer: Neuere stadtgeographische Arbeitsmethoden zur Untersuchung der inneren Struktur von Städten, I & II, Berichte zur deutschen Landeskunde, Vol. 41, 1968, pp. 277-317, and Vol. 43, 1969, pp. 261-297; M. Williams, The Parkland Towns of Australia and New Zealand, Geographical Review, Vol. 56, 1966, pp. 67-89; K. Yamori: [A historical geography of urban morphology], Jimbun-Chiri [Human geography], Vol. 17, 1965, pp. 396-414; K. T. Lata: Morphology of Indian Cities (National Geographical Society of India, Varanasi, 1971); F. Boudon: Tissu urbain et architecture: L'analyse parcellaire comme base de l'histoire architecturale Annales: Economies, Sociétés, Civilisations, Vol. 30, 1975, pp. 773-818.

[10]American: Mayer, op. cit. [note 1]; R. E. Murphy: The American City (2nd ed.; McGraw-Hill, New York, 1974); M. Yeates and B. J. Garner: The North American City (2nd ed.; Harper and Row, New York, 1976); B. J. L. Berry and F. E. Horton: Geographic Perspectives on Urban Systems (Prentice-Hall, Englewood Cliffs, N.J., 1970). British: J. H. Johnson: Urban Geography: An Introductory Analysis (2nd ed.; Pergamon Press, Oxford, 1972); H. Carter: The Study of Urban Geography (2nd ed.; Edward Arnold, London, 1975). French: J. Beaujeu-Garnier and G. Chabot: Urban Geography (John Wiley and Sons, New York, 1967). German: G. Schwartz: Allgemeine Siedlungsgeogra-

and to a lesser extent, British geographers have generally accorded the urban landscape proper status as a systematic element of urban geography; American geographers have not.[11] Thus, between 1950 and 1970 in Anglo-American urban geography the pendulum of interest had swung heavily from a morphological to a functional bias.[12]

An intimately related characteristic of this functional bias has been its strongly economic thrust, especially in North America. Residential districts, the CBD, journey-to-work patterns, industrial location, central place functions (inter- and intra-urban) and other spatial interactions have been studied for two decades in overwhelmingly economic terms: land values, economic dimensions of land use, cost-distance, utility maximization, and the popularity of rational, economic man (or woman, when it came to household consumer patterns). So divorced was this thrust from the more balanced approaches in continental Europe that, when the inevitable backlash came at the beginning of the 1970s, many American geographers jumped on the bandwagon of the "new" subdiscipline of social geography.[13] But this recent wave of American social geography has shown little awareness of the strong conceptual tradition of géographie sociale or Sozialgeographie in French and German literature; far less any attempt to confront methodological differences and hammer out a sound philosophical basis for further research.[14] So strongly behavioral has much recent work

---

phie (Walter Gruyter, Berlin, 1966; English translation in preparation); P. Schöller: Die deutschen Städte (special issue of the Geographische Zeitschrift, Beihefte 17, Wiesbaden, 1967). Japanese: S. Kiuchi et al., edits.: Japanese Cities: A Geographical Approach, Special Publication No. 2 (Association of Japanese Geographers, Tokyo, 1970).

[11]Despite controversy over urban morphology in Britain, the balanced view clearly favors its validity in geographical study.

[12]This shift was not necessarily detrimental considering the increasing repetitiveness of much morphological work in the 1950s. New advances were needed in depth of analysis and problem definition; that few came in the ensuing years may be attributed in part to the ridicule that the technical revolutionaries heaped upon morphological issues.

[13]See, for example, the tone of the preface to the textbook by J. A. Jakle et al.: Human Spatial Behavior: A Social Geography (Duxbury Press, Scituate, Mass., 1976).

[14]In some respects, the removal of applied behavioral psychology from writing by American social geographers would leave relatively little social geography. For European approaches, see P. Claval: Principes de géographie sociale (Editions M.-Th. Génin et Librairies Techniques, Paris, 1973); W. Storkebaum, edit.: Sozialgeographie (Wissenschaftliche Buchgesellschaft, Darmstadt,

in American social geography been as to render British contributions, especially to the social geography of the city, a distinctly separate if overlapping
new tradition.[15]

In some respects, there has been a narrowing of interest in the geographic dimensions of urban structure. This may appear paradoxical in the light of
heavier-than-ever borrowing from neighboring social sciences sanctioned by
interdisciplinary fervor, but perhaps this looking outwards reflects a dissatisfaction born of conceptual superficiality rather than innate paucity of fundamental questions about the geography of cities. Geographical writing on cities has
shown considerable concentration of effort on economic, locational questions to
the detriment of equally relevant social issues (until recently), and also centrifugal tendencies to study non-spatial factors only indirectly linked to man's organization of terrestrial space.

The consequences of these trends for transatlantic urban geography are
manifold. First, and most notable, has been the virtual abandonment over the
last two decades of the urban landscape as a relevant object of study. Symptoms of this outcome were morphological studies in progress during the first
flush of the technical revolution that sought to ride the inundation in the lifeboat
of quantitative methodology in apparent disregard for the subtle patterning of
the urban fabric by historical circumstances so intractable for quantitative analysis.[16] Second, there developed a decreasing ability in urban geography as a
whole to set out a coherent, logical position for integrating individual work into
the corpus of literature. Affecting functional and morphological studies alike,
this resulted in a plethora of rather isolated, often reductionist stances. Reflections of this trend can be seen in smörgåsbord textbooks and other summar-
izing vehicles conveying a highly disparate picture of the aims and purposes of

---

1969); and J. G. Hajdu: Toward a Definition of Post-war German Social Geography, Annals, Association of American Geographers, Vol. 58, 1968, pp. 397-
410.

[15]This is the tradition exemplified by E. Jones: A Social Geography of Belfast (Oxford University Press, London, 1960) and more recent work in updated
but fundamentally similar mode. See D. B. Clark and M. B. Gleave, edits.:
Social Patterns in Cities, Special Publication No. 5 (Institute of British Geographers, London, 1973).

[16]See R. J. Johnston: Towards an Analytical Study of the Townscape: The
Residential Building Fabric, Geografiska Annaler, Vol. 51B, 1969, pp. 20-32.
Many geographers who had carried out urban morphological studies for M. A.
theses or as early publications switched to functional topics for later work.

urban study by geographers.[17] Third, and more positively, a heavy investment in functional research has radically improved geographers' understanding of how cities work, so much so that conceptions of morphological processes in cities now lag far behind. Future morphological study must be predicated upon these improvements in functional perspectives. Fourth, the headlong rush towards a normative Valhalla may be linked to a decreasing interest in the full geographical reality of cities, in which cultural differences of all kinds within and between cities play significant roles. A clear symptom here has been the use of maps in the collection, analysis, and presentation of urban research, the trend in which has been towards increasingly abstract, placeless, and reductionist modes of representation and content. The not-unexpected reaction to this trend has been a minor rash of attempts at subjectivist revisionism.[18] Fifth, many urban geographers have become disdainful of pattern in the restless search for process, even to the point of refuting the mutual reflectivity and causality of both these elements. Much work in urban behavioral geography stops far short of synthesizing the representative, composite, and aggregate behavior outcomes, or patterns.[19] Sixth, urban geography in the last two decades has been heavily present-oriented, eschewing, with some notable exceptions, the role of time in molding urban conformations and calibrating rates of change.[20]

Finally, taking the first and last mentioned consequences together, it can be argued that in the neglect of the urban landscape by urban geographers it has been left to others to reinvent the wheel. Cultural geographers, social historians, architectural historians and planner-designers have not been slow to appre-

---

[17]H. M. Mayer and C. F. Kohn, edits.: Readings in Urban Geography (University of Chicago Press, Chicago, 1959); Berry and Horton, op. cit. [note 10].

[18]A. Buttimer: Values in Geography, Association of American Geographers Resource Paper, No. 24; M. E. Hurst, edit.: I Came to the City (Houghton Mifflin, Boston, 1975).

[19]For example, J. D. Porteous: Environment and Behavior: Planning and Everyday Urban Life (Addison-Wesley, Reading, Mass., 1977).

[20]Note the disinterest in evolution processes in Murphy, op. cit. [note 10], and Yeates and Garner, op. cit. [note 10]. Some important exceptions in American urban geography are A. Pred: The Spatial Dynamics of U.S. Urban-industrial Growth, 1800-1914: Interpretive and Theoretical Essays (M.I.T. Press, Cambridge, Mass., 1966); J. E. Vance, Jr.: The Merchant's World: The Geography of Wholesaling (Prentice-Hall, Englewood Cliffs, N.J., 1970); and D. Ward: Cities and Immigrants: A Geography of Change in Nineteenth Century America (Oxford University Press, New York, 1971).

ciate the importance of the urban landscape in the urban totality. Not surprisingly, though examination of the urban landscape from other perspectives is highly valuable to urban geography, others cannot be expected to provide answers to questions that arise logically from geographical objectives. This is particularly true of questions regarding the interrelations between social values, technology, and environmental constraints on land use, as reflected in their complex and changing spatial integration over time.

There are now clear signs that morphological issues are being reasserted in American urban geography—albeit in considerably more sophisticated form than before. While their increasing appeal no doubt highlights some of the shortcomings of the dominant work of the last two decades, it derives as much from external stimuli and the bandwagon effect of wide public interest in environmental quality, historic preservation, and more recently cultural resurgence, not unconnected with recognition of minorities and national celebrations.[21] It may be suggested, however, that the methodological questions arising from renewed interest in the urban landscape generally lack sufficient logical organization to cohere as a group of issues and to fit into and utilize effectively the many systematic advances that the functional era in urban geography has without question produced.

Enduring Themes in Urban Geography and the Role of the Urban Landscape

For all the experimentation with mathematical modelbuilding, economic theory, and behavioral concepts in recent years, and the apparent fragmentation of objectives, the fundamental purpose in urban geog phy continues to be the elucidation of the character of cities as discrete "open system" complexes of concrete components and forces comprising distinct regions of the geosphere.[22] As the densest and most man-made of human ecotypes, cities require particu-

---

[21] Graduate theses in North American departments with an explicitly morphological theme have jumped from two in the period 1961-65 to eighteen in the following five years and twenty-nine in the first half of the 1970s (tabulated from listings in The Professional Geographer, 1961-75). Other evidence may be deduced from P. F. Lewis et al.: Visual Blight in America, Association of American Geographers Resource Paper, No. 23, 1973; the landscape in literature session at the 1974 A.A.G. meeting; and the reestablishment of the journal Landscape to which geographers are energetic contributors.

[22] For a general discussion of the unity and diversity of modern geography from an international perspective, see H. Uhlig: Organization and System of Geography, Geoforum, Vol. 7, 1971, pp. 7-38.

136

larly diverse analysis that may be characterized under four headings.

First, the city can be viewed as a functional system in which the needs of the occupying urban society, itself part of a wider, integrated population, are catered to and accommodated within a localized physical space over time. Second, the city represents a spatial subsystem of the geosphere, the trait-complexes of which may be studied for regional variations in their generic and ideographic character. Third, the city as a temporal system is a product of continually changing process clusters that variously bequeath and supplant earlier spatial structures of functional activity and morphological accommodation for each succeeding occupation phase, thus calling for chronological treatment. Fourth, the city is a physical system composed of material structures arranged in dense patterns of culturally distinctive form-complexes. This last dimension, representing the analysis of urban landscapes, is of greatest present concern, though its relation to the other approaches is self-evidently complementary, and often undertaken in combination with one or more of the other approaches.[23] In the broad context of these four general themes for urban geography, it is reasonable to suggest that current work in the field does not adequately nor equitably cover this array of concerns. More critical is the lack of significant attempts at broad synthesis.[24] Herein lie the challenges to an enriched urban geography.

The relevance of the urban landscape as an object for study lies not only in the obvious fact that it is "there" but in its significance in interpreting the nature of an urban society in a specific habitat. The human group occupying the mature city at any one time inherits a socio-economic system which it will further refine according to its immediate needs within the constraints of sometimes long-established and often hard-to-change social mores; this blend of

[23]For a discussion of the interrelations among these distinct approaches within urban geography, see M. R. G. Conzen: Geography and Townscape Conservation, in First German-English Symposium on Applied Geography 1973, Giessener Geographische Schriften, No. 35 (edited by H. Uhlig and C. Leinau; Lenz-Verlag, Giessen, 1975), pp. 95-102.

[24]J. Gottmann: Megalopolis (Johns Hopkins University Press, Baltimore, 1961) constitutes the single exception to date. Text books on American urban geography generally have attempted no broad cultural synthesis, preferring sui generis an analytical, and at times an atomistic approach. The imminent publication of J. Vance's survey of Western urbanism, This Scene of Man (Harper and Row, New York, forthcoming 1977) may represent a significant corrective to this criticism. Regarding American cities, G. A. Wissink: American Cities in Perspective (Van Gorcum, Assen, 1962) stands as an early attempt at partial synthesis, though widely overlooked. See also B. Hofmeister: Stadt und Kulturraum Angloamerika (F. Vieweg, Braunschweig, 1971).

bequeathed values and habitual behavior on the one hand and modifications necessitated by changed circumstances on the other contribute to a particular identity of social spirit. This "personality" of the city is in some ways most effectively transmitted in the symbolism of the built environment. The urban landscape records in its morphology the patterns of aspiration, decision-making, accommodation and satisfaction (or dissatisfaction in the case of replacement) of successive generations of residents playing out their roles under particular circumstances of place. Here, particularity of place, as expressed in buildings, open spaces, or spatial arrangements of style, scale, materials and ensemble, captures and holds something of the essence of the human community. [25] More importantly, it conditions the opportunities for and constraints upon change for the community and its members.

When cities were small, compact, and clearly rooted in highly distinct regional cultures, this bonding between physical and social expressions of local identity was stronger. With supra-regional megalopoli emerging throughout the industrially-advanced world, such place particularity and unified identity of built environment and social "geist" are clearly undergoing massive alteration. Neither the diffusion of modern technology nor the nationalization of media-borne general culture is geared to preserving local identity. It is therefore an urgent question whether the urban landscape of particular places will maintain any significant symbolic distinctiveness. The question is urgent because historically valid elements of the city or townscape, once destroyed are literally irreplaceable. In interpreting the urban landscape for society at large, and city planners in particular (charged as they are with the intelligent long-term management of the environment on behalf of society), the urban geographer has an immensely relevant objective for exploring and understanding this facet of urbanism. What is the relationship between the pressure for and types of change in land use and building use on the one hand and the economic suitability and cultural symbolism of the inherited physical structure of cities on the other hand? How historically complex and locationally significant are the different districts of cities? Of what national, regional, and local significance are single buildings, groups of structures, districts, or whole cities in terms of their contribution to regional identity through the expression of their urban landscape components, and how are these factors reasonably integrated into needed

---

[25] See M. Schwind: Kulturlandschaft als geformter Geist: Drei Aufsätze über die Aufgaben der Kulturgeographie (Wissenschaftliche Buchgesellschaft, Darmstadt, 1964).

change? These appear to be some of the fundamental questions geographers can pursue in seeking to understand the rich texture of urban landscapes and the forces that mold and change them, and to contribute to their intelligent modification as new urban needs come along.

It remains only to stress that, in confronting urban landscapes in all their vast detail and unending variety, the urban geographer must of necessity adopt a morphogenetic approach. It is pointless to analyze the cityscape only in terms of present-day uses, given the inertia of physical structures. Nor can inherited structures, including even their patterns of current use, be interpreted outside the context of the city's changing socio-economic context. While emphatically true for Old World cities and towns, this is no less applicable for New World places, for what the latter may sometimes lack in age is more than compensated for in speed and scale of growth.[26]

Issues in Urban Landscape Research

The urban landscape as an inescapable visual component of everyday life in the city has not suffered neglect from the general intellectual community even if geographers have been conspicuous by their frequent absence. A vast literature, often pictorial, celebrates, records, analyzes, and interprets urban landscapes the world over from a variety of viewpoints, many of them scholarly.[27] Characteristically, the four monumental surveys of urban landscape development in history have been written by planners—Lavedan, Mumford, Egli, and Gutkind.[28] Only more recently have historians, architects, archeologists, and geographers contributed book-length surveys of townscape evolution, concen-

---

[26]Many American cities are, of course, substantially older and possibly more socially complex than European cities founded during the industrial revolution or later. Conversely, not all examples of phenomenal speed and scale of growth are American.

[27]The major disciplines with traditional interests in the urban landscape apart from geography are art history, architecture and architectural history, archeology, and town planning, and to a much smaller degree literature, anthropology, sociology, and history. Most other viewpoints may be classified as antiquarian or journalistic.

[28]P. Lavedan: Histoire de l'urbanisme (4 vols.; Henri Laurens, Paris, 1926-1952); L. Mumford: The Culture of Cities (Harcourt, Brace and Co., 1938) and The City in History (Harcourt, Brace and World, New York, 1961); E. Egli: Geschichte des Städtebaues (3 vols.; Eugen Reutsch Verlag, Zurich, 1959-1967); E. A. Gutkind: International History of City Development (8 vols.; Free Press of Glencoe, New York, 1964-).

trating in some cases on particular periods or regions.[29] These studies generally fall into two groups depending upon their principal aim. Planners and architects have been more immediately concerned with aesthetic analysis of present-day form ensembles, while geographers and historians have been interested
primarily in functional evolution of the urban landscape.[30] In the European context, historical treatments have naturally had to reach back centuries if not mil-
lennia, and in so doing rely more on ground plan evidence (often archeological)
in the absence of remaining built structures for earlier periods. In North
America, the history of townscapes is considerably less developed, and is
founded to date largely upon the work of historians of planning[31] and architecture[32] in which town plans and the building fabric are treated in isolation.[33]
There is a need to integrate the ground plan and building character of the city
together with the patterns of land and building use in order to gain a fuller understanding of the relationships among these components in the changing urban
scene. With such understanding, the psychological interplay between people
and the urban landscape as part of their external environment can then also be
better gauged.

---

[29] S. E. Rasmussen: Towns and Buildings (Harvard University Press, Cam-
bridge, Mass., 1951); F. R. Hiorns: Town Building in History (G. G. Harrap,
London, 1956); G. L. Burke: Towns in the Making (Edward Arnold, London,
1971); examples of regionally restricted surveys are H. Planitz: Die deutsche
Stadt im Mittelalter: Von der Römerzeit bis zu den Zunftkämpfen (Böhlau Verlag, Graz, 1954); M. W. Beresford: New Towns of the Middle Ages: Town
Plantation in England, Wales, and Gascony (Praeger, New York, 1967); M.
Aston and J. Bond: The Landscape of Towns (J. M. Dent and Sons, London,
1976).

[30] Among the primarily modern-aesthetic treatments, see G. Cullen: Townscape (The Architectural Press, London, 1961); and T. Sharp: Town and Townscape (John Murray, London, 1968); for functional-historical overviews, see
W. G. Hoskins: The Making of the English Landscape (Hodder and Stoughton,
London, 1955); and E. Johns: British Townscapes (Edward Arnold, London,
1965).

[31] E. H. Chapman: Cleveland: Village to Metropolis (Western Reserve His-
torical Society, Cleveland, 1964); J. W. Reps: The Making of Urban America:
A History of City Planning in the United States (Princeton University Press,
Princeton, N.J., 1965).

[32] J. M. Fitch: American Building: The Historical Forces that Shaped It
(Schocken, New York, 1973); W. M. Whitehill: Boston: A Topographical History (Belknap Press, Cambridge, Mass., 1959); and A. N. B. Garvan: Architecture and Town Planning in Colonial Connecticut (Yale University Press, New
Haven, 1951).

[33] Exceptions are Garvan, op. cit. ⌈note 32⌉, and Whitehill, op. cit. ⌈note
32⌉.

Terminological Prolegomena

Before reviewing a number of possible specific approaches to the urban landscape, it seems desirable to acknowledge a procedural problem. Much confusion reigns in geographical and other urban landscape literature regarding suitable technical vocabulary. Differences of opinion and disciplinary preferences cannot be eliminated, particularly since many new terms will undoubtedly arise as further work continues, but some fog needs to be lifted. Three pairs of terms deserve preliminary comment.

Landscape and Landschaft have often been considered synonymous, though erroneously so.[34] The English term has in practice a more restricted meaning related to the physiognomy of a place or area, whereas German geographers in the last twenty years have developed the concept of Landschaft to a new level of sophistication, best referred to as the modern theory of the region.[35] In this broader sense, the geographical region is that area occupied by a singular combination of earth phenomena constituting an open-ended spatial subsystem of the geosphere characterized by material form, functional interactions, and subject to unceasing temporal change. Thus, any geographically coherent region can be analyzed functionally, morphologically, and historically, and synthesized ultimately on the basis of all three dimensions. The landscape, be it urban or rural, is then one component of any regionalization of the earth's surface (or a part thereof), and is most effectively studied not in isolation but with the other components kept continuosuly in mind.

Another pair of terms, urban form and urban morphology, are more closely related, and while they share the same lexical meaning ("morphe" [Greek] = shape, form) they do however touch different nerves in academic minds, particularly in geography. Urban morphology, as a label that bannered the work of urban geography in the heyday of the pre-war landscape and regional research mode, has acquired the ballast of opprobrium heaped upon it by the locational analysts of 1960 vintage. Nevertheless, functionalist geographers and others, obliged by gross reality to admit the persistent importance of morphology in urban structure, have generally preferred using the term urban form. The distinction, unnecessary in any case, would be without significance except

---

[34] An early discussion of this issue is in R. Hartshorne: The Nature of Geography (Association of American Geographers, Lancaster, Pa., 1939), pp. 149-174.

[35] See E. Neef: Die theoretischen Grundlagen der Landschaftslehre (Verlag Hermann Haack, Gotha-Leipzig, 1967).

that the choice of terms generally predicts the detail and sophistication of concern.[36]

A third pairing is that between the urban landscape and the townscape (European usage) or cityscape (American usage). There are implicit scale differences between town- and city-scapes that reflect cultural history and urban mass, but otherwise their meaning is coincident. It is difficult to speak of London's or New York's "townscape," while "cityscape" might be pretentious if used in reference to a small town in rural Iowa or a market town in the Cotswold Hills of England. Hence the term urban landscape is appropriately flexible in spanning the potential range from the smallest clearly urban settlement to the whole of, or at least large portions of, Megalopolis if required. All three terms carry the same content meaning, with townscape and cityscape more particularly distinguishing scale.

The Cultural and Economic Context

A vital prerequisite for any sustained conceptual development of urban morphology is a logical organizational framework grounded in the full time-space context of relevant cultural traditions. Of clear significance here are the varying economic climates, conditions of technological change, and social values that affect, govern, and characterize the formation of urban landscapes at all times in any region. This is elementary in most of Europe where contextual blindness would produce no respectable explanation of morphogenesis whatsoever. It should be self-evident in North America too, where great cultural mixing has not yet produced a spatially homogeneous society. The great normative thrusts within geography, though, have necessitated the reassertion of this axiom of sensitivity to cultural context (at all scales), not because some general forces do not govern our society in its habitat, but because general forces are not the only elements in a full explanation of concrete situations. Elizabeth

---

[36]"Urban form" has been applied to gross city shape (outline of the complete built-up area), and sometimes to the vague texture of the built-up area, such as the general grain of the street pattern. See, for example, M. Brown: Urban Form, Journal of the Town Planning Institute, Vol. 52, 1966; C. E. Browning, edit.: Population and Urbanized Area Growth in Megalopolis, 1950-1970, North Carolina Studies in Geography No. 7 (University of North Carolina, Department of Geography, Chapel Hill, N.C., 1974). An example of extreme reductionist thinking about urban form is contained in B. J. L. Berry et al.: Land Use, Urban Form, and Environmental Quality, Research Paper No. 155 (University of Chicago, Department of Geography, Chicago, 1974). Such conceptual barrenness fails completely, of course, to represent the rich variety and scale of urban form in the real world.

Lichtenberger has recently attempted to characterize the geographical character of European urbanism in terms of its inner cultural-historical dimensions, and similar syntheses are clearly needed for the nature of urbanism in North America and other realms.[37] Each society produces its own urban landscape, working into the detailed configuration almost every assumption, objective, skill, and preference of the society at large, so while the landscape is full of "signs" reflecting the society, they will not yield answers unless the right questions are posed. Too often, the potential for interpreting this relationship has been taken for granted and ignored rather than challenged to produce the meaningful connections.[38]

The socio-economic climate that has existed at all significant stages of townscape development also requires explicit treatment in urban morphology— not necessarily to dominate the discussion but to provide explanatory clues that account for changes in the urban fabric. Two inter-related factors go far in delineating the economic context. First, functional specialization of settlements, such as trade centers, mining towns, health resorts, or educational meccas, leads to specific emphasis of some environmental needs at the expense of others, such as the massive provision of blue-collar housing, wholesaling premises, public open space.[39] What pressures do these requirements place on the income, managerial skills, local labor pools, and social harmony of the community, or the wider region surrounding such places? Second, business cycles and resource endowments (both regional and local) affect the periodicity of growth and change, particularly under changing comparative advantage.[40]

---

[37]E. Lichtenberger: The Nature of European Urbanism, Geoforum, Vol. 4, 1970, pp. 45-62.

[38]Several felicitous exceptions to such an indictment aimed at American urban morphology may be noted in W. Zelinsky: The Pennsylvania Town: An Overdue Geographical Account, Geographical Review, Vol. 67, 1977, pp. 127-147; and P. F. Lewis: New Orleans: The Making of an Urban Landscape (Ballinger Publishing Co., Cambridge, Mass., 1976).

[39]City classifications ranging from C. D. Harris: A Functional Classification of Cities in the United States, Geographical Review, Vol. 33, 1943, pp. 86-99, to B. J. L. Berry et al.: City Classification Handbook (Wiley Interscience, New York, 1972) offer the basis for ascertaining the comparative economic character of a place, but such complexions change over time, necessitating careful historical reconstruction. See E. E. Lampard: The Evolving System of Cities in the United States: Urbanization and Economic Development, in Issues in Urban Economics (edited by H. S. Perloff and L. Wingo; Johns Hopkins University Press, Baltimore, 1968), pp. 81-138.

[40]For an up-to-date study of business cycles related to urban growth in America and Europe, see M. Gottlieb: Long Swings in Urban Development

What spatial consequences can be found therefore in the urban landscape, such as the directional bias and rapidity of suburban growth or the change in building materials as wealth, local exhaustion of supplies, and new transport routes alter the decisions that fix the visual character of the town?

Technological conditions can change building construction methods, transport, utilities, and other modes of communication. Despite the obviousness of this statement, there are few studies that measure the actual impact of a construction innovation upon the geographical structure of an urban area.[41] Even studies of streetcar and automobile introduction have concentrated more on the journey-to-work and social segregation than the actual morphology of ground plan and buildings developed in the new eras. But residential building types and architectural quality often "set" the character of districts in terms of the values and aspirations of different types of people, and thereby strongly influence social segregation by their geographical distribution.

Perhaps most revealing if hardest to pinpoint are the underlying social values of an urban community constantly expanding and renewing its physical habitat. The greed of personal gain has often vied with the yearnings for social acceptance and conviviality. How have human strivings specifically shaped the physical city in terms of size and ornateness of buildings, ground coverage and placement, neighborhood homogeneity, and so forth?[42] What limits are there

---

(Columbia University Press, National Bureau of Economic Research, New York, 1976). For changing regional resource clusters, see H. Perloff et al.: Regions, Resources, and Economic Growth (Johns Hopkins University Press, Baltimore, 1960).

[41] C. Condit: American Building Art (University of Chicago Press, Chicago, 1960) documents the technical changes in building methods in American history, but can offer only an impressionistic view of the geographical impact on a city of these changes. In connection with transport innovations, S. B. Warner, Jr.: Streetcar Suburbs: The Process of Growth in Boston, 1870-1900 (Harvard University Press, Cambridge, 1962) suggests much about the geographical transformation of suburban areas.

[42] Land speculation is the obvious issue here. Indirect insights can be gleaned from such works as H. H. Hoyt: One Hundred Years of Land Values in Chicago (University of Chicago Press, Chicago, 1933), and P. H. Cornick: Premature Subdivision and Its Consequences (Institute of Public Administration, New York, 1938), but the geography of land speculation has still to be written. For some tentative probes, see J. D. Fellman: Pre-building Growth Patterns of Chicago, Annals, Association of American Geographers, Vol. 47, 1957, pp. 59-82, and C. S. Sargent: Land Speculation and Urban Morphology, in Urban Policymaking and Metropolitan Dynamics: A Comparative Geographical Analysis (edited by J. S. Adams; Ballinger Publishing Co., Cambridge, Mass., 1976), pp. 21-56.

to real property ownership and what historically has been the legacy of privacy, eminent domain, tax exemption, and government involvement in channelling the growth of cities, to mention some diverse possible questions? Some community values are legally sanctioned and protected, others informal but no less effective.[43] The urban landscape cannot be understood without thorough grounding in the social history and values of the occupying society, and by the same token understanding of the urban landscape can go far in clarifying the structure and effectiveness of those values as applied to the city as a living and working environment.[44]

The Urban Landscape from Different Vantage Points

Approaches to the urban landscape appear to fall into two broad categories based upon the landscape as an assemblage of concrete phenomena, and the landscape as a subjective human experience. The former perspective seeks to establish an inventory of "what is out there," this thing we call the landscape, and to understand the impartial processes that have produced what may be termed its objective geographical reality. The second perspective seeks to measure social awareness of the landscape in behavioral terms of perceptual biases and selectivity in observation as well as psychological attitudes towards what is perceived. The research traditions and methodological histories of the two approaches differ considerably and will be discussed in turn.

The Objective Physical Components

The urban landscape can be divided systematically into three formal components in space, arranged in a simple hierarchy of contain-

---

[43]S. B. Warner, Jr.: The Urban Wilderness: A History of the American City (Harper and Row, New York, 1972) provides an indispensable discussion of social attitudes to land and their consequences in the city.

[44]Social stratification and the location of social power naturally add a further dimension to this relationship. Elites are not the only sub-group to influence the built environment. See P. J. Hugill: Landscape as 'Gesture': The Management of Conduct by an Elite, Proceedings, Association of American Geographers, Vol. 8, 1976, pp. 99-102; also H. C. Prince: Georgian Landscapes, in Man Made the Land: Essays in English Historical Geography (edited by A. R. H. Baker and J. B. Harley; Rowman and Littlefield, Totowa, N.J., 1973), pp. 153-166. For the bottom-up approach, see H. Glassie: Folk Housing in Middle Virginia (University of Tennessee Press, Knoxville, Tenn., 1975), and P. F. Lewis: Common Houses, Cultural Spoor, Landscape, Vol. 19, 1975, pp. 1-22.

ment.[45] The most encompassing is the ground plan, usually referred to in Europe as the town plan, namely, the cadaster or matrix of land divisions functionally differentiated by legally protected ownership. Within this framework, nestles the land use pattern arising from the varying needs of the urban society for specialized use of ground and space of differing proportion, shape, and location. Third, the building fabric is contained within the land use system and contributes the physical structures needed to adapt the land ownership parcel to the specialized requirements of property use.

The urban ground plan consists of streets and other communications paths, land parcels or lots, and the ground plan of buildings which give rise to the systematic plan element complexes of street system (or street plan), lot pattern, and building pattern. These elements are distinguishable individually in terms of two factors, initial functional requirements and historical period of implementation, and together form morphogenetic plan unit complexes suitable for geographical study. Buildings likewise reflect original purpose and period of construction, being distinguishable by functional type, such as dwellings, shops, factories, etc., and socially significant architectural style—both cross-classifiable criteria in any geographical typology. Land use, on the other hand, being potentially the most ephemeral of the three urban landscape components, owes its character to immediate needs and hence breaks down along functional lines alone. These three components, then, combine in their highly varied intra-urban combinations and subcombinations to form basic geographical complexes to which the terms townscape cells or urbitopes have been applied.[46] These complexes of spatially homogeneous landscape units combine into larger urban subregions and ultimately the city as a whole.[47]

A static inventory of landscape elements and regionalization, however, is neither a worthy end in itself nor sufficient to comprehend the formative influences. A dynamic perspective on the urban landscape recognizes the changing

---

[45]M. R. G. Conzen: The Plan Analysis of an English City Centre, in Proceedings of the I. G. U. Symposium in Urban Geography, Lund 1960, Lund Studies in Geography, Series B, Vol. 24 (edited by K. Norborg; 1962), pp. 383-414. and op. cit. [note 23], p. 97.

[46]Conzen, op. cit. [note 23], pp. 97-98; K. Temlitz: Aaseestadt und Neu-Coerde: Bildstrukturen neuer Wohnsiedlungen in Münster und ihre Bewertung, Siedlung und Landscaft in Westfalen No. 9 (Landeskundliche Karten und Hefte der Geographischen Kommission für Westfalen, Münster, 1975).

[47]Thurston, op. cit. [note 5]; Stedman, op. cit. [note 5]; A. Herold: Würzburg: Analyse einer Stadtlandschaft, Berichte zur deutsche Landeskunde, Vol. 35, 1965, pp. 185-229.

needs of the occupying society over time and the translation of those needs into different periods of townscape development that mirror the functional periods of changing socio-economic organization. The investment costs of using and creating urban property are usually so great that no generation could easily afford to replace old fabric with new; adaptation of the old has been dominant, and replacement both functionally and spatially has been selective. This is especially true in Europe where long historical inheritance has been accompanied until modern times by limited technical and fiscal powers of reorganization. Even in North America, where many towns and cities are less than 150 years old and ecotechnical replacement is widespread in scale and rapid in time, the inheritance of fabric should not be underestimated.

The accumulation of structural forms not quickly demolished represents the most basic process in the urban landscape and provides most cities with some historical depth. Furthermore, the differential rate at which ground plan, buildings, and land use alter their character in keeping with ever-changing functional needs of society complicates the overall rate of morphological change of the urban landscape. In general, land and building use is subject to relatively rapid change, while actual building structures are less so (though functional modifications will be frequent), and the ground plan proves usually to be the most resistant to alteration. In Boston's North End today, for example, essentially unmodified irregular lots dating from the colonial period of craftsmens' and victuallers' shops contain large nineteenth century granite and brick warehouse buildings recently renovated for luxury waterfront apartment living. The confinement of later development (of all three component types) within pre-existing morphological frames under certain conditions may be considered, then, as one of the fundamental laws in urban landscape analysis.[48] Yet study of American urban landscapes has rarely attempted to isolate and measure systematically the differential rates of change of ground plan features, building stock, and land use in relation to each other, especially with regard to the enormous geographical variations of such change within different parts of an urban area. To know such variable rates would be to improve our understanding of the complex economic pressures on the urban environment, physical and man-made, and also the social responses to the need for physical change. Analytical

---

[48]Generally speaking, the scale factor is responsible for changing the "conformity" of change over time. The complexity and pressures of modern society together with larger technical capabilities lead to more sweeping rupture between past and present in modern city change than would have been true for earlier times.

progress in this sphere seems most likely with controlled investigations of the constituent elements, since impressionistic studies have already established some broad trends.[49] Replication of general studies such as these and dependent upon individual literary skill for synthesis may prove additive (and difficult) rather than cumulative. Past work and present possibilities may be grouped within the three broad categories of landscape components.

The ground plan. —The ground plan of cities has long been recognized as a significant indicator of historical man-land adjustments and cultural character.[50] Since the ground plan is as old as the city itself, it is best viewed in terms of its historical evolution, thereby drawing in a wide variety of factors relevant in its complete formation.[51] The complexity of the urban ground plan (as defined above) has often caused attention to be focussed upon certain elements. The most obvious of these is the general street system which not surprisingly has been the favored object of investigation for over a century, partic-

---

[49]The best examples of impressionistic studies of integral townscape change are Whitehill, op. cit. [note 32], and Lewis, op. cit. [note 38]. Though excellent general overviews written with great knowledge and insight, they do not attempt precise measurement within a tight conceptual scheme. For examples of publications featuring a wealth of information on the changing urban landscape, see J. A. Kouwenhoven: The Columbia Historical Portrait of New York Doubleday & Co., Garden City, 1953), and H. M. Mayer and R. C. Wade: Chicago: Growth of a Metropolis (University of Chicago Press, Chicago, 1969).

[50]Schlüter, op. cit. [note 2]; M. R. G. Conzen: The Use of Town Plans in the Study of Urban History, in The Study of Urban History (edited by H. J. Dyos; Edward Arnold, London, 1968), pp. 113-130.

[51]There have been two basic approaches to town plan history, one stressing changing concepts of what ground plans new towns should have (this is the common element of the references in note 28), the other tracing the origin and cumulative modifications and additions to existing towns through their individual histories. The former approach emphasizes successive intellectual vogues over broad expanses of time and place while the latter focusses upon the variations in socio-economic and cultural factors affecting individual towns or groups of towns during their particular development. The literature on individual plan developments in many languages is enormous, and often of local interest only, but three examples from one area chart the increasing sophistication achieved over the last forty years in town plan development studies. See W. Gley: Grundriss und Wachstum der Stadt Frankfurt am Main, in Festschrift zur Hundertjahrfeier des Vereins für Geographie und Statistik zu Frankfurt am Main (edited by W. Hartke; Verlag der Geographischen Verlagsanstalt Ludwig Ravenstein A. G., Frankfurt am Main, 1936), pp. 53-100; A. Beuermann: Zur Topographie der Göttinger Innenstadt, Berichte zur deutschen Landeskunde, Vol. 25, 1960, pp. 93-128; and G. Kreuzer: Der Grundriss der Stadt Regensburg, Berichte zur deutschen Landeskunde, Vol. 42, 1969, pp. 209-256.

148

ularly viewed as a unified whole together with defense walls and natural site features.[52] The outpouring of literature based on discussion of the aggregate street pattern, however, failed to rise much above individual explanations and gross classifications—a criticism now standard but not much overcome.[53] What progress there has been has centered on attempts to dissect the street system according to historical stages of implementation, functional development, or morphological inertia.[54] Those studies that focus narrowly upon aggregate street geometry divorced from the other fundamental components of the ground plan, namely, the lot boundaries and building coverage patterns, seem destined to produce limited analytical dividends.

Other special approaches to the urban ground plan have examined cadastral processes from both a morphological and functional perspective. Division of the land into parcels owned by many individuals free to transfer ownership produces over time constant "cadastral" change, the variability of which results in heterogeneity of parcel size, clustering, tenurial status, and morphological alteration. One grouping of such studies is concerned with the influence of pre-existing, often rural land divisions on the shape of subsequent urban development, demonstrating in different cultural contexts that prior ownership morphology substantially constrains later change.[55] A second grouping con-

---

[52]This genre of study is summarized profusely in Dickinson, The West European City, op. cit. [note 4].

[53]Garrison, op. cit. [note 6]; Carter, op. cit. [note 1], pp. 144-146. For examples of general studies of American street patterns, see A. J. Wright: Ohio Town Patterns, Geographical Review, Vol. 27, 1937, pp. 615-624; H. Boesch: Schachbrett-Texturen nordamerikanischer Siedlungen, Stuttgarter Geographische Studien, Vol. 69, 1957; and the more detailed study in R. Pillsbury: The Urban Street Pattern as a Cultural Indicator: Pennsylvania, 1682-1815, Annals, Association of American Geographers, Vol. 60, 1970, pp. 428-446.

[54]L. Améen: Stadsplanestudier över Kalmar [Street pattern studies of Kalmar], Svensk Geografisk Årsbok, Vol. 41, 1965, pp. 7-18 (English summary); R. J. Johnston: An Outline of the Development of Melbourne's Street Pattern, Australian Geographer, Vol. 10, 1968, pp. 453-465. Regarding the historical inertia of street systems, see B. J. Buvinger: The Persistence of Street Patterns in Pittsburgh, Pennsylvania (M. A. thesis, University of Pittsburgh, 1972).

[55]See Hoskins, op. cit. [note 30]; F. Dussart: Les types de dessin parcellaire et leur répartition en Belgique, Bulletin Sociale Belge d'Etudes Géographique, Vol. 30, 1961, pp. 21-65; D. Ward: The Pre-urban Cadaster and the Urban Pattern of Leeds, Annals, Association of American Geographers, Vol. 52, 1962, pp. 150-166; L. Dethier: L'influence de la structure foncière et du dessin parcellaire sur le développement urbain: Le quartier de Salzinnes (Namur), Bulletin Sociale Belge d'Etudes Géographique, Vol. 31, 1962, pp. 99-121;

sists of investigations of landholding patterns as the key to differential timing and ultimate morphology of development.[56] A third grouping comprises studies integrating various factors in the expansion of the built-up area through suburban extension.[57] In North America, equivalent studies have focussed heavily upon the nature of urban fringe subdivision, and the spatio-temporal process of platting and its geographical consequences.[58]

M. P. Conzen: Spatial Effects of Antecedent Conditions upon Urban Growth (M. Sc. thesis, University of Wisconsin-Madison, 1968). A major work in this area is Améen, op. cit. [note 9]. Two exemplary studies that involved major archival reconstruction of the spatial structure of property transfer in former historical times are O. Treptow: Untersuchungen zur Topographie der Stadt Siegburg: Hinweise zur Arbeitsmethode, in Die Stadt in der europäischen Geschichte: Festschrift Edith Ennen (edited by W. Besch et al.; Ludwig Röhrscheid Verlag, Bonn, 1972), pp. 701-770; and A. J. Krim: Northwest Cambridge: Report Five, Survey of Architectural History in Cambridge (M. I. T. Press for the Cambridge Historical Commission, Cambridge, Mass., 1977). For a detailed analysis of property changes along streets in already built-up areas in relation to building and architectural style, see Boudon, op. cit. [note 9].

[56]W. D. McTaggart: Private Land Ownership in a Colonial Town: The Case of Noumea, New Caledonia, Economic Geography, Vol. 42, 1966, pp. 189-204; M. H. Mortimore: Landownership and Urban Growth in Bradford and Its Environs in the West Riding Conurbation, 1850-1950, Transactions of the Institute of British Geographers, No. 46, 1969, pp. 105-120; T. R. Slater: Estate Ownership and Nineteenth Century Suburban Development [of Cirencester], in Studies in the Archaeology and History of Cirencester, British Archaeological Reports, No. 30 (edited by A. McWhirr; 1976), pp. 145-157; J. Springett: Land Monopoly and Urban Expansion in the Industrial Revolution. Paper presented at the Annual Meeting of the Institute of British Geographers, Historical Geography Research Group session, Newcastle upon Tyne, January 1977. An important influence on land ownership change, the railroad, is discussed in J. H. Appleton: Railways and the Morphology of British Towns, in Urbanisation and Its Problems: Essays in Honour of E. W. Gilbert (edited by R. P. Beckinsale and J. M. Houston; Basil Blackwell, Oxford, 1968), pp. 92-118; and T. Book: Järnvägen i stadplanen: en Nordisk inventering [The railway in built-up areas of town plans], Svensk Geografisk Årsbok, Vol. 47, 1971, pp. 143-162 (English summary).

[57]Bastié, op. cit. [note 9]; H. C. Prince: North-West London, 1814-1863; North-West London, 1864-1914, in Greater London (edited by J. T. Coppock and H. C. Prince; Faber, London, 1964), pp. 80-141; D. Wurmb: Die städtebauliche Entwicklung Nürnbergs von 1806 bis 1914: Unter besonderer Berücksichtigung von Baurecht, Bauverwaltung und städtebaulicher Theorie (Lorenz Spindler Verlag, Nürnberg, 1969); J. W. R. Whitehand: Building Activity and Intensity of Development at the Urban Fringe: The Case of a London Suburb in the Nineteenth Century, Journal of Historical Geography, Vol. 1, 1975, pp. 211-224.

[58]Fellman, op. cit. [note 42], and D. Routaboule: Aux sources de la morphologie urbaine au Québec, La Revue de Géographie de Montréal, Vol. 23,

Most ot the morphological investigation of the last twenty years has been piece-meal and conceptually fragmented. The influence of pre-existing owner-ship patterns has rarely been related to the speed and types of physical growth of the city as a whole. Fringe expansion of the built-up or platted area has been studied in virtual isolation from the detailed processes transforming the physical build of inner-city districts, and all too often the evolution of spatial patterns of urban development has lacked sufficient context of social and eco-nomic history. In general, there is as yet no conceptual unity underlying the recent improved understanding of physical growth processes.[59]

While a broad theory of cross-cultural urban morphological development is still a distant objective, however, recent investigations in England indicate the possibility of conceptual advance on several fronts, with applications in other western cultural contexts. Work on some English towns has established a complex sequence of morphological laws, hypotheses, and evident regularities that may have considerable relevance to North American cities and towns.[60] Notable among these are the "fringe belt concept" and the "burgage cycle" (best viewed as a "building intensity cycle" for American conditions) that fit within a general theory of cultural-economic change linked to building/business cycles, increasing functional specialization, and articulated in terms of three basic forms of physical growth of the urban ground plan--peripheral accretion, inter-

---

1969, pp. 88-97. A rash of graduate theses from the mid-1960s on have ad-dressed topics in this area, for example, B. L. Sukhwal: Changing Subdivision Patterns as Exemplified in Eugene, Oregon: An Aspect of the Development of Urban Landscape (M.A. thesis, University of Oregon, 1966); M. Spyrou: Land in the Suburbs: Spatial Patterns of Lots in the River Road-Santa Clara Area, Eugene, Oregon (M.A. thesis, University of Oregon, 1973); E. K. Burns: The Process of Suburban Residential Development: The San Francisco Peninsula, 1860-1970 (Ph.D. dissertation, University of California-Berkeley, 1974); and E. O. Pederson: Land Subdivision, Land Speculation, and Urban Form: An Essay on Urban Morphology (Ph.D. dissertation, University of California-Berkeley, 1974).

[59]An early attempt at synthesis is H. Bernoulli: Die Stadt und ihr Boden (2nd ed.; Verlag für Architektur, Erlenbach-Zurich, 1942; English summary and legends). Note also E. Keyser· Städtegründungen und Städtebau in Nord-westdeutschland im Mittelalter, Forschungen zur deutschen Landeskunde, Band 3 (Bundesanstalt für Landeskunde, Remagen/Rhein, 1958), and K. Yamori: [The study of city plan] (Taimeido, Tokyo, 1970; in Japanese).

[60]M. R. G. Conzen, op. cit. [note 8], and op. cit. [note 45]. Though based on case studies, this research explores in detail all features of ground plan evolution in order to differentiate as far as possible those processes and resulting patterns that may have more general applicability.

nal repletion, and selective replacement.[61] The fringe belt concept, equally appropriate in considering the land use structure component of the urban landscape, will be discussed later. The building intensity cycle is a concept that helps to interpret the changing fabric of the city, particularly in central districts where central accessibility in the traditional city has placed great pressure on the use of space. Building densities increase at varying rates in different parts of the city, both reflecting and molding functional needs for various types of space, and in central areas reach a peak sooner or later followed by slum clearance or urban renewal. The pressures on change near the city center are, of course, intimately linked to growth processes elsewhere and particularly at the urban fringe, and morphological theory should be capable of connecting them.

If modern urban landscape analysis were developed and easy to apply over broad territory, comparative study would suggest the development of morphological typologies. As it is, regionalization of variants among urban morphological processes is not far advanced.[62] Theoretically, however, there is considerable value in attempting broad regionalization of urban morphology, not as an end in itself, but as a means of approaching the key questions of cultural evolution, localization, transfer, and modification within and between geographic

---

[61]In morphological terms, accretion represents lateral extension of the urban area at its edge, variously referred to as fringe expansion, fringe subdivision, and even in a loose sense suburbanization in American writing. Repletion represents in-filling of already platted areas with additional building coverage, associated often with replatting. Replacement refers to those changes in the urban built-up area that involve substitution of former building structures with new ones. For formal definitions of these terms, see the glossary in M. R. G. Conzen, op. cit. [note 8], 2nd ed., pp. 123-131.

[62]For older attempts at urban ground plan regionalization, see R. E. Dickinson: The Town Plans of East Anglia, Geography, Vol. 19, 1934, pp. 37-50, and J. B. Leighly: The Towns of Medieval Livonia, University of California Publications in Geography, Vol. 6, No. 7 (University of California Press, Berkeley, Calif., 1939). More detailed and morphogenetic schemes are M. R. G. Conzen: Modern Settlement, in Scientific Survey of North-East England (British Association for the Advancement of Science, Newcastle upon Tyne, 1949), pp. 75-83, and J. W. R. Whitehand and K. Alauddin: The Town Plans of Scotland: Some Preliminary Considerations, Scottish Geographical Magazine, Vol. 85, 1969, pp. 109-121. See also A. Scheuerbrandt: Südwestdeutsche Stadttypen und Städtegruppen bis zum frühen 19. Jahrhundert, Heidelberger Geographische Arbeiten, Heft 32 (Geographische Institut der Universität Heidelberg, Heidelberg, 1970); H. A. Millward: A Comparison and Grouping of Ten Canadian Cities with Respect to Their Street-plan, Paper presented at the Annual Meeting of the Canadian Association of Geographers, Ontario Division, 1974; and Zelinsky, op. cit. [note 38].

regions.[63] Thus far, integration of town plan features for comparative purposes has not progressed as rapidly as single-feature regionalizations, and
even the latter are few and incomplete.[64]

The building fabric. —Geographical studies of urban buildings have not
generally advanced as far as work in plan analysis. Their lesser volume and
more fragmented coverage probably reflect difficulty in approaching the seemingly endless variety of building types and styles, the lack of widespread building inventories (as compared with the abundance of large-scale cadastral maps
of ground plan features—few countries or municipalities have taken detailed cen-
suses of morphological building characteristics), and the traditional strength of
architectural history in studying aspects of the building fabric. The limitations
of architectural history for geographers lie chiefly in the general neglect of
architectural styles and functional building types as spatially interacting regional complexes within the city.[65]

The building fabric is recognizable in two fundamental dimensions, as a
set of functional building types, such as residences, factories, shops, and as a
set of structures built in different architectural styles, such as Federalist,
Italianate, Queen Ann, and gothic, depending on historical incidence of fashion.
Not all architectural styles, however, are equally relevant to historical-geo-
graphical analysis, because they should relate to significant periods of socio-
economic evolution. Thus, in analyzing the townscape morphogenetically, several styles may occupy a single appropriate socio-architectural period. To

---

[63]Zelinsky, op. cit. [note 38], p. 102; Michael E. Bonine: Labyrinths,
Mazes and the Grid Pattern Town: The Case of the Iranian City, Paper pre-
sented at the 73rd Annual Meeting of the Association of American Geographers,
Salt Lake City, April 1977.

[64]For example, D. Stanislawski: The Origin of the Grid-Pattern Town,
Geographical Review, Vol. 36, 1946, pp. 105-120; E. T. Price: The Central
Courthouse Square in the American County Seat, Geographical Review, Vol. 58,
1968, pp. 29-60; and J. W. R. Whitehand: The Settlement Morphology of London's Cocktail Belt, Tijdschrift voor Economische en Sociale Geografie, Vol.
58, 1967, pp. 20-27. For a general discussion of the problem, see Smailes,
op. cit. [note 5].

[65]Most works in architectural history stress style characteristics of individual buildings, or at best small building groups such as market place façades,
monumental ensembles, and so forth. Even when a whole district is investigated, as in a study of a Boston area (B. Bunting: Houses of Boston's Back Bay:
An Architectural History, 1840-1917 [Belknap Press, Cambridge, Mass.,
1967]), the spatio-temporal pattern of stylistic variations within the area as a
whole is not investigated.

insist on individual categories for each style would be to abandon morphogenetic relevance for purely aesthetic purposes. Both the building type and its socio-architectural period deserve equal and preferably combined attention, though this is rarely done, especially with regard to non-residential buildings.

The most elementary studies of building types consider the current distribution pattern of building types at a given point in time.[66] While recognition of relict features in the present townscape adds some depth (suitable at least for inventory and planning purposes),[67] it is no substitute for full enquiry into the complete spatio-temporal development patterns of building types and styles.[68] Some promising work has been done in Europe where, following early attempts at detailed investigation,[69] a massive study of Vienna has set completely new standards in the analysis and synthesis of the building fabric in the city's modern history.[70] Particularly important is the integration of building types with cadastral processes, and the formulation of a conceptual model of building type evolution based upon cultural tradition, rural-urban shifts in form modification, and changing socio-economic stratification and functioning within the city. No future research on building fabric can ignore this seminal study.[71] Further

---

[66] P. Camu: Types de maisons dans la région suburbaine de Montréal, Canadian Geographer, Vol. 9, 1957, pp. 21-29; E. Jones: The Delimitation of Some Urban Landscape Features in Belfast, Scottish Geographical Magazine, Vol. 74, 1958, pp. 150-162; and P. Scott: Building Materials in Greater Hobart, Australian Geographer, Vol. 7, 1959, pp. 149-163.

[67] R. J. Solomon and W. E. Goodhand: Past Influences in Present Townscapes: Some Tasmanian Examples, New Zealand Geographer, Vol. 21, 1965, pp. 113-132; and R. J. Solomon: Procedures in Townscape Analysis, Annals, Association of American Geographers, Vol. 56, 1966, pp. 254-268.

[68] A quite successful small scale study in this regard is M. Laithwaite: The Buildings of Burford: A Cotswold Town in the Fourteenth to Nineteenth Centuries, in Perspectives in English Urban History (edited by A. Everitt; Macmillan, London, 1973), pp. 60-90.

[69] M. R. G. Conzen: The Growth and Character of Whitby, in A Survey of Whitby and the Surrounding Area (edited by G. H. J. Daysh; The Shakespeare Head Press, Eton, Windsor, 1958), pp. 49-89; I. Möller: Die Entwicklung eines Hamburger Gebietes von der Agrar- zur Grossstadtlandschaft. Mit einem Beitrag zur Methode der Städtischen Aufrissanalyse, Hamburger Geographische Studien, Heft 10 (Institut für Geographie und Wirtschaftsgeographie der Universität Hamburg, Hamburg, 1959).

[70] H. Bobek and E. Lichtenberger: Wien: Bauliche Gestalt und Entwicklung seit der Mitte des 19. Jahrhunderts (Hermann Böhlau Verlag, Graz-Cologne, 1966).

[71] Unfortunately, the Vienna study is so far available only in German. A

work is proceeding on individual building type complexes, as exemplified by a study of the evolution of court housing in Hull in which a "bye-law cycle" of residential construction is suggested to comprehend the dynamic, reciprocal relation between congested court housing development and housing legislation during the nineteenth and twentieth centuries.[72]

Geographical investigation of North American building fabric evolution has been hampered by an unfortunate division between "stylistic" and "vernacular" or "folk" architecture, and also by a long emphasis on rural housing, or at least rural antecedents of urban housing.[73] Non-residential building types have been almost completely ignored. Several recent developments offer reason for optimism, however, that new ground is being covered. Some detailed residential typologies are beginning to appear,[74] and individual building types are receiving attention, notably a study of New York skyscrapers.[75] In a number of studies, community social structure is being directly drawn upon as an important variable.[76]

---

similar work covering many English cities, though in more general terms, is I. Leister: Wachstum and Erneuerung britischer Industriegrossstädte (Hermann Böhlau Verlag, Vienna-Cologne, 1970).

[72]C. A. Forster: Court Housing in Kingston-upon-Hull: An Example of Cyclic Processes in the Morphological Development of Nineteenth Century Byelaw Housing, Occasional Papers in Geography, No. 19 (University of Hull, Department of Geography, Hull, 1972), pp. 38-40.

[73]For example, J. E. Rickert: House Facades of the Northeastern United States: A Tool of Geographic Analysis, Annals, Association of American Geographers, Vol. 57, 1967, pp. 211-238, and Lewis, op. cit. [note 44]. A sensitive, if impressionistic, overview of urban house type development in one city is Lewis, op. cit. [note 38].

[74]For example, Krim, op. cit. [note 55]. Though rural in setting, the house typology in Glassie, op. cit. [note 44], has important implications for urban counterparts.

[75]S. Zoll: Superville: New York—Aspects of Very High Bulk, Massachusetts Review, Vol. 14, 1973, pp. 447-538. See also J. Gottmann: Why the Skyscraper? Geographical Review, Vol. 56, 1966, pp. 190-212; L. R. Ford: The Skyscraper: Urban Symbolism and City Structure (Ph.D. dissertation, University of Oregon, 1970).

[76]R. Bastian: Architecture and Class Segregation in Late-nineteenth-century Terre Haute, Indiana, Geographical Review, Vol. 65, 1975, pp. 166-179, and a number of Berkeley doctoral dissertations in geography: R. T. Barnett: Suburban Subdivision: The Morphogenesis of Housing in Stockton, 1850-1950 (1973); D. J. Dingemans: The Townhouse of the Suburbs: A Study of Changing Urban Morphology and Social Space in American Suburbs, 1960-1974 (1975); Burns, op. cit. [note 58]—all the above are unpubl. Ph.D. dissertations, Uni-

Considering the inferior status of building type research in modern landscape analysis, it is hardly surprising that regional studies of urban building traits are sparse.[77] Clearly, much needs to be done before the rich regional variations in urban housing character in North America are adequately addressed. Why do row houses of various types appear in certain cities and not others? Why do triple-decker houses occur where they do? What is the morphogenetic history of the large department store and other high-bulk buildings in American cities? What has been the relation between social taste, economic pressures, and legislative actions in shaping the building types of North America?[78]

Land use morphology. —The pattern of land use in the modern city has been by far the most studied component of the urban landscape. An extended review of the literature is impossible here, but major progress has been made since World War II in land use morphology of cities. This has come through detailed mapping of land use categories and delimitation of functionally and morphologically distinct subregions of the city on the one hand, and through study of land values, population density, and accessibility on the other.[79] While models of the urban land market featuring bid-rent curves go far in accounting for land use distribution, the assumptions of unifocal accessibility demand and economic behavior do not always apply, even in American cities.[80]

---

versity of California-Berkeley. See also W. H. Rutledge: The Role of House Types in the Formation of Residential Areas in Oakland (M.A. thesis, University of California-Berkeley, 1964); and S. Openshaw: Canonical Correlates of Social Structure and Urban Building Fabric, Seminar Paper No. 11 (University of Newcastle upon Tyne, Department of Geography, 1969).

[77] A. J. Rose: Boundaries and Building Materials in Southeast Australia, in Land and Livelihood: Geographical Essays in Honour of George Jobberns (edited by M. McGaskill; New Zealand Geographical Society, Christchurch, 1962), pp. 255-276; J. W. R. Whitehand: Building Types as a Basis for Settlement Classification, in Essays in Geography for Austin Miller (edited by J. W. Whitlow and P. D. Wood; Reading, 1965), pp. 291-305; A. J. Krim, The Three Decker as Urban Architecture in New England, Monadnock, Vol. 44, 1970, pp. 45-55.

[78] Some of these issues are raised in Hofmeister, op. cit. [note 24], esp. pp. 50-70.

[79] For a discussion of the literature, see Carter, op. cit. [note 1], pp. 171-203.

[80] W. Alonso: The Historical and the Structural Theories of Urban Form: Their Implications for Urban Renewal, Land Economics, Vol. 40, 1964, pp.

Most important in broadening the scope of land use theory has been the introduction of non-equilibrium historical change into arguments concerning the evolution of land use patterns. Two issues deserve special mention, the developmental view of central business districts and the fringe belt concept.

It is now generally recognized that multi-functional but spatially-differentiated central business districts are primarily features of Western urbanism (and its diffusion), and that cities have not always had CBDs in the modern sense. Studies in the last decade have demonstrated the emergence and elaboration of CBDs in American cities over the last 120 years or so.[81] The particular form of the CBD is likely to be a function of historical inertia, frequency and timing of economic impulses, and the character of surrounding land use patterns, in addition to the normal assumptions of city size and economic specialization. Expansion of the CBD has often been held responsible for residential decline and the emergence of a "zone of transition, " a buffer zone partly blighted and much affected in recent decades by urban renewal. This process has not often been placed in full historical perspective nor linked sufficiently with other land use changes, particularly with regard to the economic rhythm of cities.

The fringe belt concept, though developed in Europe, may be applicable to American cities and provide such a broader context for understanding urban land use change. Although the basic forces leading to the emergence of fringe belts and their actual recognition were known in the 1930s, almost thirty years elapsed before the fringe belt concept was accepted and further developed in Europe, and it is only now being considered in North America.[82] Stated simply, fringe belts are initial urban fringe zones in which a heterogeneous collection of often extensive, low-rent land uses accumulate in close proximity during peri-

227-231; W. Firey: Land Use in Central Boston (Harvard University Press, Boston, 1947).

[81]D. Ward: The Industrial Revolution and the Emergence of Boston's Central Business District, Economic Geography, Vol. 42, 1966, pp. 152-171; M. J. Bowden: Persistence, Failure and Mobility in the Inner City: Preliminary Notes, in Pattern and Process: Research in Historical Geography (edited by R. E. Ehrenberg; Howard University Press, Washington, D.C., 1975), pp. 169-192.

[82]Colby, op. cit. [note 3]; Louis, op. cit. [note 7]; Conzen, op. cit. [note 8]; J. W. R. Whitehand: Fringe Belts: A Neglected Aspect of Urban Geography, Transactions and Papers, Institute of British Geographers, Vol. 41, 1967, pp. 223-233, and The Changing Nature of the Urban Fringe: A Time Perspective, in Suburban Growth (edited by J. H. Johnson; John Wiley and Sons, New York, 1974), pp. 31-52.

ods of economic doldrums when residential growth is virtually at a halt. [83]

This accumulation produces a belt-shaped urban landscape as distinctive in its own way as the CBD. Fringe belt formation alternates with residential expansion to form roughly alternating concentric belts around and away from the urban core as business and building cycles oscillate. Far from changing character and being erased, as ecological and economic models would predict, fringe belts, once locked within the expanding built-up area, often remain distinctive and consolidate their character over time by attracting further sympathetic land uses. In some European cities, generally three but sometimes four fringe belts have been discovered, the outer belts being more dispersed than those closer to the urban core. [84] The history of building and building cycles has been sufficiently different on either side of the Atlantic, both in intensity, linkages, and spatial impact, to warrant considerable testing of the fringe belt concept before it is regarded as applicable to North American cities, but preliminary indications suggest that American cities do indeed have historical fringe belts imbedded in their land use structures. [85]

The appeal of the fringe belt/residential accretion model of urban growth is that, through application of business cycle patterns to urban expansion, various elements of urban structural theory can be combined in a morphogenetic framework. The cyclical accumulation of housing is related to broad patterns of non-residential land use, and the transition zone is seen as a relict inner fringe belt intimately related to the expansion of the CBD through the "old town." [86] Other land use transformations need to be treated in a similar context; it is questionable whether the morphological processes of ghetto develop-

---

[83] For a precise definition of a fringe belt see Conzen, op. cit. [note 8], pp. 123-131.

[84] J. W. R. Whitehand: Building Cycles and the Spatial Pattern of Urban Growth, Transactions, Institute of British Geographers, Vol. 56. 1972, pp. 39-55, and op. cit. [note 57]; M. Barke: The Changing Urban Fringe of Falkirk: Some Morphological Implications of Urban Growth, Scottish Geographical Magazine, Vol. 90, 1974, pp. 85-97, and Land Use Succession: A Factor in Fringe-belt Modification, Area, Vol. 8, 1976, pp. 303-306.

[85] M. P. Conzen: Fringe Location Land Uses: Relict Patterns in Madison, Wisconsin, Paper presented at the West Lakes Division, Association of American Geographers meeting, Madison, Wisconsin, 1968; Krim, op. cit. [note 55].

[86] For example, see J. S. Adams: Residential Structure of Midwestern Cities, Annals, Association of American Geographers, Vol. 60, 1970, pp. 37-62; R. E. Preston: The Zone in Transition: A Study of Urban Land Use Patterns, Economic Geography, Vol. 42, 1966, pp. 236-259; Ward, op. cit. [note 81].

ment, for example, fit neatly into such a model or require a different treatment.

The Subjective Domain

The discussion so far has been predicated upon the assumption that the urban landscape exists as a visual component of the urban environment completely verifiable in objective terms. While this approach is appropriate for direct scientific investigation, it is certainly not the way social groups or individuals at large view the urban landscape in the course of their daily lives. People in general view the landscape, whether as a background circumstance or object of direct interest, through many, and sometimes strong, subjective filters. How particular objective characteristics of the landscape are filtered, and under what conditions, holds much significance for questions of environmental satisfaction, identity with place, and cultural roots.

Research into subjective dimensions of the urban landscape has a much shorter history than the objectively-oriented research considered earlier. Although some commentators trace interest in environmental perception to the early part of this century, intensive work on the urban landscape did not begin until after mid-century with the ideas of Kevin Lynch.[87] It is probably fair to say that this literature is considerably less developed in quantity, breadth of issues, and comparative scale than that on objective landscape. Attention here is directed towards those studies that focus on the character of the urban landscape itself, as subjectively perceived, and not on studies of the psychological mechanisms underlying the perception. Important though these mechanisms obviously are, they would require separate review, and are peripheral to the present theme.

Perception of the urban landscape can be divided systematically into three general categories of concern. The first may be termed the cultural-historical dimension and focusses upon broad interpretations of what urban landscapes have meant to people over time based upon literary and artistic evidence. The second category concerns the narrower field of landscape aesthetics in which the emotional appreciation of the landscape is more directly assessed and accounted for. The third category covers the behavioral conditions associated with particular urban landscape contexts, and deals with the results of specific filtering mechanisms by which observation, interpretation, and recall of individ-

---

[87] P. R. Gould and R. White: Mental Maps (Penguin Books, Harmondsworth, 1974), p. 28.

ual landscapes takes place. As with the earlier objective landscape components, these subjective dimensions form a simple hierarchy of containment, the cultural-historical view being the most broadly integrative of the three.

The cultural-historical dimension. —The images that people have of cities have long fascinated writers, but geographers have been slow to direct their analytical energies to this theme. Stimulus among geographers came from the works of J. K. Wright, whose call in 1946 for a field of "geosophy, " the study of geographical knowledge, set the stage for a geographical approach to imagery.[88] Subsequent writing considered landscapes in general, often with a preference for rural landscapes.[89] The approach has been to identify those general cultural traits or forces in a society that mold a landscape's image in peoples' minds, and this necessarily implies a historically-conditioned explanation specific to one culture or another. Much of this writing by geographers concerned English landscapes, but North America has also received excellent attention.[90] Recently, studies have become more comparative, and greater attention is now given to urban scenes.[91] Such work, though it often treats the interplay between man and environment with great interpretive skill, depends heavily upon a literary mode of analysis in which theoretical issues and organization remain frequently implicit.[92] Furthermore, the scale of enquiry tends to be universal,

---

[88] J. K. Wright: Human Nature in Geography (Harvard University Press, Cambridge, 1966), pp. 68-88.

[89] D. Lowenthal: Geography, Experience and Imagination: Towards a Geographical Epistemology, Annals, Association of American Geographers, Vol. 51, 1961, pp. 241-260; D. Lowenthal and H. C. Prince: English Landscape Tastes, Geographical Review, Vol. 55, 1965, pp. 186-222.

[90] Lowenthal and Prince, op. cit. [note 89]; J. B. Jackson: Landscapes (University of Massachusetts Press, Amherst, 1970) and American Space: The Centennial Years, 1865-1876 (W. W. Norton, New York, 1972). Jackson's journal Landscape has in addition provided over the years many small gems of urban interpretation. See also Lewis, op. cit. [note 21].

[91] Yi-Fu Tuan: Topophilia: A Study of Environmental Perception, Attitudes, and Values (Prentice-Hall, Englewood Cliffs, N. J., 1974); A. G. Noble: The Emergence and Evolution of Malgudi: An Interpretation of South Indian Townscapes from the Fictional Writings of R. K. Narayan, Proceedings, Association of American Geographers, Vol. 8, 1976, pp. 106-110.

[92] Tuan, op. cit. [note 91]; for an attempt at a simple ordering of themes in landscape appreciation, see Tuan: Attitudes towards Environment: Themes and Approaches, in Environmental Perception and Behavior, Research Paper No. 109 (edited by D. Lowenthal; University of Chicago, Department of Geography, 1967), pp. 4-17.

or regional where cultural differences in perception become the key variable, and the evidence is so diverse that contrary arguments may easily be made. However, Yi-Fu Tuan's conclusion that traditional societies live "in a vertical, rotary, richly symbolical world" compared with the "broad of surface, low of ceiling, non-rotary, aesthetic, and profane" world of modern man has some implications for understanding the historical layering of European towns that passed through a transition from traditional to modern sometime after 1500 (though one would question whether modern urbanized man lives any less by symbolism for being modern).[93]

The aesthetic dimension. —Writers and artists have dealt with the emotional context of perception intuitively for generations, but geographers and others are now asking about "spatial satisfaction," which, more than mere locational fitness, influences the emotional content of places for people. Ironically, the issue has produced studies that are alternatively highly practical or highly abstract.

Interest in measuring the aesthetic quality of landscapes has burgeoned in recent years.[94] Informal, individualistic methods are giving way to quantitative indexes of aesthetic content. The latter are usually attempts to apply crude numerical values to whole categories of landscape elements such as terrain characteristics, soil and vegetation cover, the emotive value of which may still vary greatly from one situation to another.[95] One application of quantitative methods to the urban landscape is a study of six American cities employing semantic-differential questionnaires administered to various occupational groups asking for their reactions, visual, aural, and olfactory, to locales on predetermined mini-walking tours (880 yards long!).[96] The results showed significant differences in the way various groups viewed the same urban vistas and also in the way similar groups viewed representative vistas in different cities.

---

[93]Tuan, op. cit. [note 91].

[94]P. Dearden: Landscape Aesthetics: An Annotated Bibliography, Council of Planning Librarians Exchange Bibliography, No. 1220, February 1977; J. H. Appleton et al.: Landscape Evaluation, Transactions, Institute of British Geographers, Vol. 66, 1975, pp. 119-162.

[95]E. H. Zube et al.: Landscape Assessment: Values, Perceptions, and Resources (Dowden, Hutchinson and Ross, Inc., Stroudsburg, Pa., 1975).

[96]D. Lowenthal and M. Riel: Publications in Environmental Perception, Nos. 1-8 (American Geographical Society, New York, 1972).

161

The technique is cumbersome, however, and has been applied to such small portions of large cities that the representativeness of the test locales, especially for intercity comparison, remains a troublesome question.

One attempt to explain the factors underlying the aesthetics of landscape is Appleton's prospect/refuge theory which argues that the fundamental biological instinct for survival (to see and not be seen) has resulted in timeless inbred desires for elements in the landscape that symbolize prospects or refuges. Thus, landscapes can be evaluated on the basis of the number, strength, and ratio of symbols representing these twin elements.[97] The symbols can be natural or man-made, making the theory applicable to urban landscapes. The theory has considerable intuitive appeal; how exact the mensuration can become may be another matter. The theory underplays the role of culture in creating differences among peoples with regard to their awareness of landscape character. Much further study will be needed before this approach can be articulated in terms of a replicative methodology.

Cognitive mapping. —No matter how skillful a scholar is in capturing the essence of a landscape experience for a group of people, there is an intuitive appeal in letting the subject express his perceptions himself. One method, by verbal questionnaire, has been touched upon already. More intrinsically attractive to geographers has been the respondent's own "mental map" of a place. A whole wave of studies has followed Lynch's initial experiments with maps derived from the spatial and landscape awareness of ordinary urban residents.[98] Lynch's assumption was that people notice and memorize only a small fraction of the objective visible characteristics of urban landscapes. Amid the limitless visual detail the resident is inclined to perceive only the gross outlines of the city's street plan, and only some of the most obtrusive buildings and land uses. Moreover, even these highlights are likely to concentrate heavily along or be visible from accustomed travel routes. Given these practical simplifications in the city dweller's grasp of the landscape, the exercise becomes one of recording the individual resident's reproduceable city image in map form, and blending it with others' to create composite maps for specific social groups. Lynch

---

[97] J. Appleton: The Experience of Landscape (John Wiley and Sons, London, 1975).

[98] K. Lynch: The Image of the City (M.I.T. Press, Cambridge, 1960) and Visual Analysis; Community Renewal Program, Brookline, Mass.: An Analysis of the Visual Form of Brookline (Kevin Lynch, Consultants, Cambridge, Mass., 1965).

derived comparative techniques for constructing mental maps based on verbal
interviews, respondent sketch maps and trained observer field study of the
city's visual structure, and coined a technical vocabulary of paths, edges,
nodes, districts, and landmarks. This approach allowed reasonably confident
comparisons to be made between resident perceptions of Boston, Jersey City,
and Los Angeles.

Subsequent work has attempted to expand the scope of this approach
through application in different cultural regions, [99] among social strata, [100]
occupational types, [101] and ethnic groups. [102] The next step appears to be research into the effects of age and growing up upon mental maps; one study has
noted the characteristic mental biases of children's home neighborhood mapping. [103] There remains a great deal to discover about the factors that expand
or diminish perception of the landscape, particularly in the areas of movement
patterns (type of locomotion, route selection), socio-psychological structure,
climate, and work habits. Two issues are difficult to deal with: the appropriate sample size for different types of analysis, given that residential location
and journey-to-work channels so limit landscape perception; and the degree to
which this type of research actually penetrates the perceived character of the
landscape. Much perception measured so far relates more to basic orientation
for movement about the city (or neighborhood) than to the specific architectural,

[99] T. Sieverts: Perceptual Images of the City of Berlin, in Urban Core and
Inner City (edited by W. F. Heinemeyer; E. J. Brill, Leiden, 1976), pp. 282-
285; H.-J. Klein: The Delimitation of the Town-centre in the Image of Its Citi-
zens, in ibid., pp. 286-306; B. Goodey: City Scene: An Exploration into the
Image of Central Birmingham as Seen by Area Residents, Research Memoran-
dum No. 10 (Centre for Urban and Regional Studies, University of Birmingham,
England, 1971); D. Francescato and W. Mebane: How Citizens View Two Great
Cities: Milan and Rome, in Image and Environment: Cognitive Mapping and
Spatial Behavior (edited by P. M. Downs and D. Stea; Aldine Publishing Co.,
Chicago, 1973), pp. 131-147.

[100] P. Orleans: Differential Cognition of Urban Residents: Effects of Social
Scale on Mapping, in ibid., pp. 115-130.

[101] B. B. Greenbie: Problems of Scale and Context in Assessing a Generalized Landscape for Particular Persons, in Zube et al., op. cit. [note 95], pp.
65-91.

[102] R. Mauer and J. C. Baxter: Images of the Neighborhood and City among
Black-, Anglo-, and Mexican-American Children, Environment and Behavior,
Vol. 4, 1972, pp. 351-388.

[103] F. Ladd: A Note on "the World across the Street," Harvard Graduate
School of Education Association Bulletin, Vol. 12, 1967, pp. 47-48.

land use, and historical character of the city's many parts. Clearly, if the urban landscape matters to residents (or visitors, for that matter), more under- standing is needed of the factors that govern the quality and variety as well as the quantity of landscape awareness.[104]

Means and Ends

An attempt has been made here to bring two highly disparate bodies of lit- erature on the urban landscape together. Research into the objective pro- cesses of formation and selective change in the urban landscape has a long his- tory but has generally lacked a sufficiently common conceptual basis to warrant practical synthesis. The accumulation of new approaches and the renewed inter- est of geographers and others in the urban landscape have made it seem appro- priate to review and in some cases reformulate concepts relevant to the system- atic analysis of this aspect of the city. Research into the experience of the urban landscape has a shorter but no less significant purpose. Without a better understanding of how individuals and groups actually perceive the character of the urban landscape, the objective knowledge remains isolated; with such under- standing, individuals and the larger community may benefit more directly by planning for objective landscape change so that identity of place and the social spirit that goes with it are best conserved, and if possible, enlarged.

For these broad goals to be pursued, the urban landscape can, in the pres- ent context, be regarded as an analytical problem in applied geography. This suggestion has two facets. First, processes of landscape change and factors in landscape experience can be drawn into public and private planning policy so that decisions affecting the urban environment can be better informed.[105] Sec- ond, and more specifically, research on the morphogenetic history of particu- lar urban landscapes can become the basis for "landscape conservation" poli- cies. This implies much more than simple historic preservation, appropriate and essential though that might be in many cases.[106] Not all historic struc-

---

[104]Perhaps the greatest limitation to date of the perceptual work on the ur- ban landscape has been its inability to measure the subjective inventory directly against the actual physical totality of the urban landscape. This relationship is generally left implicit.

[105]See J. D. Porteous, op. cit. ⌈note 19⌉.

[106]The broadening of the formal meaning of historic preservation in the last decade to include adaptive reuse, selective remodelling, and renovation as well as restoration, however, has helped dispel much resistance to this environmen-

tures or ground patterns are worth preserving; more important is the systematic blending of old and new with respect to siting, scale, and compatibility of visual design features and materials.[107] The key to urban conservation lies, of course, in a coordinated policy with appropriate education of each community sector in the long term as well as short term possibilities. Frequently, these possibilities include adaptive reuse of buildings with historic character or associations. It would be ideal if good historical and geographical survey work would precede such development decisions to avoid their being piece-meal and haphazard.[108]

Urban landscape analysis should benefit from both morphological and functional approaches, but not long ago Harold Carter noted that "it is one of the major weaknesses of urban geography that there has been a clear divorce between the study of form and function, between the study of the town as area and the town in area."[109] He spoke accurately for Anglophone urban geography,

---

tal strategy. For official views on historic preservation, see Historic Towns: Preservation and Change (H. M. S. O. for the Ministry of Housing and Local Government, London, 1967); National Trust for Historic Preservation: Economic Benefits of Preserving Old Buildings (The Preservation Press, Washington, D. C., 1976); Deutsches Nationalkommitee für das Europäische Denkmalschutzjahr: Historische Städte—Städte für Morgen (Deutsche UNESCO Kommission, Cologne, 1974); Arbeitskreis "Historische Stadtkerne" der Deutschen UNESCO Kommission: Sanierung historischer Stadtkerne im Ausland (Bundesminister für Raumordnung, Bauwesen und Städtebau, Bonn-Bad Godesberg, 1975).

[107]K. Lynch: What Time Is This Place? (M. I. T. Press, Cambridge, 1972); M. R. G. Conzen: Historical Townscapes in Britain: A Problem in Applied Geography, in Northern Geographical Essays in Honour of G. H. J. Daysh (edited by J. W. House; Oriel Press, Newcastle upon Tyne, 1966), pp. 56-78; R. M. Newcomb: Geographic Aspects of the Planned Preservation of Visible History in Denmark, Annals, Association of American Geographers, Vol. 57, 1967, pp. 462-480; P. Ward, edit.: Conservation and Development in Historic Towns and Cities (Oriel Press, Newcastle upon Tyne, 1968); R. Worskett: The Character of Towns: An Approach to Conservation (Architectural Press, London, 1969).

[108]Historico-architectural inventories have burgeoned in the last decade. The following exemplify surveys of different scales and scope: Cambridge Historical Commission: Survey of Architectural History in Cambridge (5 vols.; M. I. T. Press, Cambridge, 1962-1977); G. J. Zuidhoek: The Aim, Implementation and Results of City-block Research in Amsterdam, in Urban Core and Inner City (edited by W. F. Heinemeyer; E. J. Brill, Leiden, 1967), pp. 512-523; Plan and Program for the Preservation of the Vieux Carré Historic District Demonstration Study (Bureau of Governmental Research, for the City of New Orleans, New Orleans, 1968); Cambridge Townscape; An Analysis (City of Cambridge, Department of Architecture and Planning, Cambridge, England, 1971); K. Rodwell, edit.: Historic Towns in Oxfordshire: A Survey of the New County, Survey No. 3 (Oxfordshire Archaeological Unit, Oxford, 1975).

[109]Carter, op. cit. [note 1], p. 326.

though the statement would be inappropriate for continental geography.[110]

Some attempts to restore the dialogue between form and function may well show directions for the future.[111] The degree to which social and functional patterns can be understood in relation to morphological patterns today will depend largely upon a genetic framework that provides cultural context, and a dialectical approach to the interplay between the processes and patterns of both urban form and function.

---

[110] In modern German urban geography, there has been an unbroken tradition of integrated form/function research. See D. Partzsch: Die Entwicklung des Berliner Ortsteils Dahlem von einem agraren zu einem städtischen Landschaftsteil, Raumforschung und Raumordnung, Vol. 20, 1962, pp. 216-229; G. Abele and A. Leidlmair: Die Karlsruher Innenstadt, Berichte zur deutschen Landeskunde, Vol. 41, 1968, pp. 217-230; S. Kutscher: Bocholt in Westfalen: Eine stadtgeographische Untersuchung unter besonderer Berücksichtigung des Inneren Raumgefüges, Forschungen zur Deutschen Landeskunde, Vol. 203 (Bad Godesberg, 1971); K. Ganser: Grundlageuntersuchung zur Altstadtentwicklung Ingolstadts, Münchener Geographische Hefte No. 36 (Verlag Michael Lassleben, Regensburg, 1973); and Temlitz, op. cit. [note 46].

[111] W. K. D. Davies: The Morphology of Central Places: A Case Study, Annals, Association of American Geographers, Vol. 58, 1968, pp. 91-110; B. S. Morgan: The Morphological Region as a Social Unit, Tijdschrift voor Economische en Sociale Geografie, Vol. 62, 1971, pp. 226-233; Hofmeister, op. cit. [note 24]; H. D. de Vries Reilingh: The Tension between Form and Function in the Inner City of Amsterdam, in Heinemeyer, op. cit. [note 108], pp. 309-323.

CHAPTER 9

GEOGRAPHIC AND OTHER VIEWS OF SPACE

Robert David Sack

University of Wisconsin, Madison

Space is fundamental to all systems of thought and there may be as many approaches to its analysis as there are studies of man. Each approach may create a different conception of space; sometimes the difference being subtle and personal, other times based on broad and well organized categories such as the scientific, social scientific, artistic, and magical-mythical.

In studying the earth as the home of man, geographers have focused much of their attention on the meanings and implications of geographic space. This space has meant terrestrial physical space--described in terms of a three-dimensional Euclidian geometry. Within the scientific mode of thought and geography, the significance or evaluation[1] of physical space and its properties, such as shapes, patterns, and distances, are determined by the way in which they are causally linked to matter and energy, or, as we shall call these categories, substances. This link is expressed in lawlike (nomothetic) relationships through the relational concept of space and through action by contact.[2]

Social sciences, however, have few if any laws. Hence, there has been

---

[1] A fact or concept is scientifically significant if it is incorporated in an empirically confirmed generalization. This is the meaning of scientific significance to be used throughout this paper. For a fuller discussion of scientific significance, see M. Brodbeck: Logic and Scientific Method in Research on Teaching, in Handbook of Research on Teaching (edited by N. Gage; Rand McNally, Chicago, 1963), p. 55, and M. Brodbeck: Meaning and Action, in Readings in the Philosophy of the Social Sciences (edited by M. Brodbeck; Macmillan, New York, 1968), pp. 58-78.

[2] For a discussion of relational space in physical science, see B. van Fraassen: An Introduction to the Philosophy of Time and Space (Random House, New York, 1970), pp. 108-114; and for a discussion of action by contact, see M. Hesse: Action at a Distance and Field Theory, The Encyclopedia of Philosophy, Vol. 1 (Macmillan, New York, 1967), pp. 9-15.

confusion about the significance of space for human behavior. This leaves space in social science in a paradoxical position.

On the one hand the social sciences have received from the physical sciences a view of physical space in which all facts, including social ones, are located. This space serves as a universally accepted system for the identification and individuation of facts.

On the other hand, because of the lack of laws, the social sciences have no general view of the significance of the spatial system apart from its function as a locational system. The space which we use to locate things is not yet significantly related in the explanation of things. This lack of significance pries space and substance conceptually apart and leaves them unconnected. Laws would recombine them. But laws are only one method of conceptually recombining them.

There are other links which result from other forms of understanding, and each linkage gives space a different significance and even a different appearance. Since space is a property of all forms of understanding, its different significances become sensitive indicators of shifts in perspectives and of modes of thought. These may range from personal points of view to subtle arguments of scientific methodology, to vast differences in world views.

Until recently, the geographic profession has not directed much of its energies to meanings of space beyond the scientific mode of thought and its applicability to human behavior. The results of this research have been the identification and analysis of conceptions of space and place that come from spatial analysis, chorology, and cognitive and mental maps. These different meanings of space may be subtle when compared with the vast differences that arise from non-scientific modes. But they are the core meanings of space in a scientific human geography and in social science in general. As it becomes more evident that other conceptions of space affect behavior at the scale of landscape, and that these are not (yet) embraced by the social sciences, it becomes essential that we attempt to expand our traditional analysis and define, as clearly as possible, the links between conceptions of space and modes of thought. [3]

What follows is a sketch of a framework for analyzing conceptions of space in modes of thought of interest to geographers and a discussion of the con-

[3] Among the most influential works expanding the conceptions of space in geography are D. Lowenthal: Geography, Experience, and Imagination: Towards a Geographical Epistemology, Annals, Association of American Geographers, Vol. 51, 1961, pp. 241-260, and Yi-Fu Tuan: Topophilia: A Study of Environmental Perceptions, Attitudes, and Values (Prentice Hall, Englewood Cliffs, 1974).

ceptions of space as they appear within this framework. These modes are the physical science, the social science, the artistic, the child's, and the magical-mythical. The framework considers only those aspects of the modes of thought which are significant for understanding conceptions of space. The characterizations of the modes are based on philosophies which address themselves to questions of space. The framework stems from the empiricist tradition in geography. It is a result of extending such traditional geographical concerns as the relationships between space and substance, and the subjective and the objective views of space, into a conceptual surface, which can be used to locate the modes of thought. The framework in effect is a conceptual surface which can be used to locate and analyze other spaces. After the framework is introduced the paper discusses the different conceptions of space from the perspective of this conceptual surface.

Framework

In its simplest form, the framework has two intersecting axes or dimensions forming a conceptual surface on which the modes of thought can be placed. These axes are created by the conceptual separation of properties of reality which, when seen naively, are connected or fused. The properties are the subjective, the objective, space, and substance. When subjectivity and objectivity are conceptually separated, they form the end points of one axis and when space and substance are conceptually separated they form the end points of the other. The axes are of, and are extended by, conceptual or symbolic thought. The more abstract the concepts or symbols, the greater the separation, the longer the axes, and the greater the extent of the surface. The axes or dimensions of the surface will be labeled subjective-objective, and space-substance.

Subjective-objective

Subjectivity and objectivity are conceptually separated to form the end points of the first dimension. This dimension refers to both the objectivity-subjectivity of facts, and of analysis of facts, and follows the age-old mind-body problem. It is perpetuated by the physical scientific perspectives which view themselves as concerned with objectively analyzing facts and creating symbolic systems such as laws and theories to model them. Although recognizing that knowledge of facts is based on sensations, science is concerned with what is known about these sensations and symbolizes them through languages such as mathematics and logic. In general, science views the non-scientific as subjective. An approach to knowledge such as art is seen from a scientific perspective as concerned with the subjective abstraction and symbolization of feelings and emotions. Many artists and aestheticians share this view and also agree that science objectively symbolizes facts.[4] Both groups are aware that each has its own domain which thus far has been impervious to the incursions of the other, and thus each occupies opposite portions of the dimension; the sciences on the objective side, the arts on the subjective side.

Space-substance

Space and substance are conceptually separated and form the end points of the second dimension. This separation stems from the ancient trichotomous division of our every day, scientific, and philosophical vocabularies into terms about space, substance, and time. In the following we shall examine the oppositions between space and substance, and leave time aside.

Again, we must be reminded that the space versus substance dimension, like the objective versus subjective one, is a product of conceptual separation. It applies to the domain of imagination.

In the real world things are in places in space, and conversely, areas of space contain things, and we use the associations for identifying and individuating things. But when we think abstractly, we can remove things from their places to varying degrees. A thing at a particular place can be classified in a systematic way as an instance of a substance such as mass and can be thought of as conceptually removed from the space. Similarly, the place or area once occupied can be thought of abstractly within a system of geometric locations wherein the only differences among places are their locational coordinates. Or the shapes of things can be abstracted from the things themselves and discussed as instances of spatial concepts like squares, circles, or triangles. The most elegant conceptual separation is in physics where we have mass and energy on the one hand and space-time on the other.

These examples are of conceptual separations based on the objective factors of things and are part of the scientific modes. But the arts as well as the sciences conceptually separate space from their equivalents of substance or things and time. The arts symbolize space and its properties by creating its

---

[4]This conception of art is supported by S. Langer: Philosophy in a New Key (Harvard University Press, Cambridge, 1942), and Feeling and Form (Scribners, New York, 1953).

semblance, a virtual space.[5]

Conceptual Surface

These two intersecting axes form a surface extending the social science perspective and upon which the social sciences and other conceptions of space can be placed. Due to the limited knowledge of the social sciences, our understanding of these extensions, their degree of separation, and the links between them is limited, fragmented, and in many cases speculative. Hence, so too is our knowledge of the surface. We know little about its extent, its contours, about whether it is flat, curved, spherical, or convoluted, where precisely on it the other conceptions are projected, and how the surface itself may appear altered as we submerge ourselves in one or another mode.

Even though our current information is sketchy, it is still possible to discern the outlines of two very different patterns of thought which can be projected onto this surface, and within which the modes and their conceptions of space can be located and categorized.

Sophisticated-fragmented

The first pattern is called the sophisticated-fragmented and includes conceptions of space in modes of thought which recognize a conceptual separation of subjective and objective, and space and substance and which have made efforts to attain their syntheses. This pattern includes all the physical sciences, social sciences, and the arts. Because of the objectivity of the sciences and the subjectivity of the arts the two occupy vast but opposite sides of the space. The social sciences, however, by combining a supposedly objective methodology with a concern for the subjective feelings, attitudes, and values, occupy a space between and in part overlapping the other two.

Together these modes cover large, overlapping areas, and through their abstractions, extend the reaches of the surface. While the characteristics of the surface and the two axes may be conceived differently within each perspective, they all have in common the conceptual "capacity" for such a surface. They attempt to conceptually separate the subjective from the objective, the space from the substance, in order to represent them and their interconnections in terms of their own logic and symbolic forms.

---

[5]Langer, op. cit. 1953 [note 4], pp. 69-103.

They are sophisticated because in so doing, they handle their concepts maturely by not confusing the symbols with what they represent. The scientist realizes that the manipulations of his equations are not going to affect the things they represent, and the artist realizes that painting a landscape symbolic of feelings such as tranquility or turbulence will in no way alter the nature of the landscape. If either the painting or the scientific equations are destroyed, we may deeply regret their loss and may fail to see things in the same way, but all that has been destroyed are symbols. Nothing will happen to the facts or the feelings which they symbolize. They will still exist as before.

But the modes are fragmented because they do not encompass the entire surface and do not recombine the elements of analysis they have conceptually separated. This does not mean that they are unsuccessful, only that they are, in terms of the surface, partial and fragmented. Science does not easily embrace the subjective, and its theoretical realms still face unresolved issues about the relationship between space and substance. Problems resulting from these missing connections between the subjective and the objective and space and substance have caused extreme vexation in the social sciences.

The arts too face similar difficulties of connection. They symbolize feelings, not objects. Yet they use objective mediums as symbolic vehicles. Division of the arts into mediums of expression often makes it difficult for one branch to symbolize particular kinds of feelings, as for instance symbolizing feelings about time and movement in painting and symbolizing feelings of space and its properties in music.

These modes are partial. They all use abstract and specialized symbols which reinforce the fragmentation of the surface. The concepts of space for instance, become specialized in each mode: physical science conceiving of it in terms of a geometric system: social science in part sharing this conception but altering it through the introduction of feelings and perceptions in the forms of specific places and cognitive and perceptual spaces; and art and dream imagery creating semblances of space and shapes.

It seems that the most fundamental reason for the fragmentation of the surface, and also for the peculiar, and so far, unsuccessful, attempts of the social sciences to analyze feelings and emotions, is the fundamentally different way in which facts and feelings are symbolized, especially in the modes of thought which have specialized in such symbolism--namely, science and art. The sciences can use symbols to represent facts, and the symbols are conventionally defined. The symbolic vehicles themselves have no meaning (within science) apart from the conventional definition assigned to them. Hence an "x" in science will mean what we define it to be, and there is nothing intrinsically similar between the physical shape and appearance of the "x" and what we use it to represent. We could just as easily use any other letter in the alphabet or any other sign. But once we have agreed upon the "x," its meaning is clear and constant.

On the other hand, feelings are most successfully and naturally expressed by symbols whose meanings seem to be in part affixed to the vehicles themselves. They do not appear to be conventionally or arbitrarily decided. These symbols are said to <u>present</u> rather than <u>represent</u>.[6] Their meanings, unlike the scientific ones, are not clearly specified and stable, but rather depend on the context in which they appear. In terms of the objective side, such symbols seem to be over-determined and context dependent. Thus ensues the observation that art cannot be decomposed into invariant elements with constant meanings, but rather has to be interpreted each time anew in terms of the whole. Accordingly, there is no language of art, no vocabulary which can be combined by syntactical rules to symbolize or express. Rather the elements of an artistic creation depend on the whole for their identification and meaning.

Unsophisticated-fused

The second pattern of thought is the unsophisticated-fused and embraces those conceptions of space in modes of thought in which the conceptual separations of space, substance, objective, and subjective do not occur at a high level of abstraction, if at all. In fact as a group these modes are unaware that there could be such a conceptual surface in which to examine symbolic categories. This group includes the child's view, the mythical-magical view, and a view of space which has been associated with primitive societies.[7] These modes of thought, if placed on the surface, do not stretch as far along the axes. They

---

[6]Langer, <u>op. cit.</u> 1942 ⌈note 4⌉, pp. 79-102.

[7]For a discussion of the child's view, see J. Piaget: The Child's Construction of Reality (Routledge and Kegan Paul, London, 1955), and H. Werner: The Comparative Psychology of Mental Development (International Universities Press, New York, 1957). For a discussion of symbolic functions in myth and magic, see E. Cassirer: The Philosophy of Symbolic Forms (Yale University Press, New Haven, 1955), Vol. 2. For a non-pejorative meaning of primitive, which is intended here, see S. Diamond: In Search of the Primitive (Transaction Books, New Brunswick, N.J., 1974).

are located around the origin and occupy smaller areas than do the sophisticated-fragmented. They are unsophisticated because of their low levels of abstraction and their frequent confusion of symbols with what they represent, as when the child or the magician destroys a symbol of a thing and expects the thing itself to disappear, or creates a symbol and expects to create its referent, as in a rain dance to bring on the rain. These modes are fused because their symbols are neither highly abstracted nor primarily directed along one of the axes as in the sophisticated-fragmented. Space is not conceptually far removed from the substance or things which take form and their symbols or concepts often encompass both facts and feelings. These modes do not include a geometry, a science, and an art. Although actions and activities within these modes may be artistic, scientific, and practical, they are rarely only one of these and are not compartmentalized into these categories.

The basis for the unsophistication and fusion is the way in which objects and symbols are seen and used. [8] In these modes, the objective world is seen so intensely and closely that feelings are often projected onto it, animating the world. In such modes, the symbols only partially and tentatively separate the subjective from the objective, because they themselves are seen as sharing properties of the things they represent. By tending to appear as though they share properties of their referents, they are much like the presentational aspect of aesthetic and dream symbols. But unlike these, the unsophisticated symbols are neither specialized nor directed in only one area of the surface. They often refer to objective as well as subjective elements. Because the symbol appears to be similar to its referent, its meaning does not seem to be arbitrarily defined, and the symbol can easily be confused with what it represents. Due to the preeminence of visual stimuli the symbols of things may often be their physical spatial shape or form. Such symbols would by definition closely resemble the things they represent; hence, the frequency with which magical systems use shapes and forms as though they contained the power or the affect of the objects. In these modes the conceptions of space are not far removed from the substances, and the symbolic vehicles having shapes or forms are not conceptually distant from the things they represent and the feelings and beliefs about them. Because of the way in which symbols are used, the unsophisticated-fused view presents another range of meanings about space; a range which fuses space and substance in a pre-relational way.

---

[8]See H. Werner and B. Kaplan: Symbol Formation (Wiley, New York, 1963) for a general discussion of the function of symbols in a developmental context.

Views of Space

We turn now to the consequences of this framework for analyzing the meanings of space. We will look first at the sophisticated-fragmented pattern and the meaning of space from the objective-scientific mode.

Sophisticated-fragmented

In physical science for terrestrial events, space and substances are united in that facts are in space and time. They are then conceptually separated and recombined in terms of generalizations and laws through the relational concept of space and action by contact. The social sciences receive the view of space from the physical sciences, expecting it to be used both for location and for explanation, where the model of scientific explanation is also borrowed from science. The problem for the social sciences begins with the location of social-psychological facts in the physical space. Many are reluctant to say that categories of facts, such as the attitudes, values, beliefs, which the social sciences study are actually locatable in physical space. These, it is contended, are properties of the mind. They are internal--not external. But geographers and others have argued through operational definitions and other devices, that these mental states must correspond to overt physical states for them to be discussed objectively and publicly. Hence, these states can be indirectly located in physical space. This is what we do when we say that someone has an attitude or belief; it is what we do when we map such attitudes and beliefs. Although the mental or subjective facts can thus be "located," there has been some dissatisfaction with this approach. But we will leave it for now.

Assuming then, that the facts of the social sciences are locatable in physical space there still remains the overwhelming problem of determining the significance of this space for human behavior. That is, we would like to know what the effect of moving things around would be. What affect does separation have? What would happen if the distribution were changed? This means how are space and substances causally connected? And what meaning does space and its properties have in such a connection? The answer to this question in social science lies in the concept of social science laws, modeled after the physical science laws, and in the interpretation of the relational concept of space and action by contact within the context of a lawful social science.

In brief, the major points are these.[9] The significance of spatial proper-

---

[9] The relational concept and action by contact in geography are discussed

ties such as distance and shape are determined by laws which can be divided into two kinds: <u>geometric</u> and <u>substance</u> laws. Geometric laws determine the significance of spatial relations in a relatively closed deductive axiomatic system and do not address questions of process about the significance of spatial properties which are asked by the social sciences. Substance laws, or substance hypotheses (the difference being in their degree of confirmation), answer such questions and there are two kinds of these laws: those that <u>do</u> and those that <u>do not explicitly include physical spatial terms as part of their empirical concepts</u>. The physical science law that water freezes at 32°F at standard pressure conditions and the hypotheses that people with high I.Q.'s will most likely be successful in their freshman year at a university, are examples of laws and hypotheses which do not explicitly mention spatial terms. Coulomb's law in physics, the gravity model, and central place theory are examples of hypotheses with explicit inclusion of spatial terms, in these cases distance.

Both kinds of substance laws or hypotheses explain with equal power spatial properties of their facts. Laws without explicit mention of spatial terms state that the antecedent and consequent conditions (i.e., water, temperature, pressure, and ice; or the I.Q. and the success) all occur together in the same place. That is, they are physically spatially congruent to one another. Laws without physical spatial terms state that the facts are not congruent. They are not congruent to the degree referred to by geometric terms. In the above examples they are separated by distances. This is what geometric terms signify. Moreover, a property of space, like distance, cannot itself be a causal property in social science. Interactions among people occur through channels and media. The spatial terms, in this case, distance, must refer to the distance of the substances, channels, or media carrying the information. These substance referents must be affixed to the spatial terms if the spatial terms are to be significant in substance laws. Laws must make clear to what substances or media their spatial terms refer. If they do not, the laws would then refer to empty space as a causal property. This, however, is in violation of action by contact. Therefore, the spatial terms in substance laws must have clear substance referents. This is the relational concept of space in social science.

Although social science is presented with a space already conceptually separated from substances, this space is recombinable through laws according to the relational concept. This recombination, however, is largely hypothetical.

---

more fully in Robert Sack: A Concept of Physical Space in Geography, <u>Geographical Analysis</u>, Vol. 5, 1973, pp. 16-34.

It has not yet occurred because there are as yet no well confirmed laws of human behavior in the social sciences. The present state of the social sciences with regard to space is one of conceptual separation of substance and space. This separation is not only due to the lack of laws, but also to the difficulty of locating subjective facts in physical space. These two factors, the difficulty in locating some of the social science facts, and the lack of clarity of what a social science that is well developed will look like, have tended to pry space and substance even further apart.

On the one hand there are areas of social science which ignore spatial relations. According to the relational concept, social sciences ignore space at the risk of not having confirmable empirical generalizations. On the other hand, and in part to compensate for the lack of attention given to space by the social sciences, geographers have tended in some cases, notably the extreme spatial analysts like Bunge and Schaefer, to go overboard in the other direction and overemphasize space. [10] They have claimed that the significance of space can be determined only through special kinds of analysis, called spatial analysis, and explained only through special kinds of laws, called spatial laws. These laws have been described by Bunge as morphological laws with spatial variables, modeled along the lines of geometric laws.

Instead of arguing, as have some in the social sciences who have ignored spatial relations, that space is not necessary for determining the significance of substances, proponents of extreme spatial analysis contend that substance is not necessary for determining the significance of space. This means that space itself can have an effect, and we find this assertion in such familiar expressions of the spatial analysis tradition as finding spatial laws, finding the effect of location on behavior, determining the significance of place or shape or distance. [11]

Both ignoring space and overemphasizing it are not going to lead us to an understanding of its significance within a social science. Rather the connection between space and substance is achieved through laws--substance laws.

All substance laws would explain spatial properties of the facts they sub-

---

[10] See F. Schaefer: Exceptionalism in Geography: A Methodological Examination, Annals, Association of American Geographers, Vol. 43, 1953, pp. 226-249; and W. Bunge· Theoretical Geography, Lund Studies in Geography, Series C, No. 1 (C. W. K. Gleerup, Lund, 1966).

[11] W. Bunge: Spatial Prediction, Annals, Association of American Geographers, Vol. 63, 1973, pp. 566-568; and R. D. Sack: Comment in Reply, Annals, Association of American Geographers, Vol. 36, 1973, pp. 568-569.

sume. Thus there would be no room for expressions about the effect of space, location, and distance per se. These spatial properties would have to have substance referents. All substance laws would be spatial. To ask why something occurs where it does would be to ask why it occurs. This is the fusion of space and substance which would come about from a developed social science. It would make spatial analysis the same as social science and make social science spatial analysis. This is why Hartshorne was correct when he objected to the study of distributions and generic region or places as not by itself being geographic. [12] But we do not have a developed social science and therefore we are left with the conceptual separation of space and substance and as yet no significant evaluation of space.

There have been two modifications of the significance of physical space in social science and the way in which it is connected to substance. One has resulted from a relaxation of the criteria of explanation and results in the familiar concept of chorology. [13] The other has kept a nomothetic approach to explanation and has modified the description of space. This occurs in behavioral geography and leads to cognitive and mental maps.

Loosening our commitment to laws allows us to include more complex relationships in our analysis at the expense of clarity and certainty. Corresponding to this shift away from explanatory rigor is a shift in conception of space and place resulting in the specific place. [14] Chorology differs from spatial analysis in that it employs far more explanation sketches to link facts together.

Explanation sketches are incomplete nomothetic forms and they, like laws, require that the facts affecting other facts be in physical "contact" and that action not occur through empty space at a distance. The spatial linkages are a necessary condition for any causal relationship and chorology goes to great lengths to describe them. In the absence of lawful explanations, specifying these spatial linkages assumes paramount importance and makes it appear as though spatial configurations themselves have determined the interconnections

---

[12]R. Hartshorne: The Nature of Geography (Association of American Geographers, Lancaster, Pa., 1939), especially pp. 127-129.

[13]Hartshorne, op. cit. ⌈note 12⌉, pp. 56-57, 77-78, 91, 93, 101, 340, and 341.

[14]R. D. Sack: Chorology and Spatial Analysis, Annals, Association of American Geographers, Vol. 64, 1974, pp. 439-452.

and interactions. The degree the chorological synthesis is based on sketches is also the degree to which the spatial configurations would be specific or unique. Moreover, this uncertain linkage in chorological synthesis through explanation sketches allows intuition and feeling a far greater role in explanation than is the case in nomothetic analysis. Impressions and feelings coupled with the emphasis on "unique" spatial configuration leads us closer to "feelings" about space and "character" of place and spatial relations.[15] But this shift to "feeling" has been checked by the chorological commitment to empiricism and its eschewance of art as appropriate in chorological synthesis.[16] Hence the increased interest in sentiment toward space did not come only or even in large measure directly from chorology.

The direct confrontation of the subjective in the social sciences is the behavioral approach. This vast and diverse area of research is the logical extension of the empirical nomothetic approach to analyzing the subjective. It is founded on the assumption that decisions are made on the basis of how people perceive things to be, and hence the investigator should discover this, in addition to knowing how things actually are. The behavioral attempts to probe the subjective while adhering to the criteria of science.

The geographic bent in behavioral research is the perception of space and its properties. Perceived spatial relations may contribute more significant measures than are found in the description of physical space. This means that space, this time in perceived form, as in perceived distances and cognitive and mental maps, may be linked to substance in a significant way. There have been many empirical attempts to measure perceived distances and to compare these measures with the actual physical distances in order to discover systematic relationships between them.[17] Thus far no general relationship has been found, and moreover, from the perspective of the relational view, it is unlikely that a general relationship exists between perceived properties and actual properties of space. Rather it is far more likely that the perceptions of spatial relations

---

[15]In this regard chorology and the specific place is similar to histories "era, " or "epoch." Philosophers have frequently pointed to the use of explanation sketches in history. See A. Danto: Analytic Philosophy of History (Cambridge University Press, London, 1968), pp. 209-211, 239-239, and 272.

[16]Hartshorne, op. cit. [note 12], pp. 132-133 and 219.

[17]For a review of the relationships between physical and cognitive distances, see M. Cadwallader: Problems in Cognitive Distance and Their Implications for Cognitive Mapping, Environment and Behavior (in press).

will depend on the particular actions, substances, and individual circumstances. Moreover, the scientific significance of these perceived spatial measurements has not yet been thoroughly tested. This behavioral approach were it to succeed would connect perceived space to substance in accordance with the relational concept.

There are other ways in which space can have significance. Space and its properties, in violation of a relational concept, can find expression in other modes of thought. These connect space with the subjective. It may be expressed in the sophisticated fragmented pattern, in such modes as art and dream imagery, and in the unsophisticated-fused pattern in the child's view, myth, and magic.

Art, we have said, is the symbolization of feeling. A painting may represent an object or a person, but as a work of art, the representation of the object or person is simply a vehicle by which feelings are symbolized. A portrait of a king, as a work of art, may symbolize stateliness, power, or cowardice. It is not simply there to describe the king. This symbolization of emotion is best seen in abstract works of art, such as cubism, or in forms of art like classical music, which have little to do with the representation of conventional sounds.

In the visual arts there are two ways in which forms and shapes and space can have meaning. First, the work of art may symbolize feelings about space, such as its openness, boundedness, balance, dynamism, and so on. In these cases art creates symbols of feelings about space. But this semblance in Langer's terms, is as yet, and may forever be, untranslatable into the scientific terms of space and substance. This is because there is, as we have noted in the framework, a fundamental asymmetry in the way subjective and objective symbols refer; namely, the difference between representation and presentation. Symbols of the subjective, used subjectively, have meanings which are overdetermined and fluid. The same symbol may refer to many emotions and an emotion may be symbolized in different ways. [18]

Space and spatial properties can also have meaning in the subjective realm through the use of shapes and forms in symbolic vehicles. That is, a painter, in creating a semblance of space or of anything else for that matter, uses spatial configurations and patterns which lend meaning to the painting. Similarly, dream images, in symbolizing emotions, take spatial forms and

---

[18] Werner and Kaplan, op. cit. ⌈note 8⌉, pp. 213-232, refers to this relationship in line symbols as polysemy and plurisignification.

shapes. It appears from the artistic and psychoanalytical viewpoints, that such shapes and patterns in art and dreams possess a meaning or significance. An upward sloping line may signify happiness, a downward sloping one, sadness. A linear or circular form, especially in a dream, may refer to sexual feelings. This is why trains, umbrellas, and stairways are thought to connote similar things in dreams. In such cases shapes and forms appear to have a meaning in and of themselves. Yet, these meanings cannot be generalized from the scientific viewpoint, again because of the way in which emotions and feelings are symbolized. Their meanings are overdetermined and fluid.[19] A circle may mean something feminine, but it may mean perfection, compactness and so on. Yet these symbols do have meaning and make sense even if they cannot be generalized. Moreover, to the extent they have meaning, they give shape, pattern, and form an immediate significance, a significance which has left its imprint on our interpretation and alteration of the landscape, in effecting architecture, landscape architecture, and in effecting our images of social order manifested in utopias, planning, and even in perception. For instance, because we may associate separation with difference, we may think we see spatial separation of groups we know to be different, even if these groups are not spatially separated.[20]

Unsophisticated-fused

The quest for the significance of shapes and patterns is given a non-relational expression in the unsophisticated fused views. This realm, especially the mythical-magical mode, has had enormous impact on the interpretation and alteration of the landscape. In these views space is not far removed conceptually from substances and the subjective is not far removed from the objective. Hence, the world is seen animistically.

The importance of the child's view of the world for geography lies in its uncovering of stages which normal human beings go through in their acquisition of a practical perception and conception of the physical world. Such stages and

[19]See the concepts of condensation and displacement in S. Freud: Interpretation of Dreams, Great Books of the Western World, Vol. 54 (Encyclopedia Britannica, Inc., Chicago, 1952), pp. 253-264.

[20]Observers of Victorian Cities in England and in the United States "saw" a dichotomous segregated residential pattern which greatly simplified and obscured the complex social geography of the time. See D. Ward: The Victorian Slum: An Enduring Myth? Annals, Association of American Geographers, Vol. 66, 1976, pp. 323-336.

the temporal order of topological to metric geometry are among the observations that have been mentioned frequently in the geographic literature. [21] In
order to understand the links between objective and subjective perceptions and
conceptions of space, we need to draw attention to the following points. In the
earlier stages, the child does not have a finely developed sense of the differences between self and world, between subjective and objective. [22] The objective world is felt very strongly and feelings are often projected onto it in terms
of physiognomic seeing. As adults we do this when we see a forlorn landscape
or a weeping willow. The child, though, does it far more often than do we; he
sees much of the world as though it possessed emotions and were animated.
The genesis of symbolic functions is based on the separation of the subjective
from the objective and the introduction of the symbols to replace the direct experience of one or the other. When the child first uses symbols, the separation
between the subjective and the objective is not great, the world is felt intensely
and symbols tend to have strong connotations as well as denotations. Moreover,
the symbols tend to be thought of by the child as though they were part of the
things they represented and themselves possessed their attributes. The child,
for instance, goes through a period of believing words to be literally attached to
the things they represent, and the child often uses words to produce things, as
in word magic. [23] Equally important is that even when the child is thinking of
the world in a logical, realistic, and practical way, the thoughts of objects in
space involves curtailed sensori-motor involvement. In fact, Piaget defines
the child's ability to conceptualize spatial relations as imagining the manipulation of these objects. [24] Once manipulation is mastered and the objects and
space of the world attain a permanence, the ability to imagine things in their
spatial relations involves imagining the active engagement with these things.
Such feelings of participation are never completely removed even in the practical world view of the adult. What is meant by the child's conception of space,

---

[21]See for instance R. Hart and G. Moore, The Development of Spatial Cognition: A Review, in Image and Environment (edited by R. Downs and D. Stea;
Aldine, Chicago, 1973), pp. 246-288.

[22]Piaget, op. cit. [note 7], and Werner, op. cit. [note 7].

[23]Werner, op. cit. [note 7], pp. 357-368, and J. Piaget: La Représenta-
tion du monde chez l'enfant (Paris, 1926), p. 61.

[24]J. Piaget and B. Inhelder: The Child's Conception of Space (W. W. Norton, New York, 1967), p. 454.

and even the untutored adult's conception, is the imagining of spatial properties of things.

This view is pre-relational. It fuses space and substance because it never conceptually separated them. Because of the lack of conceptual separation of subjective from objective, and space from substance, even when the child and the untutored adult see the world and conceive of it in terms of its objective characteristics, waves of subjectivity are not far behind to immerse this space. The things that populate the world, their spatial orientations relative to our bodies (i.e., whether they are above, below, in front, behind), all draw out the subjective. But, for the same reasons that feelings about dream images and line drawings cannot be generalized, we have difficulty in generalizing about the alterations that come about when the subjective is layered over the perception and conception of space.

Most would agree that these layerings make physical space non-isotropic and that upward and frontward directions relative to the orientation of the body are positively valued, that backward and downward are negatively valued, and that such associations can be projected at all geographic scales. But these are only approximate correspondences. Positive and negative are far too narrow and brittle to signify the emotions that may be associated with these orientations. Thus, while we can suggest how space and its properties can be felt and how such feelings may alter our practical perceptions and conceptions, there are still few generalizations which come from this research.

In the mythical-magical world view we confront again, but in more elaborate fashion, a pre-relational conception of space. Confusion of symbols with referents is one of the characteristics of this mode of thought.[25] Because of the predominance of vision in human perception, a form or a shape of an object is often used to symbolize that object. For instance, a doll may symbolize a person. Because this form or shape, as a symbol, shares in the appearance of the object, it may also be thought to share in other properties of the object, both objective and subjective. Hence, the symbol may be used in place of the object wherein it is expected to have the same effect as the object and wherein altering or destroying the symbol would affect or destroy the object. The symbol, in this case a spatial form, becomes confused with what it represents. The doll, for instance, may be stuck with pins or burnt, with the expectation that the person it represents would come to the same end. This confusion al-

---

[25]E. Cassirer, op. cit. [note 7], p. 38.

lows shapes and patterns to attain a power they could not have in science. In primitive cultures the small number of people constituting a society may see and use the same symbols in the same way. They may believe the shape of the heavens from which all power emanates to be circular. By making their hearths, their huts, their corrals, and their settlements circular, they then reproduce the cosmos at each level, and each place attracts and contains heavenly powers. Not only shapes and patterns become powerful in these pre-relational and fused views, but also places attain a significance which cannot be expressed scientifically. Things have place in space. The place in myth and magic is fused with the thing. If the thing which creates awe is removed from the place, or if the thing is there only once, as in a miracle, the place becomes the symbol of the things, and, through the pre-relational fusion of things and space, the place retains the power or the awe of the thing. Thus places can become holy, magical, and infused with spirits.

This same pre-relational attitude towards place is also behind such feelings as sentiment, nostalgia, and allegiance to place. In civilizations, with large geographic areas, large populations, and class structures, the social order is not seen clearly and equally by everyone. In order to make the social order and its power real and tangible, civilizations employ the most basic and powerful tool of reification, that of location and extension in physical space. Area and power become fused and allegiance to the territorial state becomes essential.

To help assure and sustain this fusion to a specific place, nationalism and other forms of state allegiance frequently incorporate mythical-magical forms which become part of the state iconography. Myth and magic make it possible to see why this particular place, i. e. this fatherland, motherland, or homeland, is important and worth defending.

Neither art nor science can do this. Art can symbolize feelings of attachment to place, but the description of particular place is only a vehicle of this symbol. Art uses it to abstract the feeling about specific place and then severs the connection of the subjective to the objective.

Science, or social science even if it were well developed, could not symbolize and explain completely the feelings towards a specific place. The specific location of facts in social science simply serves as a means of identification and individuation. Social science laws, in explaining why things occur, would be explaining why things occur where they do.

Moreover, the social sciences, at present, have the same problem in explaining and predicting which shapes and patterns in myth and magic are significant, as they have in explaining the meanings of shapes and patterns in art or in dreams. The shapes and patterns in myth that are selected to represent the objects and express feelings about these objects are, in objective terms, overdetermined and fluid in their meanings. We may understand why a mythical and magical shape is used the way it is, but we cannot yet predict which shapes will be selected as significant ones and why.

Conclusion

Until social science develops (if it ever will) there will be no way of synthesizing these meanings of space. These meanings, though, will all continue to affect our behavior in space, to affect our interpretation and utilization of the landscape. Because these meanings of space have not been synthesized, they will often remain institutionally separated in different places. We have art in museums, science in laboratories, worship in holy places, and so on, and only infrequently and most likely unsuccessfully are they combined as in places designed to be functional and artistic. Geography must continue to explore these meanings of space, their interrelations, and understand their impacts on the landscape; for all of these meanings, their combinations and conflicts, determine the significance of spatial relations, our personal views of space, and the interpretation of the earth's surface as the home of man.

Acknowledgement.--This paper addresses itself to part of my research on space and human behavior which I am drawing together in a book Conceptions of Space in Social Thought: A Geographic Perspective. I would like to thank the John Simon Guggenheim Memorial Foundation and the University of Wisconsin Alumni Research Foundation for their support of this research.

RETROSPECT

In sum, the papers provide a multiplicity of expressions of culture or behavior and place or space. They serve to illustrate the conceptual diversity as well as the potential scope of subjective dimensions in human geography.

The introductory essay explores several of the possible, if overlapping perspectives to space, suggesting that political-institutional, social-sentimental, and symbolic dimensions enhance understanding of the economic-pragmatic sphere (Butzer). At the same time they provide a new capability for explicit cultural articulation of landscapes, and of the land ethic of different cultures. Man-environmental problems can be viewed as a behavioral problem, since choice influences behavior (Sonnenfeld). The social relationships that affect sharing, subsistence security, and control over resources profoundly influence the resource perceptions of traditional and industrial populations. Spatial organization is not limited to sedentary societies. Nomadic groups define a functional space and their cultural ecology is liable to pattern analysis. The patterns produced project a static image, one that obscures a great deal of dynamic and evolutionary potential, and that can best be examined in terms of process and outcome (Johnson). By implication, all case studies should strive to build towards a more general theory of man-environment interaction.

Landscape painting has influenced perceptions of and feelings for nature, and has contributed to a sense of place (Rees). A handful of artists has served as effective middlemen between cultures and landscapes, and the mutual stimulation has had no small impact on ecological behavior. Another neglected, aesthetic dimension is provided by the modern novel, which serves to conjure up images of a society overwhelmingly economic in orientation (Salter). The social landscapes thus described are sometimes disturbing and nearly always evocative, providing an underutilized aid illuminating many of the configurations studied by geographers.

The potential orientations to spatial organization are multidimensional in themselves. So, for example, what is ostensibly sacred space is not only symbolic but also social and even political (Tuan). This philosophical dissection of an apparently integral concept is complemented by the specific example of the self-defined cultural island of Mormonland. The ideal Mormon cosmology, while espousing the subjugation of the wilderness, sees man and nature in harmony (Jackson). Nonetheless, the character of the Mormon culture region owes more to the socio-cultural antecedents of the founders than to basic religious tenets. How appropriate the discussion of sacred space at Salt Lake City, with opportunity to view for oneself the fascinating Mormon landscape!

Urban space was by no means overlooked. Instead of overemphasizing functional attributes of urban structure, greater attention should be given to the evolution and physical expression of growth and differentiation in cities (Conzen). The complex urban imprint can best be interpreted by more sophisticated conceptual models that interrelate form, function, and culture. Finally, the traditional geographical concepts of space can be reexamined at the broadest level (Sack). Even physical space can and has been interpreted in several ways. The idea of space can be reduced to fragmented components by artists or scientists, or contracted in an unsophisticated, fused image, e.g. in the child's view of the world, in myth and magic, or by primitive societies. A degree of subjectivity also enters into the categories of scientific organization and explanation.

These glimpses of a kaleidoscope of ideas elucidate the range of what we do not understand about apparently simple, geographical configurations. These ideas also illustrate the advantages of an opening up of the mind, allowing imagination and reflection their due. In total, they make a good case against economic determinism. Geographers should learn to cope better with the world of "feeling" as it relates to environment, something most of us have been reluctant to do. The desire for systematics and certainty is understandable, but at times the things that we can measure and quantify may be less important than those we can not. This problem is not unique to geography, and besets the social sciences in general. It may explain why literature, art and religion may offer more satisfying conclusions to problems that trouble us. A preoccupation with numbers can, in the long run, be as intellectually inhibiting as medieval scholasticism or dialectic materialism.

These essays have intentionally been suggestive rather than programmatic. They represent a preliminary sorting out of many complex issues, without attempting a closure that would be premature. Paradigms evolve in the line of research, as part of the intellectual process of an intellectual community. They are formulated only after they have been shaped into a tangible, operational framework. The vistas provided by these essays may inspire a more concerted search for an integrated human geography, in which cultural and behavioral perspectives are accorded the concern they deserve.

ABSTRACTS

CULTURAL PERSPECTIVES ON GEOGRAPHICAL SPACE
Karl W. Butzer

There are intellectual limitations to the prevalent economic paradigm of spatial organization. Cultures are idiosyncratic or particularistic, and the imprint of culture on the landscape includes more than profit and loss, or distance decay. Also, culture by definition is cumulative. Geographical space can be viewed as a set of available resources, or an object of political or military control, and in terms of social identification or symbolic value. Emphases vary from one culture to another, both spatially and temporally, with increasing differentiation among more complex societies. Since culture mediates between man and environment, the land ethic of different cultures will vary with great subtlety but with considerable variation in ecological impact.

RESOURCE PERCEPTIONS AND THE SECURITY OF SUBSISTENCE
Joseph Sonnenfeld

Subsistence is secured by dependable resources or by dependable social relationships. Resources are dependable when they are abundant, renewable, or controlled. Social relationships are dependable when subsistence is shared unconditionally, and when cooperation is obligated. While randomness in the locus of subsistence deficiency reinforces a sharing ethic, persistent differentials in subsistence success tend to weaken sharing relationships. A critical variable is the control over resources provided by innovating, technical, and organizational skills. This paper considers the effects of a sharing-security-control relationship on the resource perceptions of traditional and industrial populations.

NOMADIC ORGANIZATION OF SPACE: REFLECTIONS ON PATTERN AND
PROCESS
Douglas L. Johnson

Nomadism connotes aimless movement and random ordering of space. Cartographic examination of the migration pattern and ecological setting of pastoral
nomads indicates that rationality and regularity characterize their organization
of space. This reveals that five basic spatial patterns (constricted-oscillary,
limited-amplitude, pulsatory, elliptical, complex) exist. Analogous patterns
underlie the spatial framework of other livelihoods, a reflection of the inherent
similarities between mobile livelihoods as well as a caution against facile generalizations about the variable processes that underlie discernible behavior. For
cartographic analysis projects only a static image of the complex, highly variable processes that govern nomadic space. Flexibility, mobility, diversity,
centrality, and adaptability shape a spatial organization that is more mental construct than physical reality. Resilience and flexibility permit both exploitation
of marginal resources and adaptability to political and economic change.

LANDSCAPE IN ART
Ronald Rees

Landscape painting mediates between man and environment. It stimulates the
sense of sight, organizes our vision, and heightens sensibilities. Through
paintings we acquire a sense of place and identity. As a link between us and
our surroundings, landscape painting serves an ecological function. It fur-
nishes models of the outer world and in doing so helps us to achieve, as Kenneth Clark puts it, a sense of harmony with the environment.

SIGNATURES AND SETTINGS: ONE APPROACH TO LANDSCAPE IN LITERATURE
Christopher L. Salter

One of the most signal ways in which society has identified with its landscape
has been through the visions of fiction. Whether the landscape has been given a
dominant role by elaborate development of setting, or the reader is given window to the surroundings by means of only minor comments, the space contain-
ing the drama of the work has been explicitly shaped by the author. If the reader explores the work in an attempt to answer questions dealing with the shape of
the space, the reactions of the people to these designs, and the impact of the
landscape upon the flow of the work, then the work can serve well as a source
for geographic evidence. Although landscape created in literature may not pre-

sent us with an objective recounting of spatial design, the images drawn in and from fiction do instruct us in landscape preferences and prejudices. This paper explores the ways in which geographers might derive both structural and behavioral knowledge of landscape in literary works.

SACRED SPACE: EXPLORATIONS OF AN IDEA
Yi-Fu Tuan

Experientially the sacred is that which is set apart from the commonplace, that which interrupts routine. Of course, not everything that is set aside spatially is sacred space, nor is every interruption of routine an hierophany. In addition to apartness the sacred connotes order, wholeness, purity, and numinous power. The meaning of sacred space is often ambiguous and paradoxical. In modern life the nation-state exemplifies sacred space. Other instances are the pure neighborhood and wilderness, but in these the ideas of purity and apartness are divorced from the sense of numinous, unpredictable power. The paradoxical and the mysterious are fading.

RELIGION AND LANDSCAPE IN THE MORMON CULTURAL REGION
Richard H. Jackson

The Mormon Culture region embodies the reification of values in organization of space. The region is viewed as sacred by Mormons and even non-Mormon observers maintain that the Mormon landscape is unique. Elements of this landscape image include the Mormon village, irrigation agriculture, and distinctively Mormon architectural styles. Although there are certain relic features which are recognizably Mormon in the West, they are only vestiges of an earlier occupance pattern. For the majority of the residents of the Mormon West, the cultural landscape differs only slightly from that of America in general.

The Mormon value system, developed in the nineteenth century and nurtured in geographic isolation, is primarily responsible for the "unique" Mormon landscape of the late nineteenth and early twentieth centuries. This landscape changed dramatically as transportation, and agricultural practices changed rapidly after World War I. The present Mormon landscape exists as an uneasy transitional stage between the functional pioneer Mormon West, with its simple utilitarian features, and the modern integrated economic West of split-level housing, super highways, and tall office buildings and apartments. To find the "Mormon" landscape today it is necessary to visit the isolated outlying villages, for the emerging landscape differs only in minor aspects from American suburbia.

ANALYTICAL APPROACHES TO THE URBAN LANDSCAPE
Michael P. Conzen

Functionalism has dominated the geographical study of the North American city for two decades. Far more is known about the contemporary functional side of urban structure than about the evolutionary process and physical expression of growth and differentiation. This imbalance impedes satisfactory synthesis of the geographical character of American cities, and requires a sophisticated approach to urban form at many scales, building upon functional knowledge and aimed at conceptual models of form-function interaction within proper cultural contexts. Morphological studies have been generally fragmented, narrow, and inconsequential in the absence of a general analytical framework, but new developments suggest considerable improvement. Recent work in perceptual geography promises a clearer view of the subjective observation and meaning of the landscape for urban residents, with implications for the urban planning process.

GEOGRAPHIC AND OTHER VIEWS OF SPACE
Robert David Sack

Examining the meanings of space and their interconnections from the context of geographic thought requires extending the empirical view to create an intellectual surface which conceptually separates subjectivity from objectivity and substance from space. The results of projecting conceptions of space onto this surface are that aesthetics, and social and physical sciences, range over vast areas of the surface, fragmenting and conceptually extending the surface, whereas the child's, the mythical-magical, and the primitive societal views contract the surface. The first group forms sophisticated-fragmented views of symbols and space; the second forms unsophisticated-fused views.

THE UNIVERSITY OF CHICAGO
DEPARTMENT OF GEOGRAPHY
RESEARCH PAPERS (Lithographed, 6×9 Inches)

(Available from Department of Geography, The University of Chicago, 5828 S. University Ave., Chicago, Illinois 60637. Price: $6.00 each; by series subscription, $5.00 each.)

106. SAARINEN, THOMAS F. *Perception of the Drought Hazard on the Great Plains* 1966. 183 pp.
107. SOLZMAN, DAVID M. *Waterway Industrial Sites: A Chicago Case Study* 1967. 138 pp.
108. KASPERSON, ROGER E. *The Dodecanese: Diversity and Unity in Island Politics* 1967. 184 pp.
109. LOWENTHAL, DAVID, et al. *Environmental Perception and Behavior.* 1967. 88 pp.
110. REED, WALLACE E. *Areal Interaction in India: Commodity Flows of the Bengal-Bihar Industrial Area* 1967. 210 pp.
112. BOURNE, LARRY S. *Private Redevelopment of the Central City: Spatial Processes of Structural Change in the City of Toronto* 1967. 199 pp.
113. BRUSH, JOHN E., and GAUTHIER, HOWARD L., JR. *Service Centers and Consumer Trips: Studies on the Philadelphia Metropolitan Fringe* 1968. 182 pp.
114. CLARKSON, JAMES D. *The Cultural Ecology of a Chinese Village: Cameron Highlands, Malaysia* 1968. 174 pp.
115. BURTON, IAN; KATES, ROBERT W.; and SNEAD, RODMAN E. *The Human Ecology of Coastal Flood Hazard in Megalopolis* 1968. 196 pp.
117. WONG, SHUE TUCK. *Perception of Choice and Factors Affecting Industrial Water Supply Decisions in Northeastern Illinois* 1968. 96 pp.
118. JOHNSON, DOUGLAS L. *The Nature of Nomadism* 1969. 200 pp.
119. DIENES, LESLIE. *Locational Factors and Locational Developments in the Soviet Chemical Industry* 1969. 285 pp.
120. MIHELIC, DUSAN. *The Political Element in the Port Geography of Trieste* 1969. 104 pp.
121. BAUMANN, DUANE. *The Recreational Use of Domestic Water Supply Reservoirs: Perception and Choice* 1969. 125 pp.
122. LIND, AULIS O. *Coastal Landforms of Cat Island, Bahamas: A Study of Holocene Accretionary Topography and Sea-Level Change* 1969. 156 pp.
123. WHITNEY, JOSEPH. *China: Area, Administration and Nation Building* 1970. 198 pp.
124. EARICKSON, ROBERT. *The Spatial Behavior of Hospital Patients: A Behavioral Approach to Spatial Interaction in Metropolitan Chicago* 1970. 198 pp.
125. DAY, JOHN C. *Managing the Lower Rio Grande: An Experience in International River Development* 1970. 277 pp.
126. MAC IVER, IAN. *Urban Water Supply Alternatives: Perception and Choice in the Grand Basin, Ontario* 1970. 178 pp.
127. GOHEEN, PETER G. *Victorian Toronto, 1850 to 1900: Pattern and Process of Growth* 1970. 278 pp.
128. GOOD, CHARLES M. *Rural Markets and Trade in East Africa* 1970. 252 pp.
129. MEYER, DAVID R. *Spatial Variation of Black Urban Households* 1970. 127 pp.
130. GLADFELTER, BRUCE. *Meseta and Campiña Landforms in Central Spain: A Geomorphology of the Alto Henares Basin* 1971. 204 pp.
131. NEILS, ELAINE M. *Reservation to City: Indian Urbanization and Federal Relocation* 1971. 200 pp.
132. MOLINE, NORMAN T. *Mobility and the Small Town, 1900–1930* 1971. 169 pp.
133. SCHWIND, PAUL J. *Migration and Regional Development in the United States, 1950–1960* 1971. 170 pp.
134. PYLE, GERALD F. *Heart Disease, Cancer and Stroke in Chicago: A Geographical Analysis with Facilities Plans for 1980* 1971. 292 pp.
135. JOHNSON, JAMES F. *Renovated Waste Water: An Alternative Source of Municipal Water Supply in the U.S.* 1971. 155 pp.
136. BUTZER, KARL W. *Recent History of an Ethiopian Delta: The Omo River and the Level of Lake Rudolf* 1971. 184 pp.
137. HARRIS, CHAUNCY D. *Annotated World List of Selected Current Geographical Serials in English, French, and German* 3rd edition 1971. 77 pp.
138. HARRIS, CHAUNCY D., and FELLMANN, JEROME D. *International List of Geographical Serials* 2nd edition 1971. 267 pp.
139. MC MANIS, DOUGLAS R. *European Impressions of the New England Coast, 1497–1620* 1972. 147 pp.
140. COHEN, YEHOSHUA S. *Diffusion of an Innovation in an Urban System: The Spread of Planned Regional Shopping Centers in the United States, 1949–1968* 1972. 136 pp.

141. MITCHELL, NORA. *The Indian Hill-Station: Kodaikanal* 1972. 199 pp.

142. PLATT, RUTHERFORD H. *The Open Space Decision Process: Spatial Allocation of Costs and Benefits* 1972. 189 pp.

143. GOLANT, STEPHEN M. *The Residential Location and Spatial Behavior of the Elderly: A Canadian Example* 1972. 226 pp.

144. PANNELL, CLIFTON W. *T'ai-chung, T'ai-wan: Structure and Function* 1973. 200 pp.

145. LANKFORD, PHILIP M. *Regional Incomes in the United States, 1929–1967: Level, Distribution, Stability, and Growth* 1972. 137 pp.

146. FREEMAN, DONALD B. *International Trade, Migration, and Capital Flows: A Quantitative Analysis of Spatial Economic Interaction* 1973. 202 pp.

147. MYERS, SARAH K. *Language Shift Among Migrants to Lima, Peru* 1973. 204 pp.

148. JOHNSON, DOUGLAS L. *Jabal al-Akhdar, Cyrenaica: An Historical Geography of Settlement and Livelihood* 1973. 240 pp.

149. YEUNG, YUE-MAN. *National Development Policy and Urban Transformation in Singapore: A Study of Public Housing and the Marketing System* 1973. 204 pp.

150. HALL, FRED L. *Location Criteria for High Schools: Student Transportation and Racial Integration* 1973. 156 pp.

151. ROSENBERG, TERRY J. *Residence, Employment, and Mobility of Puerto Ricans in New York City* 1974. 230 pp.

152. MIKESELL, MARVIN W., editor. *Geographers Abroad: Essays on the Problems and Prospects of Research in Foreign Areas* 1973. 296 pp.

153. OSBORN, JAMES. *Area, Development Policy, and the Middle City in Malaysia* 1974. 273 pp.

154. WACHT, WALTER F. *The Domestic Air Transportation Network of the United States* 1974. 98 pp.

155. BERRY, BRIAN J. L., et al. *Land Use, Urban Form and Environmental Quality* 1974. 464 pp.

156. MITCHELL, JAMES K. *Community Response to Coastal Erosion: Individual and Collective Adjustments to Hazard on the Atlantic Shore* 1974. 209 pp.

157. COOK, GILLIAN P. *Spatial Dynamics of Business Growth in the Witwatersrand* 1975. 143 pp.

158. STARR, JOHN T., JR. *The Evolution of Unit Train Operations in the United States: 1960–1969—A Decade of Experience* 1976. 247 pp.

159. PYLE, GERALD F. *The Spatial Dynamics of Crime* 1974. 220 pp.

160. MEYER, JUDITH W. *Diffusion of an American Montessori Education* 1975. 109 pp.

161. SCHMID, JAMES A. *Urban Vegetation: A Review and Chicago Case Study* 1975. 280 pp.

162. LAMB, RICHARD. *Metropolitan Impacts on Rural America* 1975. 210 pp.

163. FEDOR, THOMAS. *Patterns of Urban Growth in the Russian Empire during the Nineteenth Century* 1975. 275 pp.

164. HARRIS, CHAUNCY D. *Guide to Geographical Bibliographies and Reference Works in Russian or on the Soviet Union* 1975. 496 pp.

165. JONES, DONALD W. *Migration and Urban Unemployment in Dualistic Economic Development* 1975. 186 pp.

166. BEDNARZ, ROBERT S. *The Effect of Air Pollution on Property Value in Chicago* 1975. 118 pp.

167. HANNEMANN, MANFRED. *The Diffusion of the Reformation in Southwestern Germany, 1518–1534* 1975. 248 pp.

168. SUBLETT, MICHAEL D. *Farmers on the Road. Interfarm Migration and the Farming of Noncontiguous Lands in Three Midwestern Townships, 1939–1969* 1975. 228 pp.

169. STETZER, DONALD FOSTER. *Special Districts in Cook County: Toward a Geography of Local Government* 1975. 189 pp.

170. EARLE, CARVILLE V. *The Evolution of a Tidewater Settlement System: All Hallow's Parish, Maryland, 1650–1783* 1975. 249 pp.

171. SPODEK, HOWARD. *Urban-Rural Integration in Regional Development: A Case Study of Saurashtra, India—1800–1960* 1976. 156 pp.

172. COHEN, YEHOSHUA S. and BERRY, BRIAN J. L. *Spatial Components of Manufacturing Change* 1975. 272 pp.

173. HAYES, CHARLES R. *The Dispersed City: The Case of Piedmont, North Carolina* 1976. 169 pp.

174. CARGO, DOUGLAS B. *Solid Wastes: Factors Influencing Generation Rates* 1977.

175. GILLARD, QUENTIN. *Incomes and Accessibility. Metropolitan Labor Force Participation, Commuting, and Income Differentials in the United States, 1960–1970* 1977. 140 pp.

176. MORGAN, DAVID J. *Patterns of Population Distribution: A Residential Preference Model and Its Dynamic* 1977.

177. STOKES, HOUSTON H.; JONES, DONALD W. and NEUBURGER, HUGH M. *Unemployment and Adjustment in the Labor Market: A Comparison between the Regional and National Responses* 1975. 135 pp.

178. PICCAGLI, GIORGIO ANTONIO. *Racial Transition in Chicago Public Schools. An Examination of the Tipping Point Hypothesis, 1963-1971* 1977.

179. HARRIS, CHAUNCY D. *Bibliography of Geography. Part I. Introduction to General Aids* 1976. 288 pp.

180. CARR, CLAUDIA J. *Pastoralism in Crisis. The Dasanetch and their Ethiopian Lands.* 1977. 339 pp.

181. GOODWIN, GARY C. *Cherokees in Transition: A Study of Changing Culture and Environment Prior to 1775.* 1977. 221 pp.

182. KNIGHT, DAVID B. *A Capital for Canada: Conflict and Compromise in the Nineteenth Century.* 1977. 359 pp.

183. HAIGH, MARTIN J. *The Evolution of Slopes on Artificial Landforms: Blaenavon, Gwent.* 1978.

184. FINK, L. DEE. *Listening to the Learner. An Exploratory Study of Personal Meaning in College Geography Courses.* 1977. 200 pp.

185. HELGREN, DAVID M. *Rivers of Diamonds: An Alluvial History of the Lower Vaal Basin.* 1978.

186. BUTZER, KARL W., editor. *Dimensions of Human Geography: Essays on Some Familiar and Neglected Themes.* 1978. 201 pp.

178. PICCAGLI, GIORGIO ANTONIO. *Racial Transition in Chicago Public Schools. An Examination of the Tipping Point Hypothesis, 1963–1971* 1977.

179. HARRIS, CHAUNCY D. *Bibliography of Geography. Part I. Introduction to General Aids* 1976. 288 pp.

180. CARR, CLAUDIA J. *Pastoralism in Crisis. The Dasanetch and their Ethiopian Lands.* 1977. 339 pp.

181. GOODWIN, GARY C. *Cherokees in Transition: A Study of Changing Culture and Environment Prior to 1775.* 1977. 221 pp.

182. KNIGHT, DAVID B. *A Capital for Canada: Conflict and Compromise in the Nineteenth Century.* 1977. 359 pp.

183. HAIGH, MARTIN J. *The Evolution of Slopes on Artificial Landforms: Blaenavon, Gwent.* 1978.

184. FINK, L. DEE. *Listening to the Learner. An Exploratory Study of Personal Meaning in College Geography Courses.* 1977. 200 pp.

185. HELGREN, DAVID M. *Rivers of Diamonds: An Alluvial History of the Lower Vaal Basin.* 1978.

186. BUTZER, KARL W., *editor. Dimensions of Human Geography: Essays on Some Familiar and Neglected Themes.* 1978. 201 pp.

92 AU